'TIL FAITH DO US PART

'TIL FAITH DO US PART

─────────────◆─────────────

How Interfaith Marriage Is
Transforming America

NAOMI SCHAEFER RILEY

OXFORD
UNIVERSITY PRESS

OXFORD
UNIVERSITY PRESS

Oxford University Press is a department of the University of Oxford.
It furthers the University's objective of excellence in research,
scholarship, and education by publishing worldwide.

Oxford   New York

Auckland   Cape Town   Dar es Salaam   Hong Kong   Karachi
Kuala Lumpur   Madrid   Melbourne   Mexico City   Nairobi
New Delhi   Shanghai   Taipei   Toronto

With offices in

Argentina   Austria   Brazil   Chile   Czech Republic   France   Greece
Guatemala   Hungary   Italy   Japan   Poland   Portugal   Singapore
South Korea   Switzerland   Thailand   Turkey   Ukraine   Vietnam

Oxford is a registered trade mark of Oxford University Press
in the UK and certain other countries.

Published in the United States of America by
Oxford University Press
198 Madison Avenue, New York, NY 10016

© Naomi Schaefer Riley 2013

Library of Congress Cataloging-in-Publication Data
Riley, Naomi Schaefer.
'Til faith do us part : how interfaith marriage is transforming america / Naomi Schaefer Riley.
     p.   cm.
Includes bibliographical references and index.
ISBN 978-0-19-987374-6 (hardcover : alk. paper)
1. Interfaith marriage—United States. 2. Interfaith families—United States. I. Title.
HQ1031.R55   2013
306.84'3—dc23   2012030491

1 3 5 7 9 2 4 6 8

Printed in the United States of America
on acid-free paper

CONTENTS

◆

PREFACE

◆

Our first date ended with a walk around Washington Square Park. Perhaps because we had known each other for years, Jason asked me what my family would think of him. I laughed and told him everything would be fine as long as we raised our children Jewish. He looked at me, puzzled, probably assuming I was kidding. Jason, it turned out, really wanted to know how my family would feel about my dating someone black. But that wasn't something I had given any thought to. It seemed too secondary to the real issue, which was religion.

In retrospect, the topic of our future children and their religious upbringing was perhaps not first-date conversation. But it had been a bottom line in my relationships for as long as I can remember. I wouldn't say that it was inevitable that I'd marry someone who wasn't Jewish, but none of my friends or family should have been surprised.

Why did I date non-Jews? I am skeptical of the psychoanalysis of Jewish women who date non-Jewish men—and vice versa. It's not that "Shiksappeal," the Seinfeldian term for the attraction of Jewish men to non-Jewish women, is hard for me to understand. (I'm sure there are a lot of men of all backgrounds who don't want to date someone like their mother.) It's just that I don't think that's generally how people search for and meet a mate. They may talk about the characteristics they are looking for in another person ("must be a blond-haired, blue-eyed WASP") but rarely are those non-negotiable. In fact, that may be one reason why interfaith marriages are so common. The modern approach to dating is more like: "I won't know the right person until I meet him. And then everything will fall into place perfectly."

So why did I marry someone who wasn't Jewish? It's a question that my own childhood rabbi politely asked me when I interviewed him for this book. Sociologically speaking, all I can say is that, despite receiving a strong Jewish education and growing up in a Conservative Jewish household with two Jewish parents, my peer group during high school and college didn't include many Jews. (Again, you could psychoanalyze, but I won't.) And most people who study Jewish "continuity" would say that the religious makeup of my group of friends was the proximate cause of my dating habits and eventual marriage to a gentile. As sociologists correctly point out, we tend to marry from the group of people we go to school with, work with, and play with.

Interfaith marriage was actually something my friends discussed occasionally, even when we were teenagers. I remember one acquaintance in particular who was told by her parents she would be "disowned" if she ever married "out." I found the notion fairly outrageous at the time. She had not been given much in the way of religious education and hardly observed any Jewish traditions beyond attending high holiday services and a Seder. To my adolescent ears, her parents' views sounded more parochial—if not bigoted—than principled. If Judaism isn't important enough for you to pass it on to your children, why does it matter whom they marry?

I remember a conversation with a good friend—let's call him Jacob—during my senior year of high school. Jacob did have a strong religious education and his parents were very attached to the faith. They attended a Reform synagogue regularly and had a quasi-kosher kitchen. Jacob had dated girls of various backgrounds in high school, but as college approached he told me he had made a resolution. Starting the first day of his freshman year, he would only date Jewish girls. His reasoning startled me. Any of these relationships he was starting now, he explained, could end in marriage. And he had no intention of marrying someone who wasn't Jewish.

Marriage? Who was really thinking about marriage? We were seventeen-year-olds from northeastern, upper-middle-class families headed off to four-year schools to find ourselves. But Jacob already knew himself. Within the first few months of college, he had found a girl—a Jewish one—and by the time he turned twenty-three, he had married her.

I had drawn a line too, I told Jacob back then. I would marry whomever I wanted, but I would raise my children Jewish. Still, kids seemed so far into the future that the whole issue didn't merit much consideration in the short term. Moreover, since most of my friends were nonbelieving Protestants with a few Jews mixed in, it hardly seemed like it would be a difficult negotiation.

And in many ways it wasn't. When the subject came up with the couple of serious boyfriends I had in my teens and early twenties, they readily agreed to my plan—in principle. What did they have to lose?

Jason should have been harder to convince. He had grown up a Jehovah's Witness but left the faith when he was in college. Over the course of a few years he went from knocking on doors to convince others of the truth of the Witnesses' message to believing that the community was something more like a cult, revising its predictions for the end of the world every few years and forbidding members from reading anything that outsiders had written about the faith. At the very least, he determined, its apocalyptic messages—which discouraged education and indeed any kind of long-range planning for life on this earth—were incompatible with his goals in life.

So he might easily have become the type of person who wanted nothing to do with religion of any sort. And I could hardly have blamed him. But Judaism had made a different impression on him. He was more open to a religion that placed a strong emphasis on education, the kind of religion that I had grown up with. And so he agreed on that first date not only that any children resulting from our relationship would be raised Jewish but that they would be given a Jewish education. He would not convert. But the thought of asking him to never actually crossed my mind anyway.

So that was easy. I had "won" the religion discussion. And for a couple of years we went on like that.

As it turned out, there is very little that's difficult about being a young adult dating a young adult of another faith or no faith—certainly not in New York City. Before marriage (assuming you don't live together), everyone can continue to go his or her own way—attend family functions or not, participate in the other person's holiday celebrations or not, keep a home in accordance with religious laws or not.

In many cases, planning the wedding itself is the first time that the couple must confront their differences both formally and publicly. Once we decided that a justice of the peace was going to perform our wedding, and that the ceremony and reception were going to take place in a friend's backyard, we thought the difficult part was over.

But what would the justice of the peace say? Writing the ceremony was no easy task—and we're both professional writers. Jason came home from the Brooklyn Public Library one afternoon with a stack of "create your own wedding" books that ranged from hilarious to horrifying. Just because we didn't have a member of the clergy officiating at our wedding, didn't mean we were hippies—unity candles and sand ceremonies weren't going to cut it. And we hadn't become Native Americans either. Why would we use an Apache wedding blessing if we weren't going to use a Jewish or Christian one?

Why? Well, the books were right in one sense. People want to hear certain things at a wedding—eternal things, things about God, things about people who have passed away, things about the future generations. Weddings are supposed to have meaning beyond the husband and wife. What community are you a part of? What does marriage mean to you? Whose family are you trying to emulate? Why don't you just live together indefinitely? How do you know this is the right person for you? We put together a series of readings and figured out how to word things in such a way as to make our ceremony seem traditional without mentioning a religious tradition. We only had about forty guests, but we wanted to make our two families and our close friends feel comfortable. And we also wanted them to feel like they were witnessing something significant.

After that, things went back to normal. Childless interfaith marriage was not, in my experience, much different than interfaith dating. For instance, to the extent that I attended synagogue, it was still with my extended family and without Jason.

But much of Judaism happens inside the home. When I was living alone or with roommates, I never gave much thought to creating a Jewish home or even a home at all. The years after college were transient ones. Truth be told, I had little interest in being a single woman in the city and didn't want to set down any stakes in that life.

When we bought a house, Jason gave me a mezuzah to put on the door. I began to think more frequently about lighting candles on Shabbat, about picking up a challah somewhere, about finding a synagogue to attend. But it never seemed urgent, and occasionally it seemed awkward. Should I light candles alone? Should I announce what I was going to do so Jason could choose whether to stay or not? Should I go visit family for Passover or host my own Seder? Would I do it by myself? Should he come home early from work to help?

When our daughter was born, all of these choices began to seem more important. First, I wanted to have a baby-naming ceremony for her. Which meant I really did have to find a synagogue. I tried a couple, but felt strange attending by myself. I found one in a lovely, rural spot about twenty minutes north of us. It seemed very welcoming and small. Very informal, too. It was a do-it-yourself crowd, with families bringing their own food for the kiddush after services. For a wealthy commuter town near New York, surprisingly little attention was paid to attire. They didn't have a full-time rabbi but were very enthusiastic about hiring one, and the members told me that anyone who wanted to be involved in the recruitment process could be.

So we had Emily's baby-naming there. And then I never went back. I ran into one of the members a couple of months later, shortly before Passover, and asked if the community was planning anything for the holiday. I was told that no, everyone did their own thing and it was just too small a membership to plan something. But I should check out the local Chabad.

And then I realized that as much as I liked the idea of belonging to a small religious institution where everyone pitched in and nothing was too formal, I was going to need the support of a much larger institution if I wanted my family to have a Jewish identity. I wanted a nursery school, kids' services, activities on the weekends and during the week. I was happy to help where I could, but I wanted my kids to grow up feeling part of a Jewish community. I wanted a calendar of options. I wanted a place where Jason felt welcomed but also, realistically, I wanted a place where I could show up just with the kids and know everything would already be set up.

Once we got over paying the synagogue dues—something that often comes as a surprise to non-Jews and Jews living on their own for the first time—I found myself at a larger version of the shul I had grown up in: a big, suburban, Conservative synagogue. It might not have been ideal for the Jewish person I was in my head. But it was practical for the life I was planning to lead.

Then I started to notice that Conservative Judaism had changed since I was a teenager. It's not that interfaith marriage was a constant topic of conversation at the synagogue of my youth or the Hebrew school I attended a few hours a week in high school. But after the famed 1990 Jewish Population Survey—revealing that the intermarriage rate for the population had surpassed 50 percent—I do remember hearing a sermon on the dangers of assimilation. And mixed families were simply not common in the Jewish community where I grew up.

But twenty years later, there I was chatting with the senior rabbi at my new synagogue, and he expressed, oddly in my view, no sense of surprise or disapproval that I was married to a non-Jew. There are a number of interfaith couples here, I was told by other members of the community. Of the local Conservative Jewish day school, I was given the same impression. "Oh, interfaith couples are nothing. They have lesbian couples there now." Who knew it was a sliding scale?

Interfaith marriage has become more common and more accepted in the dozen years since I had left my parents' home. No one at synagogue asks where Jason is. His presence at preschool events is welcomed, and no one makes a special effort to explain Jewish traditions or holidays to him. And we have never been subject to any derogatory comments by other members of the community, let alone by its leaders.

The challenges of being an interfaith family—or at least a faith/no-faith family—are no longer about fitting in. They are much more subtle, and they are ones that I still struggle with. How do we talk to our kids about God? How do we talk to them about holidays? About the differences between Mom and Dad? What do we say about death? And which one of us should field these questions?

And those are just the questions of our nuclear family. How should we explain the beliefs of Jason's family to our children? Why don't their aunts and uncles and cousins know about the kinds of things they learn in preschool? Why won't they come inside a religious building other than their own? And what about my family? Why do their grandparents keep kosher but we don't? Why do their cousins wear yarmulkes and tzit-tzit (ritual fringes)? Are we still as Jewish if we don't do those things?

These questions are hardly insurmountable obstacles in bringing up children. And I dread them no more than questions like "Where do babies come from?" But I am anxious to find the right answers. The answers that will leave them comfortable with their identity, happy with the choices we have made for them, and excited to find out more about their religious roots and traditions.

Perhaps this sounds naïve, but being the partner who "won" the religious argument is actually a lot more work than I expected. It can also be emotionally taxing. When I take my children to Tot Shabbat and I look around and see whole families—fathers like the boys I grew up with, who know all the prayers and who are just as comfortable inside a Jewish setting as I am—I am lonely. If religious life for me is more about being in community than about my personal relationship with God, then going to religious services alone is not fulfilling in the way I'd like. I imagine sometimes that it will get easier as my children get older—they will share in a spiritual life with me. But I know there is also a sense in which it will never be quite the same.

When I look at our family, I have no regrets. Our children are growing up with parents who share the same sensibilities about the world, who want the same things for their children in the long term. Our children, I hope, are helping to shape a world in which religious and racial differences do not keep people separated. They are gaining an intimate and not just superficial knowledge of people from truly different backgrounds. They are being taught to understand that faith is something to be taken seriously and respected, and that the differences among religions cannot be papered over.

This book is not a memoir or a self-help treatise. I am not wise enough nor (I'd like to believe) old enough to write a book-length account of my own adult life that would be particularly interesting. As a woman who has been married for less than ten years and whose children have barely begun elementary school, it would be hard for me to claim enough expertise on the subject of marriage (interfaith or any other kind) to be dispensing advice.

I am a reporter, though, and this book represents the results of interviews with close to two hundred members of the clergy, marriage counselors, and interfaith couples. But in order to talk about interfaith marriage, a nationwide phenomenon that is growing larger each year, it is also necessary to look at the big picture.

So I commissioned an Interfaith Marriage Survey.[1] The respondents consisted of a nationally representative sample of men and women as well as an additional oversample of members of interfaith couples. Not only did I want to get a handle on where and how interfaith marriage was growing, I also wanted to find out how public attitudes toward it were changing. In addition, I tried to draw on a large enough sample of interfaith husbands and wives to get a sense of their views and habits—what they believed about religion, how they practiced it, how they were raising their children, and even their own level of marital happiness. How did they compare in all of those areas with same-faith couples?

Interfaith marriage is on the rise. My survey showed an interfaith marriage rate of 42 percent. That number included mainline Protestants who married evangelicals but it did not include members of different denominations who were both mainline or both evangelical—mainline Baptists married to mainline Methodists were not counted. The rate was 36 percent if you count all Protestants as one faith.

Compare that to the data from the General Social Survey, which reported in 1988 that 15 percent of U.S. households were mixed-faith. That number rose to 25 percent in 2006. (Those numbers counted Protestants as one faith.) This trajectory seems likely to continue: Less than a quarter of the eighteen- to twenty-three-year-old respondents in the National Study of Youth and Religion think it's important to marry someone of the same faith.[2]

Certainly different regions of the United States have different religious histories. Waves of immigration have changed the religious landscape in a variety of ways. And the different cultures of our regions may encourage or discourage interreligious mixing. What's interesting, though, about inter-faith marriage in the United States is that it is happening across the board.[3] It is true that religious diversity in America has continued to grow during the course of the twentieth and twenty-first centuries, thereby increasing the odds that people would marry out randomly. But as Robert Putnam and David Campbell calculate in their book, *American Grace*, "that factor plays at most a supporting role in the trend [toward a higher rate of interfaith marriage]."[4]

My survey results show that marriages between people of two different faiths are becoming more common in every area of the country, and for men and women regardless of educational status or income level. None of these factors will significantly change the likelihood that a person will marry someone of another faith.

Members of some religious groups are much more likely to marry out than others. Broadly speaking, Jews are the most likely and Mormons are the least likely to marry members of other faiths. Muslims fall somewhere in the middle.[5] Because different dynamics are at work in these different communities, it may be possible to identify particular practices—Jewish summer camp, Mormon missions—that make intermarriage more or less likely. But almost no demographic factor or childhood practice seems to change the likelihood that a marriage will be an interfaith one. The one ex-ception is the age at which people get married. The older you are when you wed, the more likely you will marry out.

Public opinion has also shifted on this issue. I looked in my survey at the change in one generation, comparing the responses to a question about how concerned your parents were that you marry someone of the same religion with a question about how concerned you are that your children marry someone of the same religion. The numbers fell noticeably in every religious group.

The rise of interfaith marriage is a bittersweet trend for American reli-gious groups. On the one hand, it means that they are moving away from traditional practices, that their children will be less likely to be observant members of their faiths. On the other hand, it means that they are being thoroughly accepted into American society. Not only do large numbers of Americans seem happy to marry members of other religious groups, but when they do, they take their extended families along with them. Americans tend to have fonder feelings for a particular religious group after they have married one of its members. In general, the more contact someone has with a member of another religious group—through friendships or extended-family relationships—the more likely they are to have warm feelings for the group as a whole. Interfaith marriage has become an important vehicle for assimilation and a major driver of religious tolerance.

I cannot claim to be an impartial observer of these trends. Nor am I rooting for the all-out victory of any one of them either. America's history of assimilation and tolerance is the reason that I, the grandchild of Jewish immigrants from Eastern Europe, can have the life I do today. It is the reason I could marry the man I wanted to, without fear of being ostracized or worrying about whether my children would ever fit in.

But the strength of America's religious communities is also an important contributor to this country's generosity and compassion, not to mention some of its most important founding principles. In other words, I would be sorry to see the waning of those religious traditions as a result of interfaith marriage. And it is certainly true that interfaith families are less likely to raise their children religiously. Those who do must often make real compromises on the way a faith is practiced. These are difficult trends for religious communities to weather.

Then there is the institution of marriage itself, which has experienced its own decline in recent decades. My survey suggests that interfaith marriages are generally more unhappy—with lower rates of marital satisfaction—and often more unstable, with particularly high divorce rates when certain religious combinations are involved.

My interviews, meanwhile, suggest that few Americans are aware of this problem. Interfaith couples tend to marry without thinking through the practical implications of their religious differences. They assume that because they are decent and tolerant people who don't have anything against people of another faith—and even commendably appreciate religious diversity in their communities—that they will not encounter difficulties being married to someone of another faith. Unfortunately, being in an interfaith marriage provokes conflicts and requires compromises that merely living near, working with, or being friends with someone of another faith does not.

We might think of recent enlightened attitudes toward interfaith marriage as part of the racialization of religion—the belief that faith, like skin color, is a trait that need not divide us. Indeed, there are those who believe that only a bigot would pass over a spouse on religious grounds. But religious identity—even in a completely tolerant society—can and should be considered more substantively than racial identity.

Like religion, marriage is also an important foundation of American life, and I would be sorry if too many people entered into marriages that were unhappy or unstable. For my own selfish reasons, as well as what I think are more broadminded ones, I hope it will be possible to find a balance—to keep religion and marriage strong while fostering a tolerant society. But there is reason for skepticism. Perhaps only a different vision of pluralism would be able to coexist with efforts to strengthen religion and marriage in the United States. Such a pluralism would seek to genuinely tolerate difference and cultivate a sense of civility between groups without falling prey to the idea that all religions are equally true or valuable—and would not minimize the importance of forging marriages around common beliefs and behaviors. I hope what follows here will give us a sense of whether that vision is ultimately possible.

ACKNOWLEDGMENTS

I have been nattering on to colleagues and friends on the topic of interfaith marriage for the better part of a decade. They in turn have generously suggested interviews, recommended books and articles, and offered countless insights on this topic. I am extraordinarily grateful to have such thoughtful interlocutors, who are so willing to indulge me in these conversations.

I have spent much of my career criticizing college professors. Let me just say here that if universities were filled with scholars like David Campbell, I would never have another negative word to say about them. Dave's help constructing the survey and analyzing the statistical data in this book has been invaluable. He is the consummate professional, regularly delving further into the material than I had asked, even if it meant creating more work for himself. His intellectual curiosity seems boundless and his warmth and kindness make me wish I were one of his students.

It is possible to write any number of short, off-the-cuff books on the subject of interfaith marriage. But thanks to the generous support of Roger Hertog, the Bradley Foundation, and the Earhart Foundation I was able to travel extensively for interviews and conduct the kind of survey that will, in my view, give readers the statistical information that has not been previously available on this topic.

I owe my interview subjects an enormous debt of gratitude. Thank you for opening up yourselves to my often-intrusive questions. I hope you will find that your thoughts and feelings have been accurately represented in the pages that follow.

I'd like to thank my editor at Oxford, Theo Calderara, for his painstaking work on the manuscript and my agent, James Levine, for his help with the proposal. Christine Rosen and Abby Wisse Schachter offered great feedback on the manuscript. And Christine Whelan Moyers generously let me use her students as guinea pigs for some survey questions and helped me think more clearly about this topic.

And finally to my family. Thanks to Emily, Simon, and Leah for their love and laughter. And to Jason: It would be hard to imagine a more supportive partner in work and in life.

'TIL FAITH DO US PART

Introduction

———✦———

WHEN JUDY WAS SIXTEEN, SHE WOULD ARRANGE TO HAVE A Jewish boy come pick her up from her house in the Squirrel Hill neighborhood of Pittsburgh.[1] Then she would sneak off to see Bob, an Irish-Catholic boy she knew from school. Judy's Jewish family had no idea she was dating Bob until one night when there was a knock on the door from the police. Bob had been racing Judy's car through the streets nearby and got pulled over. It was not an auspicious start to their relationship. But even if Bob had been a more careful driver, Judy's parents would not have approved.

In 1964, at the age of eighteen, Judy and Bob ran off to West Virginia to get married. No one they knew in Pittsburgh would marry them without their parents' permission. So Bob's brother drove them over the state line and waited around the corner while they tied the knot. How did Judy's parents feel about her marrying a Catholic? "They didn't like it. They really didn't like it," she tells me one fall afternoon while sitting at the dining room table in the small but well-preserved house she grew up in. And Bob's parents "weren't too thrilled at all," she adds.

Judy is a tired-looking woman with a smoker's cough. But her face lights up remembering her illicit romance with that young steel-mill worker almost a half-century ago. Bob passed away suddenly a few years back, just months into his first term as mayor of Pittsburgh, and so Judy is left to reconstruct the beginnings of their relationship. Her three grown children—Heidy, Terry, and Corey—are with her too, and they are learning some new things about their mother's past.

When I ask Judy who performed her wedding ceremony, Terry tells me it was a "justice of the peace." But Judy quickly interjects to say to her son and me that no, the place she got married was a church. "Was it?" Terry asks incredulously.

At the time of their wedding, Judy and Bob did not know a single other interfaith couple, and both of their religious communities were skeptical about the union, to say the least. So they decided to just celebrate the holidays at home and avoid dealing with his parents' parish and her parents' Conservative synagogue. When they were first married, Judy agreed to raise any children they had as Catholics, but in retrospect she thinks she just told Bob that "to make him happy." And he didn't press the issue, at least at first. Their children weren't baptized, but they didn't have a circumcision or Jewish baby-naming ceremony either. Bob and Judy offered their children very little in the way of religious education or formation. Bob did become more religious as he got older, even acting as a Eucharistic minister in church. And once, according to family lore, he even secretly took Heidy to a priest to have her baptized, but the priest refused because Bob and Judy hadn't been married in the Catholic Church.

They sent Terry to a Catholic high school, but Judy says that was more for the quality of the education than for any religious reason. Whatever their intentions, Terry subsequently became a priest. Heidy tried out a number of different denominations with her husband who grew up in a black Baptist church. Her children were baptized in the Episcopal Church, but now they don't have any church affiliation. Corey, the youngest, is circumspect about religion. He's dating a Catholic girl and attended a Catholic high school and college "but hasn't yet been baptized." He considered it when Terry became a priest (he thought of it as a sort of surprise gift in his brother's honor), but decided he wasn't really sure. Judy is proud of her children. But she has regrets, too. "Why didn't somebody pick Jewish?" she asks her children searchingly.

They have no answer. They marvel at the racial and religious diversity they see in their family, and they joke that it was more than a little useful when their father was campaigning for office. No matter what ethnic neighborhood he visited, there was someone in his extended family who could relate. Over time, both Bob's and Judy's parents became more comfortable with their arrangement. And Judy and Bob even lived with her parents for a time. Judy's sister became an Orthodox Jew as an adult, and she lives nearby. Their family gatherings include intense but friendly religious arguments between Terry and his cousins about the finer points of their respective faiths. In some ways, though, Terry's Catholic orthodoxy means that he has more in common with his Jewish cousins when it comes to his attitude toward religion than he does with his siblings.

"There are so many rules," Heidy says of her aunt's Jewish observances. "After going through a whole bunch of different religions," Heidy asks rhetorically, "who am I to say which ones are right, which ones are wrong, which one is best? Who knows, really?" Terry teases his sister a little about her "relativism." He is sure about his faith, but, in his way, no less humble. "Thank God that the Lord called me and the spirit led me to the fullness of the faith which is the Catholic Church." But it is not God alone who has brought him to this point. He also credits the "values" his parents taught him.

When Bob passed away, there was a mass at St. Paul's Cathedral in Pittsburgh led by the Archbishop of Washington DC. Terry offered the homily, and Corey led the mourners in the Pittsburgh Steelers' anthem. Bob was then buried in the cemetery of the archdiocese. There is a place next to him for Judy. Over his is a cross. Hers has a Star of David.

The public face of Bob and Judy's interfaith marriage was nothing less than heartwarming. Their marriage, happy in and of itself, had the added benefit of bringing together two extended families that might never have come into contact. A family of Orthodox Jews counts a Catholic priest among their close relatives. According to some scholars, this kind of contact may create warmer feelings and improve the perception of the other religious group as a whole—on both the Catholic and the Jewish sides of the family.[2] Their community in Pittsburgh, meanwhile, can see how a family with members of different religious groups can get along. The example of interreligious harmony can have positive effects all around.

But this community has remained largely unaware of the rough beginnings of their marriage and the pushing and pulling that continued, particularly as Bob felt himself tugged more toward Catholicism. In some ways, they are one of interfaith marriage's success stories—managing to stay married while at the same time allowing for Bob's religious development. But theirs is a story with difficulties too. Judy sounds almost mournful as she wonders why her own faith doesn't appear to hold any appeal for her children.

And what of her own spiritual journey? Did she give it up for the sake of a happy marriage? What would have happened if she too had decided to become more serious about religion? Looking at her family, she undoubtedly feels the tradeoff was worth it, but did it have to be this way?

Since Judy and Bob were married, the rate of interfaith marriage in the United States has more than doubled. About 20 percent of couples married before the 1960s were interfaith matches. Of couples married in the past decade, 45 percent were. The 2001 American Religious Identification Survey reported that 27 percent of Jews, 23 percent of Catholics, 39 percent of Buddhists, 18 percent of Baptists, 21 percent of Muslims, and 12 percent of Mormons were married to a spouse with a different religious identification.[3]

Judy and Bob's match seemed exotic in the era when they got married. In 1955 when sociologist Will Herberg published *Protestant, Catholic, Jew,* he made the case that America had become a kind of "triple melting pot" in which people, rather than settling into one big stew, had dropped the ethnic part of their identities and maintained the religious part.[4] So Irish Catholics and Italian Catholics could be in one pot. And so could German Jews and Russian Jews. But the religious barriers remained largely stable.

Sixty years later, those barriers have plainly broken down. Today, Jewish-Catholic couples are not uncommon—they're not even uncommon in a traditionally religiously segregated place like Pittsburgh, where I interviewed several others. Interfaith marriage has come to involve and affect a much larger swath of the public.

For most of the second half of the twentieth century, intermarriage was a topic that seemed to concern Jews more than other religious groups. Particularly after the Holocaust, many Jews worried that intermarriage would only further diminish their numbers and the likelihood of group survival. Today, other religious minorities now have the same sets of concerns that Jews did fifty years ago when they worried that too many young people marrying out would lead to the dissolution of the faith. And even some churches have come to worry about the effect of intermarriage on the spiritual life of their Christian congregants.

Our ways of thinking about interfaith marriage have evolved significantly as well. Most Americans are now very accepting, if not welcoming, of interfaith mixing. They see it as a confirmation of American tolerance, of our progress as a society. But as the friends and family of these couples, and even as their religious leaders, we have become content to merely notice this mixing, smile, and move on. We don't ask too many questions before the wedding. And once it happens, we leave the nuts and bolts of interfaith marriage to the husband and wife. We leave them with the tensions about their own religious pursuits. We leave them with little guidance in how to raise children, how to celebrate holidays, how to interact with extended families. We are not sure how to bring them into our religious institutions, and so we often leave them out.

The rise of interfaith marriage is but one way that marriage has changed since the 1950s. Recently, we've seen a spate of books and articles about people delaying marriage, choosing cohabitation instead, or even settling on the single life.[5] But what is often overlooked is how, for those who do marry, the approach to marriage has shifted, from something that was supported (if not arranged) by communities to something that is based entirely on personal preference. It is this individualistic ethos that actually leads people to partners of different faiths. And then a whole new series of challenges arises as they try to reconcile their personal choices with the demands of participation in a religious group. In that sense, interfaith marriage is a striking case study of the tensions between American individualism and the search for community.

✧ ✧ ✧

Today, Amy and Farid are pushing the boundaries the same way that Bob and Judy once did. The two live in a rural area of Rochester, NY. They welcome me into their living room, which doubles as Farid's office. He has taken their son, who is almost two, to see his grandmother a couple of miles away so we can talk.

Amy, a warm and ebullient woman, was raised not too far from here, in a suburb of Buffalo. Her mother was Catholic and her father Presbyterian, but the family attended a Catholic church. During high school Amy became disenchanted with Catholicism. She recalls being invited to a youth group at a Presbyterian church by a friend. From that it was a quick leap to a regular Bible study. At the end of high school, she estimates that she was reading the Bible for one or two hours a night. She fully embraced evangelical Christianity and went on two mission trips when she was eighteen—one to Juarez, Mexico, and one to the Dominican Republic. And then she enrolled at Oral Roberts University in Tulsa, where she was "introduced to a more charismatic version of Christianity." She described people speaking in tongues and the power of the "healing" services: "It was a very demonstrative religion . . . It is on the exact opposite end of the Christian spectrum from Catholicism."

Amy spent three years after college working as a campus minister at a college in Pennsylvania. And then her religious enthusiasm began to fizzle. She says she did not believe less, but that, as Farid interjects, "She didn't want religion to be her full-time job." Between the ages of twenty-two and twenty-eight, Amy went to graduate school, tried stand-up comedy in New York City, and eventually found a job in Human Resources closer to her family.

When I ask Amy how she met her husband, she responds immediately: "He bamboozled me, for sure." The two met on Match.com. He went by the name "Frank" and didn't say anything in his profile about his religion. He said he was twenty-five, but Amy was suspicious. "He looked younger," she insists. He still does. So on their first date, Amy asked to see his driver's license. "I didn't want to get in trouble for dating someone underage," she jokes. Then she noticed the name on his identification was Farid and the questions started flying. "Where are you from? Are you a Muslim?"

Farid is a little more reserved about his story. He shrugs often, more reluctant than Amy to reflect on how he got here. He moved from Afghanistan to the Rochester area with his mother when he was three. His mother wasn't very religious, but Farid remembers that when his father joined them three years later, the Muslim faith became a more important part of their lives. Every Sunday he would spend five or six hours at a religious school where he would learn how to read Arabic. "I was terrible at it," he recalls, laughing. He was thirteen but reading at the third-grade level when he stopped. After that, he would occasionally go to the mosque with his father. In high school, he dated a few girls who weren't Muslim, but always kept the relationships from his parents. "If they knew they would worry that I would marry someone outside the faith." After college, Farid joined the U.S. army, though his parents wanted him to become a doctor instead. And then, four years later, he too returned to upstate New York.

Farid acknowledges that even three years after 9/11, he didn't feel comfortable advertising his religion and ethnicity in his online profile. "As I got older, religion became more of an issue for people [that I dated]. But it really wasn't something that defined me. I put in my profile that I was neutral toward religion. Because I really am neutral toward religion." Amy said that she listed herself as Christian. And also she wrote that she was "looking for a Christian." Farid acknowledges that he didn't look at her profile that closely. He just sent emails to a number of the new girls who came on to the site and waited to see which ones responded.

A smart tactic, in retrospect. The relationship quickly became serious, and for the first time in his life, Farid brought a girl he was seeing to meet his family. His parents didn't pull their punches. "They said they thought I was making a poor choice and that I should go find a Muslim girl to marry and forget about dating Amy." According to Farid, their "top fear was having nonbeliever grandchildren."

Still, he says it was easier for him to deal with these issues because he was a man. Islamic law allows a Muslim man to marry a non-Muslim woman, so long as she is from a "people of the Book," that is, as long as she is Jewish or Christian. (Women are strictly forbidden from marrying anyone outside the faith.) The idea is that Islam is passed down patrilineally, so if the father is Muslim, the children are automatically Muslim as well.[6]

That's not the way Amy and Farid saw it. They began talking about the question of how to raise children very early on. And even though they now have a child, they say the discussion is still "ongoing." As Amy says, "We're still making it up." From the beginning she thought it was important to focus on the beliefs they had in common.

"I think we both believe there is a God," says Farid. "Yep," agrees Amy. "We both believe we're supposed to do good work here on earth." "Yep," she repeats. Then Farid pauses. "I think that's pretty much it." They rarely go to church or to mosque on their own, but each one accompanies the other's family to religious services on holidays. They say that they practice their faith through good works, like buying presents for underprivileged kids on Christmas. And before their son was born, Farid worked as a volunteer EMT. Neither one believes God is an active presence on earth. "I think man is kind of on his own," says Farid. Amy sees heaven and hell "as a metaphor for the life we live now."

These are two individuals who have given significant thought to their own religious beliefs, but like so many other couples I interviewed, they didn't give a lot of consideration to how their religious lives would fit together. Certainly, they came to no agreements. Rather, they simply muddle through the challenges of interfaith marriage, from the day-to-day conflicts to what to expect as their children grow older and begin to ask questions about faith.

Amy and Farid dated for more than three years before marrying and almost broke up several times. Both families continued to register their disappointment with the match. Farid's family even staged what he called an "intervention" shortly after they were engaged. His parents asked him to come over one afternoon, and when Farid arrived he found his entire extended family, aiming to talk him out of marriage. After that incident, Amy was ready to end things. "I'm not walking into a family where I'm the outsider for the rest of my life," she told him.

The two went to see a couples therapist, who told Amy not to worry, that even though Farid did not tell his parents that he was going to do whatever he wanted, he had proved able to stand up to them in the past. His parents had threatened to disown him when he joined the army and he did so anyway.

Their wedding was actually two weddings. One was a traditional Muslim Nikah ceremony with both sets of parents and ten male witnesses and their wives. Then, a few days later, they had what they call their "American wedding," with a pastor presiding. Most of Farid's extended family didn't show up for the latter ceremony, though he is still not sure whether they were offended at the idea of attending a Christian ceremony or whether they were just very late, as is, he says, the Afghan cultural tendency. The reception was a bizarre conglomeration of Afghan and American food, an Afghan live band, an American DJ, and two groups of people who didn't quite know how to interact. Amy says it was a "circus" and insists they should have gone with her original plan of running off to Las Vegas. Still, she was touched by the toast her father gave, in which he emphasized that he sees no differences between his family and Farid's.

No doubt Amy, Farid, and many of their wedding guests breathed a great sigh of relief upon hearing these words. The public face of interfaith marriage seems to be a harmonious one. Some interfaith couples see the wedding as the biggest hurdle they will have to get through—"if we can get our parents to get along for one afternoon, we're home free." But as meaningful as such ceremonies are, they are also orchestrated. We can pick prayers that will appeal to everyone, traditions that will offend no one. But the rest of life is not quite so scripted.

Four days after the birth of their son, Farid's family showed up in what Amy describes as a "caravan." The men came into the living room, started pulling up chairs, and began to pass the baby around, each one reading a passage from the Koran and then "blowing on him." Amy remembers her mother-in-law asking if she had anything sweet to eat since that was part of the ceremony. Amy hadn't been shopping and offered them granola bars. "I had no idea what was going on." In retrospect, she says, she didn't object to the ceremony; she just wished she understood it. "I was just like, 'How come you didn't tell me so I could get the camera because this is an important moment in our lives?'"

Amy and Farid feel that it is good for their son to be exposed to both religions. "Because I know how informative religion was in my development and how important it was to me," explains Amy. But they are still unclear on any specifics. The two have encouraged their respective parents to expose their son to as much religion as they'd like, bringing him to mosque or church, teaching him about their beliefs. Farid jokes: "They can sort it out. We're not going to get involved."

✧   ✧   ✧

In some ways, Amy and Farid's marriage is also a success story. Only in America could an evangelical Christian woman be happily married to a Muslim man with so little difficulty. (This narrative might not go over as well at a meeting of Amy's Oral Roberts University alumni association.) They have not been ostracized. They are on good terms with both families.

And their story is more representative than one might expect, starting with the age at which Amy and Farid married. The average age of first marriage in the United States is twenty-seven for a woman and twenty-nine for a man.[7] Interfaith marriages are more common among older couples. According to my survey, 48 percent of people who were married between sixteen and twenty-five are in interfaith marriages, compared with 58 percent of people who were married between the ages of twenty-six and thirty-five and 67 percent of people between thirty-six and forty-five.[8]

In part, these statistics can be explained by the fact that very religious people are more likely to marry young and less likely to marry outside their faith. But the rising age of marriage in America may also be indirectly responsible for the higher interfaith marriage rate. The period between when a child leaves his or her parents' home and when he or she starts a family has long been a religious downtime. Young people move around, date different people, drop in and out of school, try out different jobs. They have few institutional ties, religious or otherwise. But when the time comes for a marriage ceremony—or, at the very latest, nursery school enrollment—young adults return to church.

At least that's been the case historically. This picture of religious demography is rapidly changing. As these "odyssey years"—what New York Times columnist David Brooks has dubbed the time between college and marriage—grow longer, the attachment to faith grows more and more tenuous. Indeed, after several years of living in a kind of single netherworld, many young people don't think of themselves as religious at all. They are meeting their mates at a point in life when they have been away from religion for a long time. And while they may not mean to misrepresent themselves, they may not realize that someday they will want to return to faith.

Amy's heavy involvement in a strongly Christian community might have led her to marry young. But once she got into her mid-twenties, things would have become more difficult. Evangelical churches have a significant gender gap. Some estimates put it at 60–40. According to David Murrow, author of *Why Men Hate Going to Church*, in virtually every form of church-related activity, women constitute from 60 to 80 percent of participants.[9] And as a result, women in these communities are more likely to "marry out" as they get older.

Farid, too, is, in his own way, representative of today's trends in interfaith marriage. To begin with, Muslims in America are marrying outside their faith at a rate comparable to many other religious groups. While estimates of interfaith marriage among small population groups like Muslims are tricky to make, the raw data from the Pew Religious Landscape Survey suggests that, in round numbers, about one in five American Muslims have married outside their religion.[10]

The different standards of modern times meant that Amy and Farid dated a lot longer before marriage than Judy and Bob did. They even lived together while they were engaged. Their meeting online is also obviously a modern phenomenon—and a means of dating that allows people from different backgrounds to come into contact much more easily.

In principle, all of this should mean interfaith couples today are more aware of the difficulties they might face, but for the most part they seem no less naïve than previous generations. If anything, they may be more so. Cohabitation and long periods of dating seem to give couples the illusion that they know their future spouse inside and out. But being a childless cohabiting couple with two faiths is a fairly easy prospect. Each person can continue to live almost autonomously.

The fact that Amy and Farid have effectively outsourced much of their son's religious education to his grandparents suggests that they have not made any deliberate decisions about how they want their son to be raised religiously. Both couples' attempts to square the circle of their religious differences "by exposing children to both" may likely result, according to clergy and marriage counselors I spoke with, in children who have no particular attachment to either faith.[11] In fact Amy and Farid's decision to try to compromise on their faiths is fairly uncommon among American interfaith couples. Only 4 percent of interfaith couples, for instance, reported having two or more religious leaders of different faiths officiate at their wedding. And less than a quarter of interfaith couples indicated they plan to raise their children in both faiths. A surprisingly large number of the couples I interviewed commented on the sheer impracticality of it.

✧　✧　✧

Despite the widespread social acceptance of interfaith marriage, a higher percentage of married Americans believe it is "very important" for a happy marriage that a husband and wife have the same religion (21 percent) than say they should have the same level of education, the same race, or the same political views. They seem aware that the more a couple has in common, the more likely their marriage will be to succeed. And to the extent that religion is a significant part of one's identity, having the same religion will make things easier.

So, instinctively, Americans realize that interfaith marriage can be problematic. Yet the growth in interfaith marriage shows no signs of slowing. Why do Americans believe one thing and then do another? No doubt there are simply cases where a young couple falls in love, and they are convinced that they will be the exception, that religious differences will not become an issue in their own marriage. Of course, love, and young love in particular, has always been blind. But our cultural messages today seem to reinforce the idea that marriage is a purely individual choice. And that the most ideal matches are the ones that occur by happenstance. Making a list of traits (including religion) that one is looking for in a mate and then searching methodically for someone who matches them is not as likely to appeal as simply finding one's "soulmate" in a crowded room.

But there are pressures other than romantic ones—namely the cultural pressures of pluralism—that are pushing people toward interfaith marriage. Or, to be more precise, letting them fall into it. Some young Americans even pride themselves on marrying someone very different from themselves. One woman I spoke to, who was brought up Catholic, recalls her thoughts on dating when she went off to college: "To limit yourself to only people of your own religion seemed bigoted . . . There is a whole world of people that I don't know." To write them off as potential partners before she even met them "seemed rude." The language is revealing. It's as if our society's institutional rules about hiring an employee or admitting someone to college have morphed into rules for dating.

Some young people have adopted the idea that we need diversity in our marriages. It seems to go against our national grain now to ask people about their religious beliefs on a date, even if we suspect it will affect the long-term prospects for our marriages.

Ten years ago, Philip Weiss wrote in the *New York Observer* that Jewish objections to interfaith marriage are "racist."[12] And today, young people of all faiths are bending over backward to make sure that they don't appear as such. Former megachurch pastor Lee Strobel writes that Christians should not give off the wrong impression when they turn down a date from a non-believer. "Don't send the subtle message: 'I'm good, you're bad, so stay away from me.'" The positive connotation of the word "discriminating,"—having good judgment—has been lost to the ages.[13]

Finally, it seems that many Americans believe that religious differences can be bridged if a couple hold other guiding principles in common. In my survey, we asked respondents to choose between the following:

1. It is better for everyone involved if a husband and wife have the same religion.

2. What really matters is that a husband and wife have the same values, regardless of their religion.

An overwhelming majority (79 percent) of married Americans chose the second.

In other words, when asked directly, Americans see the advantage of having two spouses of the same faith. But they are not willing to put religion ahead of "common values," a more inclusive-sounding phrase.

Common values, I found in my interviews, is a phrase that stands in for one of two things—treating other people with respect or giving back to the community. There is nothing wrong with such values, obviously—in fact, one would be hard-pressed to find anyone walking down the street who *does not* subscribe to them.

But they are awfully generic. How much should you give back? How comfortably should you live before you start giving back? To whom should you give back? Does everyone deserve respect? Is some behavior worthy of disrespect? One wonders: Are these common values ultimately enough of a basis on which to build a successful marriage? Is there anything more specific that couples might want to teach their children?

The substance and the specifics of "values" often come from religion, but in order to get along, many members of interfaith couples simply stop practicing the specifics of their religion very much. Indeed, those who marry outside their faith tend to take religion less seriously or lose their faith entirely. What had been a temporary state of religious disinterest when a person was single now becomes a permanent one.

But faith is a tricky thing, and it sneaks up on people. The death of a loved one, the birth of a child, the loss of a job, a move to a new city—all of these things can give people a sense of religious longing, a desire to return to the faith of their childhood. Some people will pursue that desire, occasionally to the detriment of their marriages. Others will suppress that desire and thwart their own spiritual journeys. One man I spoke with felt that the more involved he became in his Catholic church, the further he was pushing himself away from his Jewish wife and their children. So he stopped going altogether, telling me that though his desire to pursue his spiritual path was important, people in a marriage are not "sovereign selves." Another woman was devastated when, on the way home from the hospital after the birth of her second child, her husband announced he could no longer come to church with her because he was converting to another faith. Her family's whole life had revolved around church and now all that would have to change.

These are not the kind of stories that people want to share with their families or their friends. There is, in some cases, a fear of the "I told you so" from a parent who didn't want them marrying outside the faith. There is also a sense that spouses should not be publicly airing their disagreements. Or even that disagreements about faith—unlike those about money, for instance—are less legitimate. And finally, the cultural pressures to be an example of how well diversity works can also play a role. No one wants to say, "I just couldn't make it work with my husband because he's Jewish." Or, "My wife and I are fighting all the time because she wants me to go to church and I won't do it."

These relationships are complicated in ways that most people, including and especially interfaith couples, may not fully appreciate. But our obsession with tolerance at all costs makes discussing the problems of interfaith marriage taboo. That needs to change.

CHAPTER ONE

◆

Defining Holy Matrimony

IN 1973, KALMAN PACKOUZ HAD JUST GRADUATED FROM THE University of Washington and was on his way to law school when he decided to spend part of the year in Israel. He had grown up in a Reform Jewish household in Portland, Oregon, and was curious to find out more about his faith. Like not a few young Jews who make the pilgrimage to Israel, Packouz says he "started finding answers as far as the direction I wanted to go in life." He studied Torah and the various rabbinical commentaries in a Jerusalem yeshiva and "came to conclusions on the truth of the Torah and the relationship I wanted to develop with the Almighty."

At the same time, Packouz's brother back in the United States was engaged to a woman who was not Jewish. In a long phone interview with me, Packouz described this confluence of events as "amazing." "Here it is, I'm finding this [return to my tradition] so meaningful and fulfilling, yet my brother is separating himself from the Jewish people. Not just himself but future generations." Packouz decided that he needed to make a last-ditch effort to stop his brother's marriage. He flew home and asked his brother to come and study Torah with him for two weeks. "You should know what it is you're giving up," Packouz told him.

His brother, not surprisingly, dismissed his concerns, according to Packouz, and told him something along these lines: "Love will conquer all. I'll do what I want. We'll raise the kids with the best of both religions and let them choose."

"Then," Packouz responded bluntly, "they will get the least of either."

Packouz concluded from this exchange with his brother and subsequent conversations with others in similar situations that high rates of Jewish intermarriage are not simply the result of assimilation, a fading of Jewish identity in the wider American "melting pot."[1] Rather, Packouz blames "ignorance." He explains, "You can't love what you don't know." Of course, these two explanations are not mutually exclusive, but he argues that if Jews understood their history, their traditions, and their laws, they would be more reluctant to give them up.

His brother got married, and Packouz returned to Israel. After years of study, he was ordained as a rabbi in Jerusalem. In 1976, he self-published a book called *How to Prevent Intermarriage: A Guide for Parents to Prevent Broken Hearts*, and for the past four decades, Packouz has been one of the Jewish community's most consistently outspoken opponents of interfaith marriage.[2] There are other Orthodox rabbis who are equally adamant in their opposition to interfaith marriage, but Packouz speaks to a wider audience.

In the late 1970s, he returned to the United States and started a branch of Aish Ha'Torah in St. Louis, Missouri. With centers all over the world, Aish is an Orthodox organization (somewhat like Chabad) with a strong Zionist impulse that encourages Jews to learn more about their faith and to develop a connection to Israel. Much of Packouz's work remains fighting the trend against Jewish intermarriage. Visitors to his website, Preventintermarriage. com, can download the latest edition of his book and read his weekly email newsletter. He monitors the issue closely both in Jewish communal discussions and in secular and Jewish media.

There are plenty of Conservative, Reform, and secular Jews who would dismiss Packouz as a kind of crazy uncle. Sometimes he might say more bluntly what others are thinking—that interfaith marriage is eroding the Jewish community and that something should be done to stem the tide. At other times, he seems to wander further off the reservation, advising parents of children who enter interfaith marriages to act as if their kids are dead. Still, unlike many of the rabbis and other Jewish leaders with whom I spoke, Rabbi Packouz begins any discussion of intermarriage with the text of Jewish law.

Packouz cites a number of passages from the Torah and its commentaries to support his argument against interfaith marriage.

The first is from Deuteronomy 7:3, which states, "Do not intermarry with them, giving your daughters to their sons or taking their daughters for your sons."[3] The prohibition is also mentioned in the book of Nehemiah (10:30): "We will not give our daughters to the peoples of the land or take their daughters for our sons."

The Mishnah, a set of rabbinical commentaries on the Torah, based on the Jewish oral law tradition, states: "When a Jew engages in relations with a woman from other nations, [taking her] as his wife or a Jewess engages in relations with a non-Jew as his wife, they are punished by lashes."

In another section from the Mishnah, it is written that although marrying outside the faith or engaging in sexual relations with a non-Jew is not punishable by death, "it should not be regarded lightly, for it leads to a detriment that has no parallel among all the other forbidden sexual relations." A child conceived through any other union (even out of wedlock) is considered the father's son with regard to all legal matters and is considered a member of the Jewish people. But if he has been born to a gentile woman, he is not considered a Jew. This law is derived from Deuteronomy 7:4, which warns that the gentile "would turn away your children from following me, to serve other gods."

Although today there is obviously no legal punishment in America today meted out for the violation of the prohibition on intermarriage, Packouz argues that the lashes indicated in the Mishnah do suggest the seriousness of the offense. Violating the commandment against intermarriage, he says, is one of the worst transgressions a Jew can commit because "you're cutting yourself off from the Jewish people."

There are, of course, instances of biblical figures who married out. Moses is the most prominent. After he slays the Egyptian taskmaster for beating an Israelite slave, Moses is forced to flee Egypt for Midian. It is there that he meets and marries his wife, Zipporah, a non-Jew. Not only is there no mention of a conversion by Zipporah, but Moses maintains a very close relationship with the non-Jewish family he marries into. We are led to believe that his father-in-law, Jethro, becomes a kind of mentor to him. On the other hand, it is worth noting that it was not Moses's son Gershom who carried on his legacy. Rather, it was Joshua who led the Israelites into the Promised Land.

Esther, though not a biblical figure, is a seminal woman in Jewish history. Her marriage to the king of Persia has traditionally been explained as exceptional—she did it to save the whole Jewish community and therefore was justified. Some scholars have suggested that because she was a woman it was less of an issue. Thanks to the principle of matrilineal descent, her children would have been Jewish regardless. But modern Jewish authorities do not make an exception to the ban on interfaith marriage for women.

The Book of Ruth is perhaps the most famous story of intermarriage. The gentile Ruth did convert, but not until after her Jewish husband died. Then she decided to follow her mother-in-law, Naomi, who is also a widow, saying: "Do not press me to leave you or to turn back from following you! Where you go, I will go; where you lodge, I will lodge; your people shall be my people, and your God my God. Where you die, I will die—there will I be buried. May the Lord do thus and so to me, and more as well, if even death parts me from you" (Ruth 1:16–17).

"Anyone prepared to follow Ruth's example of total loyalty," says Packouz, "will be accepted into the Jewish faith with open arms." If a non-Jew wants to convert to Judaism before the marriage, Packouz has no objections, but it must be an Orthodox conversion. He explains that "to convert you must believe that there is a God, that God gave the Torah to the Jewish people and you must promise to fulfill all of the 613 commandments of the Torah." He acknowledged, "Nobody's perfect, nobody's infallible, but this is a commitment that it is God's word." He says it's like becoming a citizen of the United States. You can't say, "I'll keep all the laws of U.S. except for red traffic lights, I won't stop at them. No. You have to accept all the laws."[4]

Packouz emphasizes repeatedly that he does not oppose intermarriage because he has anything against non-Jews. Rather, he says, "we feel strongly because the Jewish people have a mission. We have a covenant with the Almighty—to perfect the world and be a light unto nations, to bring morality to the world." The notion that the Jews have been "chosen" to lead the world to greater goodness, that they have a special obligation that non-Jews do not, has been the source of much controversy historically. And it does not sit well with modern liberal sensibilities. But Packouz does not shy away from it. This view is not, in Packouz's estimation, bigoted. In fact, he says, "if non-Jews all had hangnails and bad breath, no one would intermarry. It's because non-Jews are fine people that Jews want to marry them."

Parents of Jews who want to marry non-Jews regularly consult Packouz for advice. (He says his email list includes 100,000 subscribers.) He tells them that they must have "bottom-line consequences" for their children. Whether it's skipping the wedding or "sitting shivah" (mourning for the child as if he or she were dead), parents, in Packouz's view, must confront their children about their actions and stick to their guns. These parents are by no means mostly Orthodox. In fact, many of them are facing the issue of intermarriage precisely, in Packouz's view, because they have raised their children with very little in the way of Jewish identity at all.

He tells the story of one woman who came to him crying because her son was going to marry a non-Jew. Packouz asked what she was going to do about it, and she replied, "Nothing."

"In that case," he told her, "get a good psychologist and get used to it." What should parents do? Packouz offers a sort of sample lecture to the intermarrying child: "Understand that this is not the way we raised you, this is not what we stand for. You have free will, but there are consequences. If you drop a glass, it breaks. Know that you are cutting yourself off from your family. There are other children and we want them to marry Jews. This is what we did for 150 generations. We gave up our lives rather than convert. Don't think you'll be able to drive a wedge into this family. You do what you want, but you have to live with the consequences you create." Parents who speak like this, Packouz says, will have an effect on their children's choices, or at least the choices of others in the community who will see their example.

In addition to biblical injunctions against intermarriage, Packouz, like many religious leaders, has become familiar with the psychological and sociological issues associated with intermarriage. He tells people who consult him: "You want to be happy? You want to marry someone and be happy? I want that for you too." He tells them that they will have a higher likelihood of divorce if they enter an interfaith marriage. He believes that many interfaith couples have not sufficiently thought through all of the potential conflicts that will arise in their marriage. Citing *Pirkei Avot* (a collection of maxims from medieval rabbis) he says, "Who is the wise person? He who foresees the consequences."

At one point during our conversation, Packouz seemed to go off the rails. He tells me he believes that intermarriages are less likely to succeed in part because there are "many differences historically between the way Jews were raised and non-Jews were raised." What does he mean by this? "I always tell people, 'when someone [a spouse] gets drunk and calls you a dirty Jew,'" he can't take it back. "You can't put Humpty Dumpty back together again. They have revealed something deep down, a disdain for who you are. You'll never look at your spouse the same again."

For Packouz, it is clear that God's commandments are foremost in his mind when he is telling people not to intermarry. But it is hard to square his concern about non-Jews uttering drunken anti-Semitic slurs with his claim that "non-Jews are fine people" and that's "why Jews want to marry them."

While Kalman Packouz tries to get his message out to the entire American (and world) Jewish population, his views most closely align with those of the Orthodox community, which makes up about 10 percent of the American Jewish population. The 2001 National Jewish Population Survey estimated the intermarriage rate for Jews at about 47 percent, but for the Orthodox it was only 5 percent.[5]

Packouz is a modern, entrepreneurial sort. He launched the first Jewish dating service in 1980. And before his email newsletter, he sent out his thoughts by fax. But his views more closely represent a previous generation of American Jews when it comes to interfaith marriage. While there are other Jewish communal leaders who take seriously the biblical and rabbinical injunctions against marrying outside the faith, they are less likely to use these theological arguments in persuading their congregants to marry other Jews.

For Christians, the injunction against marrying outside the faith comes primarily from Paul. "Do not be yoked together with unbelievers," he wrote. "For what do righteousness and wickedness have in common? On what fellowship can light have with darkness? What harmony is there between Christ and Belial? What does a believer have in common with an unbeliever? What agreement is there between the temple of God and idols? For we are the temple of the living God" (2 Corinthians 6:14–16, New International Version).

In his book *Surviving a Spiritual Mismatch*, Lee Strobel, a former pastor at Saddleback Community Church in Southern California (the megachurch founded by Rick Warren), tries to explain Paul's words. Strobel speaks not only as an evangelical Christian leader but also as someone who has been in an interfaith marriage himself. "If you've experienced the anguish of being a Christian wed to a nonbeliever, you can readily understand why God has prohibited his followers from marrying outside the faith. He loves us so much that he wants to spare us from the emotional anguish, the clash of values, and the ongoing conflict that can result when one spouse is Christian and the other isn't." Strobel tries to make his audience understand that the barriers God has placed before them are not without reason. "His goal isn't to unnecessarily limit our choice of prospective mates but to lovingly shield us . . . ."[6]

"Equally Yoked" has become such a common part of the Christian lexicon that there is a Christian dating service with that name. The phrase originates in a command from Deuteronomy against harnessing different kinds of animals to plow a field. "The yoke," Strobel writes, "was a rigid wood and metal device that was fitted around the necks of two animals. If the animals were of the same kind and similar strength, they would work harmoniously together, equally sharing the load. But if they were from different species, like an ox and a donkey . . . their out-of-sync gait would cause the yoke to pinch and choke them, bringing severe pain."[7]

Which is, figuratively speaking, what happened to Strobel and his wife, Leslie. When they married, religion was not important for either of them, though Strobel says he was a staunch atheist while Leslie was an agnostic with happy childhood memories of her mother singing traditional hymns to her. A few years into their marriage, Leslie became friends with a neighbor who subsequently invited her to church. Leslie found church, in her words, "exciting," but Lee had no interest. He recalls the condescending things he would say to her. "Look, if you need that kind of crutch—if you can't stand on your own two feet and face life without putting your faith in a make-believe god and a book of mythology and legend, go ahead." But he told her she could not give any money to the church and she should not try to get him to attend services with her. "I'm too smart for that [bleep]."[8]

After a few years, Strobel had a conversion of his own, but his book, written with Leslie, is filled with advice about the ways in which a Christian spouse can continue to live a godly life even if he or she is married to a nonbeliever. Some of these suggestions may seem obvious (and hardly specific to interfaith relationships): don't disparage your spouse in front of the children; don't try to harangue your spouse into believing what you do; learn how to compromise.

Theologians and religious leaders speak much less about the dangers of straying from the faith if you're married to a nonbeliever than the dangers to the marriage itself. The unequally yoked are making their own lives difficult and leaving themselves unable to act in harmony. This may raise problems for God, but it will more immediately raise problems for the couple themselves.

As a secondary concern, there is also a sense in which the prohibition on interfaith marriage is intended to protect the faith of the believer. Too much (or too intimate) contact with nonbelievers can be problematic for the faithful. For Jews, because there is no commandment to proselytize, there is no need, in principle, for Jews to encounter and mix with non-Jews.[9] Christians, on the other hand, are specifically told to spread the Gospel to nonbelievers. The admonition to "be in the world, but not of it" has produced mountains of theological commentary. But it has also presented individual Christians with a difficult decision about how much to become involved with the wider world of nonbelievers.

Some sects, like the Jehovah's Witnesses, warn members even against becoming friends with non-Christians. American evangelicals, meanwhile, seem to be moving in the opposite direction in recent years. They have embraced their roles in the world and tried, if not surreptitiously then at least more subtly, to bring the Gospel to neighbors, friends, and coworkers. Indeed, it is precisely this new level of involvement in the world that has made the issue of interfaith marriage more pressing in the evangelical community today.

David Slagle, an evangelical pastor in Atlanta, says that as the culture has moved further away from traditional Christian beliefs, many Christians have moved in one of two directions. Either they become "jerks or jellyfish." The jerks, he says, become more militant. The jellyfish, on the other hand, settle for relativism. They say of Christianity, "this is my truth. It may not be your truth. In the end it will all work out. God is a mountain and there are many ways to climb up." Those are the people who are more likely to end up in interfaith marriages in the first place, and perhaps over time to find that their own convictions become more "squishy," in Slagle's words.

The question of how Christians can be steadfast in their own faith while remaining active and welcoming in the world is not easy to begin with, but it is made more complicated by the issue of interfaith marriage. Over the past several years, I have interviewed many young evangelicals who have proudly told me that they are not the type of people who share their faith by standing on street corners handing out pamphlets or knocking on the doors of strangers. They don't feel this is an effective means spreading the word—it is too impersonal. They prefer getting to know people before talking about faith.

So how can you become close enough with someone to feel comfortable sharing your views on faith, while at the same time maintaining a distance so that you are not influenced by their beliefs? How will you work with non-Christians and socialize with them while at the same time keeping them and the other people you meet through them off your list of potential mates?

The Mormon Church has long recognized the issue of interfaith marriage as one that could affect the beliefs of individual members and the strength of the community as a whole. But to understand the theology behind the Mormon injunction against interfaith marriage, it is first important to understand the views of the Church of Jesus Christ of Latter-day Saints on marriage itself. Mormons believe in something called "celestial marriage," a union that lasts for eternity and which allows both husband and wife to achieve the highest level of exaltation in the afterlife.

According to a passage in the Doctrine and Covenants (132:7 15–18), part of the divinely received scripture for the LDS Church, "In the celestial glory there are three heavens or degrees; And in order to obtain the highest, a man must enter into this order of the priesthood [meaning the new and everlasting covenant of marriage]; And if he does not, he cannot obtain it."

Celestial marriage in earlier Mormon history implied a polygamous union, but today it refers to a husband and wife who are both members in good standing of the faith and become "sealed" to each other in the temple. (Both members must receive what is called a "temple recommend" from their local bishop, certifying, among other things, that they attend religious services regularly, that they tithe, and that they generally behave in accord with the tenets of the church.) Not only does a temple marriage mean that the couple will be able to live together for eternity, but any children that arise from that union will also be a part of the family in the afterlife. So, in a sense, when it comes to marrying inside the faith, the stakes are actually significantly higher for Mormons. (The words "'Til death do us part" do not appear in any Mormon wedding ceremony.) And they tend to have the lowest rate of intermarriage of any religious group in the country.

In a statement on celestial marriage, Russell M. Nelson, one of the twelve Apostles, the LDS Church's governing body, compared finding a spouse to shopping: "Wise shoppers study their options thoroughly before they make a selection. They focus primarily on the quality and durability of a desired product. They want the very best. In contrast, some shoppers look for bargains, and others may splurge, only to learn later—much to their dismay—that their choice did not endure well."[10]

A couple in love, writes Nelson, can choose a marriage "of the highest quality or a lesser type that will not endure." Citing a passage from the Doctrine and Covenants to the effect that "thy duty is unto the church forever, and this because of the family," Nelson explains that "[t]he noblest yearning of the human heart is for a marriage that can endure beyond death.

Fidelity to a temple marriage does that. It allows families to be together forever. This goal is glorious. All Church activities, advancements, quorums, and classes are means to the end of an exalted family."[11]

Just like those of other faiths, Mormon religious leaders explain that they want marriages to succeed, to be happy. Elder L. Whitney Clayton, a member of the Presidency of the 70 (disciples of the church charged with spreading the Gospel), tells me that, first and foremost, "We believe in families. That's one of the first things that anyone who wants to understand the LDS faith needs to understand. Families make people happy and have the opportunity to be the source of great personal satisfaction."

In fact, Clayton suggests that celestial marriage, also called eternal marriage, means that "couples will go at things differently. We hope they'll never be divorced. We don't see marriages ending at the time of death. This framework imbues the entire system of marriage."

It's hard to say whether the idea of living with a spouse eternally makes people more likely to take marriage seriously than if they merely have to live together for, say, forty or fifty years, but one can see how the church's emphasis on the importance of marriage and family might have an effect on people's attitudes about picking spouses, making them more careful shoppers, as it were.

Interfaith marriage is rare but it is not unheard of in many Mormon communities. And many of the non-Mormon spouses do seem to convert after a time. In fact, Clayton and his wife both grew up in such situations. His wife's mother was a member of an LDS church, though she did not attend frequently. His wife's father was a Presbyterian. When his wife was old enough, she decided on her own to attend the LDS church. The community, according to Clayton, did not treat her any differently because she was the product of a mixed marriage. And the bishop of the church encouraged her to attend her father's church sometimes as well, in order to fulfill the scriptural command to love and honor your father. Clayton acknowledges that there is the potential for confusion here for the kids (which is why the church discourages such marriages in the first place), but once such a match is in place the church leaders would like to lessen the disharmony if possible.

Clayton himself had a very similar experience. When his parents married, neither was a Mormon. Sometime between the wedding and Clayton's birth, his mother was baptized into the LDS Church. His father remained a Presbyterian and Clayton went to his father's church as often as his mother's for the first ten years of his life. Around the time he turned eleven, his father, according to Clayton, "began to feel a stirring of his faith and responsibility to his sons." (Clayton has three younger brothers.) His father was baptized, and his parents' marriage was sealed in the temple. His entire family was sealed together in the temple shortly thereafter. A child, Clayton notes, can never be sealed to just one parent. It must be to both together.

More than one observer has remarked on the unique ability of the Mormon Church to maintain a theologically conservative approach to many issues while at the same time ensuring that its members are both comfortable and successful (despite being in a religious minority) living and working in a pluralistic society. Their approach to interfaith marriage seems to embody this tension. Interfaith marriage is discouraged. But those who enter them are rarely shamed. The greatest form of exaltation is denied to interfaith couples and their children (even if the children are being raised entirely in the LDS Church), but the nonmembers are welcomed into the community with open arms.

✦　✦　✦

If you think the LDS Church takes a strict view of intermarriage, have a look at the Eastern Orthodox churches. This religious group maintains no connection with the nonmember spouse or children of intermarried couples. More surprisingly, the Orthodox Church also effectively excommunicates the Orthodox spouses themselves.

For members of the Orthodox churches, marriage to a non-Christian is simply not permissible. According to an article by Greek Orthodox priest Charles Joanides and University of Athens theologian Lewis Patsavos, "Marriage with a non-Christian or non-believer is not mentioned at all [in the Orthodox commentaries], except in the case of a pre-existing marriage, where one of the spouses had subsequently espoused the Orthodox faith. The continuation of such a marriage is permissible, if so willed by the believing spouse."[12]

Orthodox Christians rely for guidance not only on the Old and New Testaments, but on the commentaries of Church Fathers, which suggest that even marriage to other Christians is a questionable prospect. According to Canon 72 of the Council in Trullo, "An Orthodox man is not permitted to marry an heretical woman, nor an Orthodox woman to be joined to an heretical man." What is a heretical man or a heretical woman? As Joanides and Patsavos write, "The claim of the Orthodox Church to be the One, Holy, Catholic and Apostolic Church has as its result the deep reluctance to ascribe to another Church 'ecclesial reality' in a formal documentable way. No official statement has been issued in this regard even during the present days of ecumenism on the part of the Orthodox hierarchs, theologians, episcopal synods or local Orthodox Churches. If, therefore, no ecclesial reality is recognized in another Church, neither can its sacraments be recognized."[13] If the sacraments (including marriage) of another church cannot be recognized then, strictly speaking, a marriage between an Orthodox Christian and a non-Orthodox Christian is not in the theological realm of possibility.

This denial of an "ecclesial reality" has proved most problematic between Orthodox and Roman Catholics who want to marry. The churches are in many ways quite similar and the hierarchy of each speaks regularly of wanting to reach some kind of unity with the other. The idea that Catholics would be considered "heretics" to members of Orthodox Churches and therefore barred from marrying them is a bit hard for Catholics to swallow.

Since the nineteenth century, though, certain allowances have been made for these unions. Marriages between Orthodox Christians and other Trinitarian Christians (that is, other Christians who subscribe to the doctrine of the Trinity) may be allowed as long as the wedding is performed by an Orthodox priest in an Orthodox church, the children of any such union are baptized and brought up in the Orthodox Church, and any marital problems that arise are adjudicated by the Orthodox Church. If these conditions are not met—for example, if a Catholic man married an Orthodox woman in a Catholic church—the Orthodox member would be effectively excommunicated.

As Joanides and Patsavos explain, "The issue at stake here is the reception by an Orthodox Christian of a sacrament outside the communion of the Orthodox Church. For the Orthodox spouse of an 'interchurch marriage,' marriage sought outside the communion of the Orthodox Church is tantamount to the denial of one's ecclesial affiliation." In other words, marrying in another church signals that you are rejecting your own church. The only way to restore the Orthodox spouse to his or her former relationship with the church is to perform the marriage again in the Orthodox Church. This ceremony would actually be preceded by the sacrament of penance, in which the Orthodox spouse expresses his or her "intention for reconciliation with the Orthodox Church."[14]

Joanides became interested in the issue of interfaith marriage a few years ago and eventually decided to do a survey of his community as well as some

in-depth interviews. He found that almost 70 percent of the Greek Orthodox in America are marrying outside of the Orthodox Church, and most of
those were deciding to raise their children in another faith. There were a
variety of reasons for this. In many Orthodox churches, the liturgy is still
primarily in another language, for instance, which can be off-putting to
those who don't understand it.

But Joanides became convinced that his church's attitude toward their
members marrying in another church was not helping the situation. He
hopes that the church might at least develop a policy whereby the Orthodox
spouse who marries out could maintain some relationship with the Orthodox Church. Right now, "they lose all access to the sacraments," Joanides
tells me. And if they ever wanted to reconnect with the church for themselves or their children, that option has been effectively cut off to them.

In addition to the fact that the church is all but bleeding members thanks
to interfaith marriage, Joanides believes it is important to examine these
doctrines as part of a broader approach to its work on "ecumenical affairs."
For instance, he and Patsavos write that church leaders need to "find ways
of affirming and celebrating Orthodox theology, while also avoiding dispar-
aging remarks about non-Orthodox faith groups."

For its part, the Roman Catholic Church has taken a very different approach
to the question of interfaith marriage, at least in recent decades. In the early
part of the twentieth century, "the idea of a Catholic marrying outside the
faith was practically unheard of, if not taboo," acknowledges an article on a
marriage website run by the U.S. Conference of Catholic Bishops. "Such
weddings took place in private ceremonies in the parish rectory, not in a
church sanctuary in front of hundreds of friends and families."[15] It is interesting that despite the fact that these ceremonies were not celebrated like
same-faith marriages, Catholic clergy were still willing to perform them
and to do so inside of the church building. Still, there were certain conditions for interfaith weddings. First and foremost, the non-Catholic spouse
had to promise that any children arising from the marriage would be raised
in the Catholic faith.

As it did with many issues, the Second Vatican Council provided the inspiration for the alteration of the Catholic Church's approach to interfaith marriage. Today, there is little difference between the wedding ceremony of a
Catholic to another Christian and a Catholic to a Catholic. Both may be

married within the church sanctuary (and inside the Communion rail). It is true that Catholics who are marrying other baptized Christians must receive special permission—known as a "dispensation from disparity of cult"—from their local bishop. But there are few cases in which it is not granted. And now it is the Catholic spouse who must promise to raise children in the Catholic faith, while the non-Catholic partner need only be made aware of this promise.

What was behind these changes? How did the Catholic Church go from seeing interfaith marriages as an embarrassment or "taboo" to celebrating them as holy sacraments? It began first with *Unitatis Redintegratio*, which starts with the words: "The restoration of unity among all Christians is one of the principal concerns of the Second Vatican Council. Christ the Lord founded one Church only." While the bishops affirmed that there are real disagreements among Christians that are not to be papered over, the document continues, "The children [from other denominations] . . . who grow up believing in Christ cannot be accused of the sin involved in the separation [from the Catholic Church], and the Catholic Church embraces upon them as brothers, with respect and affection. For men who believe in Christ and have been truly baptized are in communion with the Catholic Church even though this communion is imperfect."[16]

In 1963, while the Council was still in session, Pope Paul VI issued a decree, *Pastorale Munus*, giving local bishops the power to issue the aforementioned dispensation. Previously this could only be granted by Rome and was much more difficult to obtain.[17]

After the conclusion of the council, the Congregation on the Doctrine of the Faith issued instructions for marital preparation for mixed marriages, thereby codifying the practice. In 1970, Paul VI published an apostolic letter called *Matrimonia Mixta*, in which he instructed Catholics on their obligation to raise children in the Catholic faith even if they were in a mixed marriage. "The faithful must therefore be taught that, although the Church somewhat relaxes ecclesiastical discipline in particular cases, she can never remove the obligation of the Catholic party . . . The faithful should therefore be reminded that the Catholic party to a marriage has the duty of preserving his or her own faith. Nor is it ever permitted to expose oneself to a proximate danger of losing it . . . Furthermore the Catholic partner in a mixed marriage is obliged not only to remain steadfast in the faith, but also, as far as possible, to see to it that children be baptized and brought up in that same faith and receive all those aids to eternal salvation which the Catholic church provides for her sons and daughters."[18]

What prompted the Vatican to charge only the Catholic partner with this responsibility instead of both, as had been the policy previously? This change also had its roots in Vatican II. As Nicholas Cafardi, a canon lawyer and a professor of law at Duquesne University in Pittsburgh, explains, the Second Vatican Council took seriously the question of "religious freedom. They realized that you can't force the Protestant party to make promises. You have to respect the consciences of other persons."

The greatest change in the Catholic approach to interfaith marriage, though, came when marriage between Catholics and other baptized Christians was recognized as a sacrament. While this idea had its roots in earlier documents, it was formalized in the 1983 Code of Canon Law, according to Cafardi. Since the marriage between a Catholic and another Christian is a sacrament, the ceremony is the same as if it were between two Catholics. It must be performed in a Catholic church. It may not be co-officiated (another religious leader may be present, but cannot participate in the marriage ceremony itself). The parties must complete a Catholic premarital counseling course.

It is interesting to pause here for a moment and compare the way the Catholic Church views Eastern Orthodox partners for its flock with the way the Eastern Orthodox view Catholics. In *Matrimonia Mixta*, Pope Paul VI goes out of his way to explain that his Eastern brethren "possess true sacraments, above all the priesthood and the Eucharist, whereby they are joined to us in a very close relationship."[19] The Catholic Church does recognize marriages performed by a member of the Eastern Orthodox Church to be valid sacraments as well (though, again, a dispensation is required).

But what about marriage between Catholics and non-Christians? These marriages are not sacramental. A priest who performs a marriage between a Catholic and, say, a Jew or a Muslim, is acting in his civil capacity, not his religious one, according to Cafardi. The church does recognize these marriages in the sense that they are a "natural bond." The church would see as valid the "contractual obligation" that the husband and wife have to each other. While his understanding is that only marriages between two Christians are supposed to take place inside of a church, he acknowledges that local bishops may make exceptions. "While there is meant to be a unity of belief in the Catholic Church, there is not always a unity of practice."

Vatican II had perhaps one final point of influence on the Catholic view of intermarriage. In particular, because the church affirmed that God's covenant with the Jewish people was not "superseded" by Christianity and that

Jews were not responsible for the Crucifixion, the church began to take a more sensitive view of Catholic-Jewish relations in general and Catholic-Jewish marriages in particular. Bishops now give dispensation for Catholic-Jewish marriages to be held at "neutral" sites—that is, outside of churches. They also allow for a rabbi to preside, though again, a dispensation must be given in order for the church to recognize such a marriage as valid. Finally, a report from the U.S. Council of Catholic Bishops (USCCB) in 2004 concluded that "[a]ttempting to raise a child simultaneously as both Jewish and Catholic . . . can only lead to violation of the integrity of both traditions." But it does not go on to say that therefore a child must always be raised Catholic.[20]

In the USCCB website on marriage, an article explains: "The question of what faith in which to raise children must be an ongoing topic of dialogue between the couple and during marriage preparation." It even adds that "traditionally, Jews consider any child of a Jewish woman to be Jewish." In the case of Catholic-Jewish matches, it seems that the church is not simply respecting the conscience of the Jewish partner but suggesting that there may be a good argument for raising the children in the Jewish faith exclusively.[21]

The church's sensitive approach to the question of these matches provides an interesting contrast to its view of Catholic-Muslim marriages. In 2004, Pope John Paul II issued a statement warning Catholic women against marrying Muslim men. The Pope suggested that when a Catholic woman intends to marry a Muslim man, "bitter experience teaches us that a particularly careful and in-depth preparation is called for." He also wrote that there are "profound cultural and religious differences" between Catholics and Muslims, highlighting what he suggested was a poor record of protecting women's rights on the part of the latter. Women, he wrote, are "the least protected member of the Muslim family." While the Pope did suggest that the two faiths have elements in common and that such marriages have the potential for holiness, he warned Catholic women to avoid signing Islamic documents or swearing oaths, including the "shahada," Islam's profession of faith.[22]

There may be many reasons why the Catholic Church worries more about marriages to Muslims than marriages to Jews, not least of which is the stated concern for the rights of Catholic women. But there are others too. Of course, Muslims are much more numerous and as their numbers grow in Europe, intermarriage between the two groups will presumably become more common. Moreover, Muslims are actually permitted by their own law to marry out. That is, Muslim men are allowed to marry women who are members of a "People of the Book"—Jews and Christians. The Catholic Church hierarchy probably also realizes that Jewish leaders will present more objections to interfaith marriage than the church ever would.

✧   ✧   ✧

Let's turn now to the Muslim community, which, though probably not on the verge of any Vatican II–like changes to its doctrines about interfaith marriage, is engaged in small-scale theological discussions about the issue.

One issue not under discussion is the idea that marriage between a Muslim and someone who is not Jewish or Christian is simply considered "*void ab initio*" (of no legal effect), according to Alex Leeman, a law student who authored an article in the *Indiana Law Journal* on "Interfaith Marriage in Islam."[23] Almost no scholars believe that Muslims are permitted to marry outside of the Abrahamic faiths.

It is possible, according to Leeman, that a change in one partner's religious status may affect the marriage. In contrast with Christian practice, if two non-Muslims get married and one converts to Islam, this may threaten the status of the marriage. In other words, unlike in Christianity, the preservation of the marriage does not take precedence over the demands of the faith. Also, if one of the partners leaves Islam, then charges of apostasy may apply and that will also threaten the marriage.

Again, there is not much disagreement about this. Where questions begin to arise is in the rule that Muslim men can marry Jews and Christians, while Muslim women cannot. There are three passages in the Qur'an that are often cited to support this idea:

> And do not marry the idolatresses until they believe, and certainly a believing maid is better than an idolatress woman, even though she should please you. (Qur'an 2:221)
>
> This day the good things are allowed to you . . .; and the chaste from among the believing women and the chaste from among those who have been given the Book before you (are lawful for you); when you have given them their dowries, taking (them) in marriage, not fornicating nor taking them for paramours in secret . . . (Qur'an 5:5)
>
> O you who believe . . .; and hold not to the ties of marriage of unbelieving women, and ask for what you have spent, and let them ask for what they have spent. That is Allah's judgment; He judges between you, and Allah is Knowing, Wise. (Qur'an 60:10)[24]

Jews and Christians are different from other unbelievers in the eyes of Islam. They are followers of a legitimate divine message, albeit one superseded by Muhammad's revelation. In short, God is the same, the history is similar, but Jews and Christians just have an incomplete account of the world because they do not accept Muhammad as the Prophet.

There are Muslim scholars who have argued that because nothing is said in the Qur'an about Muslim women marrying non-Muslims, then it is permitted. But the traditional schools of thought are almost uniform in their belief that because the Qur'an dictates that men need express permission to marry Christians and Jews, so must women. And because it is not mentioned in the Qur'an, it must therefore not be allowed.

One theory about this difference is worth mentioning. When a Muslim man marries a Christian or Jewish woman, she is not required to curb her own practice of her faith, except insofar as the children must be raised as Muslims. Mashood Baderin, a professor of law at the University of London, has written that "[u]nder Islamic law, a Muslim man who marries a Christian or Jewish woman has a religious obligation to honour and respect both Christianity and Judaism. Thus, the woman's religious beliefs and rights are not in jeopardy through the marriage because she would be free to maintain and practice her religion as a Christian or a Jew. Conversely, a Christian or Jewish man who marries a Muslim woman is not under such an obligation within his own faith, so allowing a Muslim woman to marry a Christian or Jewish man may expose her religious beliefs and rights to jeopardy."[25]

Compare this statement with the Pope's thoughts on why Catholic women shouldn't marry Muslim men. Muslim and Catholic theologians apparently both believe that the rights of "their" women will not be protected in a marriage with the other. Both Catholic and Muslim leaders, though, suggest that they are under their own religious obligation to protect the rights of women of other faiths. None of this is to suggest that either is empirically right. Given the treatment of women in much of the modern Islamic world, the Pope probably has more cause for concern, but the parallel theological statements are noteworthy.

✦   ✦   ✦

Still, there are reasons that Muslim leaders, especially in the United States, would like to have a serious reconsideration of the issues surrounding interfaith marriage. In a later chapter, we will examine the dynamics at work in the Muslim American community in depth, but suffice it to say that allowing

Muslim men but not Muslim women to marry out produces a severe gender imbalance among the community's singles. There are two solutions to this— either ban intermarriage altogether, an answer that does not find much support in the Qur'an or later Islamic commentaries, or allow women to marry out as well.

Some scholars suggest that because the status of women is different today—in the West, anyway, they are considered equal partners with their husbands—there is less cause for concern that they will compromise their faith simply because the man, the "head of the household," instructs them to do so. Imam Khaleel Mohammed, a professor of religion at San Diego State University, argues that conditions are different for Muslim women today. And that if "women have legal rights, and that those rights include placing conditions on a marriage . . . an inter-faith marriage can take place on condition than neither spouse will be forcibly converted to the other's religion."[26]

Some Islamic scholars suggest that it is time to use the practice of *ijtihad* (which roughly translates as the exercise of personal judgment regarding Islamic law) when it comes to interfaith marriage. After surveying the field, though, Leeman does not foresee much possibility of change in the immediate future. Nor does he seem to be pushing for it.

"It is not unreasonable," he writes, "to conclude that social conditions of the time underlie the Qur'an's interfaith marriage prohibition for Muslim women. Unfortunately, humanity has not yet universally eliminated many of the concerns that existed at the time God revealed the Qur'an." Indeed, he suggests that the traditional and the reformist positions on intermarriage "are both equally valid, and perhaps each is more valid than the other in certain conditions and cultures." What's missing from this analysis is some sense of where or when Jewish and Christian men are failing to respect the rights of Muslim women to follow their own consciences.

Religious leaders in the Abrahamic faiths have debated particulars of interfaith marriage—if it is allowed, when it may be allowed, how it could be allowed—for ages, but one wonders to what extent the messages are heard by the people in the pews. Do they understand what their faiths say about intermarriage? And how closely does it match their own views?[27]

In general, it seems that almost half of Americans believe that, according to the teachings of their religion, people should marry someone of the same religion. Twenty-four percent said it was very important in their religion and 23 percent said it was somewhat important. Given that 14 percent said they didn't have a religion, it seems that most religiously affiliated people are well aware of their faith's teachings on the subject.

Not surprisingly, though, the number varied significantly from religion to religion. For mainline Protestants, only 9 percent said it was very important according to their faith's teachings to marry within their religion. Among Catholics that number is 30 percent. And among evangelicals, it's 40 percent.

The importance placed on avoiding intermarriage has been falling among Americans for decades. Gallup poll questions about marriage between a Catholic and a Protestant and a Jew and a non-Jew showed approval rates of 60 percent in 1968 and nearly 80 percent in 1982.[28]

Our survey supported the idea that the importance people place on marrying in the faith seems to be slipping. We asked people "how important is it to your parents that you marry someone in the same religion?" Thirty-nine percent said it was very or somewhat important to their parents. And 35 percent said it was very or somewhat important to them that their children do so.

We can also break down this generational slipping by religious group, as in tables 1.1–1.2 below. Among Jews, there is quite a drop-off, with only 21 percent of Jews saying it is very important that their children marry someone

TABLE 1.1   How important is it to *you* that your children marry someone of your own faith?

	Very Important	*Somewhat important*	*Not very important*	*Not at all important*
None	3	7	18	72
Evangelical Protestant	32	29	23	15
Mainline Protestant	7	27	35	31
Black Protestant	24	28	33	16
Catholic	14	29	30	27
Jewish	21	31	28	21
Mormon	52	18	22	8

TABLE 1.2   How important is it to *your parents* that you marry someone
of your own faith?

	Very important	Somewhat important	Not very important	Not at all important
None	8	13	22	57
Evangelical Protestant	28	27	25	20
Mainline Protestant	9	27	28	36
Black Protestant	26	27	28	19
Catholic	21	28	27	25
Jewish	44	23	19	14
Mormon	58	15	15	12

Jewish, compared with 44 percent who said it was important to their parents that they marry someone Jewish. There was even a drop-off among
Mormons, with 58 percent saying it was very important to their parents
compared with 52 percent saying it was very important to them that their
children marry in the faith.

To what extent, one might reasonably ask, does the level of concern about
children marrying out of the faith fall on the shoulders of the clergy? Few
Catholic priests or evangelical pastors seem to preach directly on this issue,
but there are other ways that their messages could get through. For one
thing, evangelicals place a lot of emphasis, starting in the teenage years, on
finding the right partner. And this message could be coming through in
youth groups or in adult singles groups.

The two groups that stand out for the importance their followers believe
that they place on marrying within the faith are Jews and Mormons. Fifty-
five percent of Jews and 64 percent of Mormons say that, according to the
teachings of their religion, it is very important to marry someone of the
same religion.

However, there are interesting divergences between the teachings of a
religion and believers' opinions (table 1.3). For example, only 14 percent of
Catholics say that it is very important to them personally that their own

TABLE 1.3   Comparison of religious teachings and respondent's opinion

	Religious teachings say it's important	Think it's important for my children[i]
None	33	9
Evangelical Protestant	71	61
Mainline Protestant	39	34
Black Protestant	62	52
Catholic	69	43
Jewish	85	51
Mormon	89	70

[i] These numbers combine those who answered "very important" or "somewhat important" to the question.

children marry a Catholic (compared to 30 percent who said their religion teaches that same-faith marriage is very important). Jews are also out of step with their own religious teachings: 21 percent of Jews say it is very important to them that their children marry a fellow Jew (compared to 55 percent who say it is very important within their religious teachings). Evangelicals and mainline Protestants are in close accordance with the perceived importance placed on same-faith marriage within their religions (32 percent of evangelical and 7 percent of mainline Protestants say it is very important). Mormons stand apart from every other group, as 52 percent say it is very important that their children marry within their religion—less than the 64 percent who say their religious teachings place this much emphasis on it, but still much higher than any other group.

To be sure, interfaith marriage is by no means the only issue on which people may be aware of their faith's teachings and yet choose not to pay much attention to them. Catholics know what the church thinks of artificial contraception, but its use is fairly widespread among them. Jews know that bacon isn't kosher, but the percentage of Jews who observe the dietary laws is relatively small in America.

It certainly seems to be the case from my interviews that fewer clergy want to talk about this topic, particularly in sermons. In that way, interfaith marriage has become a little bit like divorce or abortion or premarital sex. Except in the most restrictive of communities, clergy realize that many of their congregants have had personal experience with these issues. And so any criticism will have to be put delicately. They don't want to push people away by suggesting that those who have engaged in these activities are to be shunned by the community. Hating the sin but loving the sinner is a hard message to get across to a large audience. Similarly, as congregations include more and more interfaith couples or at least relatives and friends of inter-faith families, religious leaders are having a more difficult time taking a hard line on the subject. But that, in turn, means that even if believers understand that interfaith marriage is not in accord with their religious tradition, they do not understand why.

CHAPTER TWO

◆

The Road to Marriage

BRIAN AND ALISSA WERE SITTING AT A BAR EARLY ON IN THEIR relationship, when Brian turned to his now-wife and asked out of the blue: "Is it a problem that I'm Jewish?" Alissa, who says she didn't realize how serious Brian was about her, quickly replied, "Not on our second date." In the days that followed, Alissa said Brian made clear "he wasn't happy about my flip answer."

The two had found each other with the help of Alissa's brother, John. He and Brian occupied seats close to each other at Pittsburgh Pirates games and Brian had, over time, become close with John's family—John's kids even called him Uncle Brian. Alissa met him at a baby shower when she was visiting from out of town and the two hit it off.

But why was Brian raising the topic of religion on their second date? Brian had grown up in the heavily Jewish Squirrel Hill neighborhood of Pittsburgh in a "completely non-observant home," he says. "We lit Chanukah candles and went to High Holiday services—essentially because of my grandmother." He said his parents did express a "clear preference for me marrying within the faith." But looking back he would say to them—they're both deceased now—"you raised me with almost no Jewish background, you really don't have much credibility."

Still, when Brian was dating in high school and college, his mother would always ask him two questions about his romantic partners: (1) Is she Jewish? and (2) What does her father do? Brian says his answers were "almost always as bad as you could get in her eyes." Not only did he date mostly gentiles, but he was more likely to go out with the daughters of coal miners than those of doctors or lawyers. The subject came up as usual when he started dating Alissa. "You can hardly come up with a worse answer than daughter of Presbyterian minister," he says, laughing.

But there she was. And maybe that's why Brian saw trouble coming on his second date. Whatever his romantic past suggested, Brian explains, "I had this very strong feeling that my children had to be Jewish." He says that "[a]t least some dimension of that was the Holocaust and the idea of perpetuating the religion and not turning my back on it completely." What would the daughter of a Christian clergyman make of this?

Alissa, who was twenty-seven at the time, actually expressed a fairly typical reaction to a question about religion so early in the relationship—a total lack of concern. "I'd never thought about it." What was on her mind at the time? "I thought, 'Wow, he's a great guy and this is really fun and I hope it works out.'"

Despite being a minister's child, going to church every Sunday when she was growing up, and being active in her youth group, once she got to college Alissa attended church only a "handful of times." Alissa had lived in Boston for a few years after college and had never found a church there she felt comfortable in. Her three older siblings had similarly fallen off and so her parents weren't all that surprised by her behavior, she says. In her twenties, she had dated a few Catholics, but mostly didn't give any thought to the faith of her romantic partners. By bringing up faith so early in the relationship, Brian caught Alissa off guard. She had not expected that kind of long-term talk.

It is not because they are not interested in marriage or children that most couples do not have discussions about religion early on in their relationships. It is rather because they are not at all certain these relationships are headed toward marriage.

The road to matrimony has lengthened considerably in recent decades, and it's become quite a bit more winding as well. In order to understand why we have so many more interfaith couples headed to the altar, we need to look first at a map of that road.

The amount of time that we date before marriage now has grown longer, to the point where many young people do not make much of a connection between the people they choose to date and the people they will eventually marry. There are more than fifteen years between when the average teenager will go out on his or her first "date" and when he or she will send out wedding invitations.

It is difficult to measure how many significant relationships young people have in the interim. But there are some statistics that can shed light on the mindset of young men and women before marriage. First, the average age of marriage has risen to an all-time high of twenty-seven for women and twenty-nine for men. Those numbers are even greater for young people who have graduated from college.

So what happens before marriage?

We know that 95 percent of Americans had their first sexual encounter before they were married and 84 percent of people between the ages of eighteen and twenty-three have had sex.[1] We also know from the 2002 National Survey of Family Growth that, of people ages eighteen–thirty-five who are married, most have had partners other than their spouses. Sixty-four percent have had two or more sexual partners besides their husbands or wives.[2]

But these days sex is not necessarily, for better or worse, the measure of a significant relationship. According to data from the Survey of Marital Generosity, which was conducted in 2010 and 2011, 64 percent of husbands aged eighteen to forty-five lived with a significant other once prior to tying the knot, and 22 percent have cohabited with multiple partners. Of the wives, those numbers are 60 percent and 18 percent respectively. Since people generally don't see cohabitation as having the same degree of permanence as marriage, they get used to the idea of having multiple significant relationships.

But where do you cross the line between significant relationship and future spouse? When does couplehood start to look like it will become 'til death do us part? When do issues like our religious worldviews begin to matter to our partners? When should we discuss the faith of our future children?

There are plenty of people who will say religion is not important in their lives at all. As we will see later, they may sometimes misjudge or misrepresent themselves. But those who do consider religion a somewhat significant factor in their lives will reasonably ask: If I have no intention of marrying the man I date in college, why does his faith matter? If cohabitation may not result in marriage and kids, why should we talk about these things? If I have no intention of marrying the woman I met at a party a few weeks ago, should I even mention my beliefs?

Indeed, many parents of young adults employ a similar logic. Brian's parents certainly seem to be the outliers here, asking about the religious backgrounds of his dates as early as high school.[3]

More common are the attitudes of Sharon's parents. Sharon grew up the youngest of seven kids in a traditionally Catholic family in Rhode Island. She attended a Catholic school and her family went to mass every Sunday. She even became the organist at a nearby chapel. And yet despite this devotion to the faith, Sharon regularly dated non-Catholics in high school and college. "My prom date was the only Jewish boy in high school," she jokes. But she says her parents never made an issue of it.

Mary Ann tells a similar story. A "cradle Catholic" from Atlanta who attended mass every week and Catholic schools as well, Mary Ann recalls that her mother and father "were very open and were never judgmental about me dating someone outside the faith." When she began a serious relationship in college with someone who was Jewish, her parents said nothing. "They probably sensed that I was still many years away from marriage so they weren't concerned about it." She can't remember any religious leaders talking to her about the issue either. "It's interesting," she recalls, "I don't think I've been in too many environments where people . . . felt comfortable counseling or advising me about that."

No doubt many parents and clergy didn't want to start talking to young people about marriage too early. They don't want to place more importance on a relationship than it merits. And they don't want to seem like throwbacks to another era, when marriage occurred much earlier. The desire of parents, beginning with the boomer generation, to appear nonjudgmental has had an enormous impact on the kinds of romantic choices that their children make. They generally emphasize that their children should find someone they love and who brings them personal fulfillment. But they are reluctant to say more. In some cases, the people I interviewed said their parents were divorced and felt it would be hypocritical to offer any marriage advice. Whatever the reason, they don't generally push a timeframe for marriage and would be even more reluctant to say that marriage to a person of a particular faith would be preferable. The rose-colored glasses through which the young tend to see romance and marriage may not be new, but the approval of this view by their elders is a recent phenomenon in human history.

✦   ✦   ✦

David Slagle, the pastor of Veritas, a small, nondenominational evangelical church in Atlanta, says that people often fail to reflect seriously on their own relationships and where they're headed. Sometimes they are hesitant to acknowledge the issue of faith. He tells the story of one woman in her late twenties whom his wife knew from Bible study. The woman became friendly with a man living in her apartment complex. Slagle and his wife inquired whether the two were dating. "No. We're just hanging out," they were told. The man was an ardent atheist and the young woman announced, "I'm not going to date him. He's just a good friend. I could never date someone who didn't value what I value ultimately." A few months later she announced that they were dating but she would not get engaged to him "unless he becomes a Christian." A few months after that, according to Slagle, "she did an about-face on that one too."

Slagle, who often goes to speak to groups of local college students about marriage, says that the issue is one of "intentionality." "Young people today are intentional about their education, their career, thinking through the possibilities for an occupation and where they want to live and buying a home." But, he says, "our romantic view of marriage precludes intentionality."

The way our culture sees marriage, he says, is this: "We believe it's inevitable. It's going to happen. We're going to move through life and we'll eventually meet the right person and we'll know it when it happens. It will be magical and it will all happen before I'm 30." As Mark Regnerus and Jeremy Uecker write in their book *Premarital Sex in America*, "Many lose sight of the fact—or more commonly, realize it too late—that there is a marriage market out there . . . It's a pool that does not grow deeper or more impressive with age. Just like the NBA draft, optimal candidates tend to get selected earlier rather than later."[4]

While Regnerus and Uecker do not advise getting married "before one is prepared to," they are concerned about the way that finding a life partner has become a secondary concern for most young people. "Marital-partner seeking in college has diminished considerably . . . Marriage now serves emerging adults' other interests and plans rather than the other way around. It is clearly no longer the principal institution of adult life as families are considered additions (even accessories) to the unrivaled unfettered individual."[5]

Listening to a public radio show recently, I heard a caller explain how she had always placed her personal life on the back burner in order to work longer hours, but now, in her mid-thirties, she was ready to make time for dating. Her friends, she reported, seemed to think that her new focus on finding a spouse was strange.

So we put years of planning into other aspects of our lives, but marriage is supposed to just happen. In fact, the more intentional a match is, the less "romantic" it is. We enjoy movies about love blossoming by happenstance—a man finds an item lost by a woman in the back of a taxi, a woman meets a man at a friend's wedding and then bumps into him again on the street ten years later. How do they know they're right for each other? The music swells at just the moment their eyes meet.

Liza Minelli once sang of a woman at the ripe old age of thirty-one who was not yet married. She traveled the world, determined to "haul me home a hus' if it's the last thing I do." It's a comic—perhaps downright unattractive—image. But then, magically, effortlessly, she meets a man along the way who happens to live in the apartment next door and, of course, he falls for her too.

This is our understanding of modern love—it will happen when we stop looking, when we stop trying so hard. So when David Slagle or some other religious leader encourages nineteen-year-olds to be intentional about marriage, to actually make a list of the qualities they are looking for in a spouse, to figure out what are their "non-negotiables," it doesn't sound romantic. Perhaps for women, in particular, it sounds like they will turn into high-maintenance nags, the types men aren't interested in anyway.

Because many young people take so long to find a husband or wife and because even the ones who do care about faith are not particularly intentional about what they are looking for in a mate, they tend to simply drift into what will be the most serious relationship of their lives. In an article in the *Wall Street Journal*, a woman in her early forties describes why she has not yet married and had children. She writes that she did not put her career first or feel that she was not ready. Rather, she writes, she "craved something less logical." She confesses, "I believe in soul mates."[6]

Of course soul mate is a term whose origin is religious. The Yiddish word "bashert," meaning destiny, was meant to signify a match pre-ordained by God, that the two souls were like puzzle pieces that fit together. And there is even some basis in the rabbinical literature for the idea that "marriages are made in heaven."

But that is not what most people mean by soul mates today. In fact, it has, if anything, a decidedly secular connotation. If soul mates were ordained by God we would, presumably, look for help from our religious leaders and family in finding them.

No, today's soul mates are pre-ordained by some mysterious force called love. As Simon May writes in his book *Love: A History*, religion has been replaced by love as the highest good in modern Western society. "The religion of love," he notes, "is no less attractive to the diehard atheist than to the agnostic or the believer. Many atheists find in love a taste of the absolute and the eternal that they rigorously deny to any other realm of life."[7]

The people who are looking for soul mates in the popular sense of the term, it turns out, tend to wait longer to marry than those looking for the one God intended. It is the most religious people who marry while young. According to my survey, people who report marrying between the ages of sixteen and twenty-five attend religious services more frequently than people who marry at any other age, except those who marry over age fifty-five (a very small portion of the population).

Of those respondents who married between the age of sixteen and twenty-five, 52 percent were same-faith matches and 48 percent were interfaith. In marriages that occur between the ages of twenty-six and thirty-five, interfaith marriages account for 58 percent of the total. And for those who marry between thirty-six and forty-five, as many as 66 percent are in interfaith relationships. As the ages get higher, the couples are also more likely to be in their second marriage. And those, too, are more likely to be interfaith marriages.

This dynamic can affect even the deeply religious. If they don't find someone of the same faith in their early twenties, they are more likely to go searching outside of their religious institution for an eligible partner. Church-going women in their late twenties and beyond complain that they don't find many eligible bachelors at church. And so they end up leaving that environment in order to find a husband.

In doing so, they are becoming part of a larger religious trend as well. As people enter what sociologists now call "emerging adulthood" (the period between ages 18 and 25), faith seems to become less of a priority.[8] Among young adults, there has been a steady decline in church attendance across geographical, denominational, and class boundaries in the past forty years. As Princeton professor Robert Wuthnow explains in his book *After the Baby Boomers*, there are about three hundred thousand religious congregations in the United States; the loss in membership since 1970 (if you divided it evenly) would amount to twenty-one young adults each.[9] Some scholars, like Baylor's Rodney Stark, point out that at least as far back as the 1930s, young adults have left religious institutions. And he suggests that there is little reason for alarm since they tend to return eventually.

But others, like David Kinnaman, president of the Barna Group and author of *You Lost Me: Why Young Christians Are Leaving Church and Rethinking Faith*, suggest that there is something fundamentally different about the millennial generation when it comes to their willingness to engage with institutions of any sort. (This is the same noncommittal group who RSVP "maybe" to every Evite they receive.)[10]

Stark argues that the "Barna [group] has [unnecessarily] scared the heck out of people." But, even if Stark is right that young people have always strayed from the church before marriage, practicing a religion is a matter of habit and the longer that young adults are out of that habit—that is, the longer they spend as singles—the less likely they are to pick up the habit again. Despite what these singles may say about returning to the fold once they are settled down, according to Wuthnow, only about half do so.

✦　✦　✦

Many parents and religious leaders assume that the young adults who intermarry are people who were never particularly attached to their churches in the first place. And they also assume that interfaith marriage is more likely to occur among those who did not have a religiously observant childhood. In other words, we can blame the parents for their straying children. But my survey suggests that these notions have little evidence to support them.

Childhood religious experiences, it turns out, are not very good predictors of who will marry out. My survey showed that *none of the following things will significantly alter the likelihood you will marry someone of another faith*:

- You attended religious services frequently growing up (table 2.1).
- You received some kind of religious schooling (table 2.2).
- You characterize your upbringing as "very religious." (table 2.3)

That fact that people in same-faith marriages and interfaith marriages were equally likely to say they attended Sunday school or the equivalent "very often," to characterize their family growing up as "very religious," and to say they attended religious services "every week" suggests that there is something other than a religiously detached childhood causing the rise in interfaith marriages.

TABLE 2.1 How often did you attend religious services when you were growing up, if at all?

	Same-faith marriage (%)	Interfaith marriage (%)
Every week	48	46
Nearly every week	19	21
2–3 times a month	8	9
About once a month	4	4
Several times a year	8	6
About once or twice a year	3	4
Less than once a year	5	5
Never	6	7

TABLE 2.2 When you were growing up, did you attend Sunday school or religious education classes very often, sometimes, rarely, or never?

	Same-faith marriage (%)	Interfaith marriage (%)
Very often	55	60
Sometimes	25	22
Rarely	10	8
Never	11	11

TABLE 2.3 In general, how religious was your family when you were growing up?

	Same-faith marriage (%)	Interfaith marriage (%)
Very religious	32	31
Somewhat religious	43	44
Not very religious	16	20
Not religious at all	9	6

There could be any number of reasons why religious education doesn't seem to affect the likelihood of interfaith marriages. It's possible that the religious practices in childhood are simply too far removed in the minds of young adults thinking about marriage. However frequent the church attendance, however significant the Sunday school curriculum, and however fervent one's own family, these factors may be no match for the ten years or more that elapse between leaving a childhood home and marriage.

It is not just the number of years between when they start dating and when they start thinking about marriage that accounts for this drift. It may also be the result of geographic mobility. According to 2008–2009 U.S. Census data, the most mobile segment of the population are people between the ages of twenty and thirty. Of twenty- to twenty-four-year-olds, 27 percent had moved to a different house in the past year. For twenty-five- to twenty-nine-year-olds, it was 25 percent. While they don't seem to be much more mobile than previous generations at this age, my interviews suggest that moving away from home does give young adults a greater sense of freedom in whom they date.

A few years ago, a movie called *Failure to Launch*—the story of a thirty-five-year-old man who had an interesting job and a nice car, but who lived with his parents—became the symbol of what many saw as a new trend among twenty- and thirty-somethings. They earned the name "boomerang generation" because of their increased likelihood of returning home after college.

Those boomerangs who stay home seem to have a largely different relationship with their parents than did the young adults living with their parents a half century ago. As Katherine S. Newman notes in *The Accordion Family*, "the relaxed attitude toward intimate relations between the sexes" preceded the rise of this boomerang generation. "What is different now is that the intimate lives of the coresident generations, the boomers and their kids, are carrying on under the same roof . . . The new arrangement is born from a desire to support and admire the new person this adult child has become."[11] In other words, the judgmental attitudes that parents might have had in the past toward the dating habits of their children have all but disappeared. And those young adults who live at home have much more freedom than their previous counterparts would have.

By historic standards, though, the portion of young adults living at home is not particularly high. The percentage of young adults between the ages of twenty-five and thirty-four who live in "multigenerational households" fell gradually from 27.7 percent in 1940 to 11 percent in 1980 and then went gradually back up to 21.6 percent by 2010.

So what happens to those four in five young adults who are not living with their parents, especially those living a considerable distance away? First, social ties begin to loosen. If we live close to home, our friends and family will meet our significant others in the normal course of events. If we do not, dating can go on for a long time without the watchful eye of people you know. Many of the people interviewed for this book describe being in a relationship for months, if not years, before their spouse-to-be "flew home" to meet their families. Just think of the movie *Meet the Parents*, in which the character played by Ben Stiller is forced to make the acquaintance of his longtime live-in-girlfriend's family only when he wants to propose to her. And even that meeting is prompted only by the fact that his potential father-in-law (played by Robert DeNiro) is a lunatic former CIA operative who is so old-fashioned as to expect Stiller to ask him for permission to marry his daughter first.

Second, ties to religious institutions may loosen as well. Being away from one's childhood congregation may mean that someone no longer feels obligated to come to church on Sunday or the mosque on Friday. It is no longer a habit. It means that young adults are less likely to meet their mates in a religious setting (since they don't find themselves in one as often) and it means that any potential mates will not see them as particularly observant. This falling off of religious faith in young adulthood is an important factor leading to interfaith marriages.

After growing up in California, Maria went about as far away as she could get from her traditional Filipino Catholic family. When she graduated from college, she joined the Peace Corps and helped to train other volunteers in Chad, the Central African Republic, and the Congo. While in Cameroon, she was introduced by one of her colleagues to the Church of Jesus Christ of Latter-day Saints. After she returned to the United States, she looked into the beliefs of Mormons further and decided to convert, much to her parents' disappointment. Being away from her family, she recalls, clearly opened her up to other religious possibilities.

But her conversion to Mormonism happened almost in a vacuum. While most converts think about their change in the context of a community—becoming friends with the other members of the church, getting to know religious leaders through study and fellowship—Maria was baptized in California and then immediately moved to Washington, D.C., for graduate school. Not long after that she left again, this time to work for an NGO in Morocco. That's where she met her now-husband Ahmed, a Muslim.

While his six siblings stayed in their remote village in Morocco, Ahmed decided to leave home for university. His childhood home wasn't terribly devout. His father says he doesn't go to mosque because he hasn't done anything wrong that he needs to ask forgiveness for. But his mother is more traditional. She used to call Ahmed and ask if he was praying regularly. Ahmed did not seem to take her concerns very seriously, however. His attitude seemed to be "out of sight, out of mind."

Ahmed and Maria were both living away from their communities when they met. In Maria's case, she had already left the faith of her family. But she wasn't living among her new coreligionists either. When the two of them speak about what it was like getting to know each other, it sounds as if they were completely autonomous beings. Ahmed acknowledges he knew very little about any faith other than his own. "Anything besides Islam is, they are infidels and we judge them before we know." Having grown up in an insular, religiously homogeneous community, he was only aware that Christians and Jews existed, but that was the extent of his knowledge.

Maria says she was somewhat aware of the basics of Islam because she had lived in Africa. But mostly what she noticed when she came to Morocco was that Mormonism and Islam shared similar practices. "I already didn't drink or smoke. I already dressed modestly. I already knew about fasting because we fast too." Without family or community nearby, any filter through which they would process the beliefs or practices of the other person was gone.

To some, the way that Ahmed and Maria encountered each other is the ideal way to get to know other people—without, as they say, baggage. They had no one giving them information or misinformation about the other's faith, no one to suggest they keep to their own kind. And they also had no religious obligations standing in their way. Neither one of them was regularly attending a prayer service and neither one had a family nearby to check whether they were. Neither had to meet the other's parents and make awkward dinner conversation. They existed in their own world.

Maria and Ahmed's case is extreme, but many of the people I interviewed describe how being away from their families freed up their dating lives. Ruth attended Rice University but lived at home with her parents, who were fairly traditional Catholics. They said the rosary and went to mass. She met Sam, who is Jewish, when she went to live with a high school friend in

New Rochelle, New York, for the summer. Sam was a student at Dartmouth, and the two dated surreptitiously for several months. Upon graduation, though, Sam was drafted to go to Vietnam, and the two decided to marry quickly. Each thought the other's parents were going to be a problem. Neither set was thrilled, but Ruth said she had the feeling Sam's parents would have "paid me $10,000" to hit the road. Their distance from each family allowed them to cement their relationship in place before getting input from the outside world. Presenting a relationship as a fait accompli—by moving in with a partner, getting engaged, or simply dating for a long period of time—makes it harder for parents or friends to object.

✦   ✦   ✦

There are other ways to consider the question of how geography might affect one's likelihood to marry outside the faith. There are some slight regional differences in the prevalence of interfaith marriages in America. They are most common in the West, where 47 percent of all marriages are interfaith. That compares to roughly 40 percent in the other three regions. In the region that the Census Bureau refers to as the Pacific (which includes California, Oregon, Washington, Alaska and Hawaii), the rate is 49 percent.

No single metropolitan area in my survey had more than twenty-five married respondents, which makes for tenuous estimates within any given community. Nonetheless, it does appear that there is a high rate of interfaith marriage in both Portland and Eugene, Oregon. In the Eugene-Corvallis-Medford area, thirteen of twenty-one marriages were interfaith. In Portland, it was eleven of sixteen. The Denver-Boulder area of Colorado is similar: fourteen of twenty-two.

The Northwest does tend to be a more secular area of the country, which could account for the difference. But it is also a "newer" area of the country. Many of the people who live there are transplants, people who have come during the tech boom of the '90s or even more recently. And many have left the constraints of family and religious community thousands of miles behind.[12]

Jay Rosenbaum, the rabbi of Herzl-Ner Tamid, a Conservative synagogue on Mercer Island near Seattle, was not surprised by this trend. He knows many people who have "left behind a more traditional world on the East Coast or even in the Midwest and have come out to this place where you don't have family ties and you don't have the same kind of community ties that bind a person to a tribe."

Rabbi Rosenbaum, whose wife grew up in the Seattle area, says he has always been struck by the "culture of tolerance there." His wife went to a multiracial and multiethnic high school where people seemed to get along—from her descriptions of it, he says it seems like "a Camelot in the '60s and early '70s." Today he also notices a lot of interracial marriage around him. Indeed, according to a report from the Pew Research Center, among all new marriages in 2008, 22 percent in the West were interracial or interethnic, compared with 13 percent in both the South and Northeast and 11 percent in the Midwest.

For Daha, a Sikh[13] man from Vancouver Island in Canada, and Haimi, a Hindu woman from nearby Port Alberta, living close to their respective parents and religious communities didn't present a barrier to their relationship. Now residents of a small suburb outside of Seattle, they both came from very traditional families, though his had lived in the area for four generations, while hers had only immigrated from India recently. After college, the two were performing traditional Indian music at different events and had plenty of time to see each other at concerts in other cities, away from their parents' watchful eyes.

They told their parents they were just friends, and maybe they had convinced themselves of that as well. But when Haimi told Daha she was going to visit some family in India, he became convinced she was being sent there for an arranged marriage and decided it was time to express his interest. Haimi insists that her parents had never planned such a marriage for her, though they certainly expected her to marry in the faith.

And what did Haimi herself expect? She knew that she would marry someone of Indian descent because she wanted someone from a similar cultural background. About half of her friends growing up married "Caucasians," and she says she has seen serious cultural tensions in their relationships.

Daha and Haimi seem caught between two worlds, that of their traditional parents—who come from a culture where dating of any sort is frowned upon and arranged marriages are common—and a Western one in which young adults are free to make their own romantic decisions. Daha and Haimi emphasize their shared values, particularly, respect for one's elders, and especially one's family. "Respect is big in both of our cultures," she says.

But when it came to their own relationship, they were clearly crossing some lines. Consider the way Daha spoke to Haimi's father about their relationship. "I just told him, 'I'm going to marry your daughter. I want to make sure that's okay with you.'"

"Would you like to rephrase that?" Haimi's father asked, clearly taken aback by his future son-in-law's boldness.

And with his own parents, Daha recalls, "I didn't ask their permission. I just told them, 'This is who I am meant to be with.'" Daha's words—both the way he told their parents of his intentions and the idea that he and Haimi were somehow destined for each other—suggest that they have decided which world they plan to live in. They have chosen the romanticism and the individualistic ethos of America over the demands of the communities that they have come from.

For young people from more traditional religious families, the introduction to and the subsequent adoption of the American popular understanding of romance and marriage often happens during high school and particularly during college.[14] At secular schools, students can show a serious fall-off in their adherence to faith. It is not merely that they are exposed to ideas about other faiths that may be foreign. There are also all the temptations of college life, from drinking and drugs to unmonitored contact with the opposite sex.

In decades past, what many religious parents worried about was finding a campus with a sufficient population of coreligionists for their children. Were there enough Jews? Enough Catholics? Was there a "Campus Crusade" branch? A decently staffed Hillel? Underlying these inquiries was the question of whether those students would find a mate there.

That concern is no longer a primary one for most parents. As one Notre Dame professor told me, parents who send their kids to that bastion of Catholicism are more worried that their kids are going to come home engaged than that they will be having casual sex. Many of these parents would prefer that their children find personal fulfillment in the form of a career first before they settled down with a spouse.

Still, there are some religious communities that worry about the influence of college, particularly sending young people *away* to school. They are well aware of the influence that being away from home, in a more liberal and diverse social setting, can have on their children's religious practices and their choice of romantic partners.

Jihad Turk, the director of religious affairs at the Islamic Center of Southern California, says he regularly gets phone calls from parents thinking of sending their children to UCLA or the University of Southern California, inquiring about the campus atmospheres. He divides the Muslim community into three groups—those who are "very concerned and don't let their daughters go away to college," those who are moderately concerned and try to find some circumstances (i.e., a large Muslim population on campus, the availability of halal food) that they feel comfortable with, and those who say "I've raised my daughter and I trust she'll make good decisions if I send her away to school."

Imam Steve Mustapha Elturk of Troy, Michigan, told me that his own son met his first wife, a Christian woman, while in college. Though Elturk was adamant about his son marrying within the faith, he says that "when our children are developing relationships . . . they're not necessarily thinking about the future."

The growth of Muslim Student Associations on campus has facilitated more in-group socialization. There is no data I know of on the average age of American Muslim marriage. Because of the high percentage of immigrants in the population, many would have already been married before coming here. Anecdotally speaking, though, it seems that American Muslims are still getting married younger than most of their classmates. Elturk says most of the Muslim women he knows, even the ones who go to college, are married by the age of twenty-two. And Munira Ezzeldine, the author of *Before the Wedding: 150 Questions for Muslims to Ask Before Getting Married*,[15] jokes that MSAs are sometimes referred to as Matrimonial Student Associations.

✦   ✦   ✦

The years of dating before marriage would seem, in some ways, to be the ideal means of finding out everything there is to know about a potential marriage partner. When asked about why they are living together before marriage, many young adults answer that they are intent on getting to know their partners thoroughly before getting engaged. According to a *USA Today* poll in 2008, half (49 percent) of Americans said living together makes divorce less likely; 13 percent said it makes no difference.[16]

But sociologists have found again and again that cohabitation does not improve the prospects for making a marriage last, and may perhaps diminish the likelihood of long-term success. As Brad Wilcox, a sociologist at the University of Virginia, told me, "People think that cohabitation is a great way to practice or test a relationship. In reality, we know that cohabitation tends to set people up for marital failure—both in terms of high rates of divorce, but also in terms of more conflict in their marriage and less happiness."

Young adults want to find out what it will be like to live with someone, how they will interact when they have to see each other all the time, what it will be like to share responsibility for chores or to pay bills out of the same accounts. And they also think about less practical issues, like whether they can tolerate each other's families and friends. Or even whether they agree on the issues that come up in the news or in their personal lives. Even before we start dating someone, we are able to now access a huge trove of information about them—including their political preferences, sexual preferences, dating history, and so on.

So then it is particularly surprising that more than half of interfaith couples said they did not discuss the religion of any future children before they were married. And that does not include the 20 percent who did not plan to have children. Which makes you wonder: What do they talk about? Are they following the traditional prohibition on discussing religion or politics at the dinner table?

It is hard to imagine that young adults don't share their political views with their partner before tying the knot. What is it about religion that makes people particularly reticent? One explanation is certainly that when emerging adults are dating they may not be thinking about religion very much.

But another possibility lies in the way in which we think about faith. It is possible that this gets back to the issue of not wanting to appear "discriminating" when choosing a mate. But it is also possible that emerging adults consider religion to be a pursuit of the individual. The modern emphasis on "personal spirituality," even when it is part of an organized religion, may suggest that what you believe is between you and God. Maybe checking in on one's partner's beliefs seems too personal—more so than what kind of toothpaste they favor or how they behave in the bedroom.

It is also conceivable that young men and women don't see religion as an important element to explore in their relationships because they come from families where different faiths existed or even thrived. One of the most clear predictors of whether a person will enter an interfaith marriage is whether he or she was raised in an interfaith household.

Of people I surveyed who had two parents of the same faith, 22 percent entered into interfaith marriages. Of those whose parents were in an interfaith relationship, though, 28 percent were in an interfaith marriage. That is a gap of 6 percentage points—not enormous, but still statistically significant.

Furthermore, the effect comes from simply being raised in an interfaith home and not because interfaith homes are less religious. In a model predicting interfaith marriage, we looked at three childhood factors: parents in an interfaith marriage, religious attendance, and attendance at religious classes (e.g., Sunday school). Only being raised in an interfaith home has a statistically significant effect on the likelihood that an individual will marry outside his or her faith. Even children who grew up religious in interfaith homes were more likely to enter an interfaith marriage.

Sally is a good example. She was only somewhat aware of the details of her parents' relationship before she reached adulthood. Her mother was Russian Orthodox and her father was Catholic. Every Sunday for the entire length of her childhood, Sally and her entire family attended a Catholic church. She remembers sitting at mass week after week, though no one in her family actually sang the hymns aloud.

One morning when she was in college, Sally got a call from her mother. During the course of their conversation, Sally realized that it was Sunday and that her mother wasn't in church. And then it came out: When her parents married, her mother had agreed to attend Catholic church with her father as long as their children were home. Twenty-odd years later, the kids were both living elsewhere, and her mother had stopped accompanying him. For all those years, Sally had been completely oblivious to their agreement. But she did understand that her mother "was not a religious or spiritual person in any way." For a woman to attend church every Sunday for two decades and to be described that way is telling. It is not that Sally remembers her mother criticizing the church or even seeming particularly reluctant to observe the rituals of the faith. Her mother had just made this impression on her in some subtle way.

Sally didn't really think much about her own parents' match as she became involved with her now-husband David, a Jew. She did know that her mother wouldn't mind her dating a non-Christian, while she was convinced her father would. Her father had intended to present a "united front" to their children when it came to religion. But somehow the message was garbled. Sally did have an attachment to her faith when she met David, but over time that turned into an attachment to *his* faith. The two are raising their children in the Jewish faith alone, though Sally, like her mother before her, did not convert to her husband's religion.

Even in families where the mother and father are from the same faith background, children can often see very clearly that their parents have different views of religion. It was surprising to me how often this came up in my interviews with individuals in interfaith relationships. They would tell me immediately that it was their mother who dragged their father to church or (occasionally) vice versa.

If being the product of an interfaith marriage will make it more likely that a person will end up marrying outside the faith himself, we might wonder why this didn't actually have a more significant influence. Why isn't there a bigger gap between same-faith and interfaith couples on the question of whether they were raised in an interfaith home? One reason is that "interfaith" only refers to mothers and fathers coming from different denominations or traditions. It does not account for the phenomenon whereby one parent (usually Mom) is devout and the other is not.

Hassan was born in Iran, but his father was a diplomat and so he grew up all over the world: Washington, San Francisco, London, and New Delhi. Hassan is descended from ayatollahs—senior members of the clergy—on both sides of his family. But in his own family, the situation was different. "Religion was very unimportant to my father and very important to my mother," he says. His mother prayed several times a day and even went on a pilgrimage to Mecca. His father, on the other hand, was actually a Communist in the 1940s when he was in college. The anti-religion attitude of the party stuck with him, Hassan reports. "So I grew up in this very mixed kind of thing," says Hassan. "Not that my father would walk around saying you can't believe in God. Nor did he ever criticize or make fun of my mother and her praying."

Hassan met Isabelle, a lapsed Methodist from the Midwest, while he was living in New York City. When I went to visit them in their Brooklyn loft, the two had a six-month-old boy, and they told me they would work out some approach to faith in which they would expose their son to a variety of different ideas and beliefs. They seemed confident that such a plan would not confuse their son in any way. And thinking about Hassan's "mixed" background, it is easy to understand why.

There is one last type of family that seems, anecdotally anyway, to produce children who eventually enter interfaith marriages: families that switch faiths. Michael can't remember beginning a meal without a prayer when he was growing up in rural Arkansas. His parents both spoke about faith regularly. During the course of his childhood, Michael attended Nazarene, Assemblies of God, Methodist, and Seventh-Day Adventist Churches. All of them fell broadly within a certain tradition of so-called holiness churches, but Michael grew up with the impression that religion, while important, was "unstructured." Even after he was married and had children, his parents joined a new church and wanted Michael and his brother to get baptized there. The pastor said that they should undergo the ritual as a family. For Michael, religion was always changing.

Michael's marriage to Vanessa, a Catholic whose parents are from Cuba, was certainly not typical of people who grew up in this environment. Michael even acknowledges a latent anti-Catholic sentiment in his parents and his community. But he was open to learning more about Vanessa's background and, during the couple's marriage, Michael's views have continued to evolve. After a long period of discernment, he converted to Catholicism.

Michael is part of another trend in American religious practice today—the now-common practice of religion switching. According the Faith Matters survey conducted for *American Grace*, "roughly 35–40 percent of all Americans . . . have switched at some point away from their parents' religion."[17] Seeing religious institutions as something that one can dip into and out of seems to have an effect on the way people view interfaith marriage as well. As we will see in the case of those who have married out of their own religious tradition, faith in America today is seen as fluid. It is not a barrier between people.

The road to marriage, the period of emerging adulthood, and the period immediately afterward, we have come to understand as ones of personal exploration. Finding the right career, going back to school, figuring out where we want to live and with whom have all become matters of individual discernment. Parents rarely want to interfere and generally encourage thinking about all of these issues, as well as romance and marriage, as steps on the path to personal fulfillment. Religious leaders generally do not advise about marriage when addressing adolescents and teenagers—it seems too early—and by the time their congregants are young adults, they have stopped attending religious services anyway.

But thinking about marriage and family as a purely personal choice can have its downsides, even for young people who like to think of themselves as autonomous beings. Though it is true that the millennials are generally considered noncommittal when it comes to their engagement with institutions, they are also referred to as the "relational generation." And not just when it comes to using Facebook and Twitter. Often as a result of moving away from family or leaving religious institutions, people in their twenties and thirties are thought to be living in "urban tribes," as David Kinnaman of the Barna Group described them to me. In other words, emerging adults are not islands. They value community deeply. And when they cut themselves off from it, they may come to deeply regret it.

Indeed, my interviews suggest that one of the things that interfaith couples missed most was a community where they and their children could feel comfortable. Many were surprised by the difficulties this presented them. The question of how religious communities treat interfaith couples will be taken up in a later chapter, but for now it seems worth noting that the modern road to marriage, with its almost total emphasis on individual preferences, is not a particularly good reflection of the kinds of experiences and challenges that marriage itself presents.

CHAPTER THREE

✦

The Vows We Make

IT DOES NOT TAKE MANY VIEWINGS OF *SAY YES TO THE DRESS* or *Bridezillas* to realize that Americans spend a great deal of time dreaming about the perfect wedding. Over and over, brides will gush: "I've always wanted to look like a princess on my special day." "I've known this was our song since we met." "I've always pictured myself having a big wedding." Sometimes there are deeply felt regrets about the impossibility of having one's dreams fulfilled. "I only wish my grandmother could be here." "I always imagined my father walking me down the aisle." Underlying these fantasies and sorrows are the weddings we have all witnessed in our lifetimes.

The religious element of a wedding tends to determine its structure and some of its most meaningful moments. We expect to walk down a church aisle and see a crucifix at the end. We look to see the chupah (wedding canopy) being held up over the bride and groom by their family and friends. We imagine a full mass before the ceremony. Or maybe the minister who baptized the groom as a baby offers a blessing. We expect the prayers to be in Persian or in Hebrew or maybe we listen for a particular passage from Song of Songs or First Corinthians. Perhaps the bride will circle the groom seven times. We already know in our minds what words we will use to wish the couple well and what traditional dances will be performed at the reception. For some of us it will be a Big Fat Greek (Orthodox) Wedding; for others a small, reserved Methodist one.

When an interfaith couple begins to discuss their own wedding, these fantasies can come crashing down.

Jonathan and Beth knew each other as far back as high school. Jonathan's father was a Lutheran minister in a small town in Iowa and Beth came from a strong Catholic background—she and her five older siblings attended mass weekly and sometimes daily. Jonathan and Beth were students together at Iowa State when they began dating seriously. They had both started to fall off in their respective religious practices in college and didn't see their denominational differences as much of an issue.

They got engaged at a particularly difficult time in Beth's life. Her mother was dying of cancer. The couple moved the wedding up so her mother would be able to attend. The two had planned to be married in a Catholic church in deference to Beth's family, but Beth's mother had one other request. She wanted the wedding to be accompanied by a mass. Jonathan's parents were not happy. A Catholic mass, they felt, would have made them "uncomfortable," Jonathan says.

The issue of whether to have a mass before the wedding ceremony is often a sticking point when Catholics are marrying non-Catholics. In general, the mass is not a mandatory part of the service and priests who are officiating at interfaith ceremonies will generally advise against it. In order to receive communion at a Catholic mass, you must be in communion with the Catholic Church.[1] To receive the Eucharist is to profess a belief in transubstantiation, to say, as one Catholic writer put it, "Yes, Lord, I believe that this truly is your Body, Blood, Soul, and Divinity."[2] Catholics would argue that it makes no sense for a non-Catholic who doesn't believe this to receive communion. In fact, some Catholics would suggest that if non-Catholics receive the Eucharist without truly believing, it amounts to idolatry and blasphemy.

This is the theological reality, but it is not one that most of the people in the pews of Protestant or Catholic churches give much thought to. Until, that is, there is suddenly a large contingent of non-Catholics (including the parents of either bride or groom) who are not welcome to participate in a significant part of the ritual of a family wedding. Then, feelings are hurt.

I attended a wedding in Oklahoma many years ago in which the bride and groom were both converts to Catholicism. When the time came for communion, the priest politely but firmly warned the room full of Baptists and Methodists (and me, the lone Jew) that they were not invited to participate. The awkwardness that followed was palpable. But at least it was felt on both sides of the church equally.

Beth was still agonizing about the decision of whether to have a mass at the wedding until a week before the big day. She finally determined that even though it might alienate her new in-laws she couldn't deny her mother's dying wish. "The key to marriage is unity," the Rev. Eric Andrews, a Paulist priest in Southern California, tells me. Having a service where only some can participate is a sign of "disunity." He explains: "If the first meal—if you will—as husband and wife is the Eucharist and one can eat and one can't eat at that table, what message is that?"

Though feelings can run hot on this issue, skipping the mass is actually one of the easier compromises of interfaith weddings. (It does not make the marriage any less valid in the eyes of the Catholic Church.) The most important and first decision that a couple has to make is who will perform the ceremony in the first place—a religious official or a civil one. According to my survey, more than half (53 percent) of people in interfaith couples report that their wedding was conducted by someone representing one religion (compared to 67 percent of people in same-faith marriages).

We often tend to imagine interfaith weddings as having two officiants—that both the bride and groom's traditions are represented equally, perhaps symmetrically. The New York Times wedding announcements do seem to mention a disproportionate number. But weddings with religious leaders from different faiths are rare: only 4 percent of interfaith (and, surprisingly, 2 percent of same-faith) couples employ them. Instead, interfaith couples are much more likely to have used a civil official (43 percent vs. 31 percent for same-faith couples). In other words, interfaith couples rarely try to incorporate both religions. Rather, they compromise by picking one or neither.

Decisions about who will preside over a ceremony seem to have significance for a couple's relationship and their family's religious practice beyond the day of the wedding. My survey found, for instance, that if a couple picked one religious leader to conduct their ceremony, they were more likely to raise their children in that faith. This could be correlation, of course, not causation—that is, couples who were more likely to lean toward one faith for the wedding would lean toward the same faith for the childrearing. But it could also be that the wedding sets the religious tone for a marriage. Only 8 percent of couples who had one religious official at their wedding raise their children in a faith other than the one represented by that person. Another 7 percent of couples raised children in both faiths and 21 percent raised them in no faith at all.

For interfaith couples who procured the services of a judge or other civil official to preside over their wedding, the situation differs dramatically. Forty-one percent of interfaith couples who had a nonreligious official at their wedding ceremony are not raising their children in any religion. One needn't have a member of the clergy present in order to have religious elements in one's wedding, but it does mean that what many would consider the most important religious symbol was missing. Still, having a civil servant perform a ceremony does not seem to suggest that the couple never intend to raise children in one faith. More than one in five couples in this situation went on to do so.

What effect does the presence of clergy at a wedding ceremony, or lack thereof, have on future children's religiosity? As rough as it is, church attendance is the easiest way of measuring to what extent families are actually involved with a particular faith. Children of couples who were married by one member of the clergy attended religious services on average of thirty-two times per year, that is, between two and three times per month. Children of couples who were married by civil officials attended services about twenty-two times per year, or a little less than twice a month. The difference in these two groups is not as wide as one might expect. And it certainly suggests that those who choose to get married by a civil official are not saying they don't care about faith at all. Rather, it seems in many cases that they could not agree on one faith for the purpose of their wedding.

The number of respondents whose weddings were performed by representatives of two faiths was fairly insignificant (only 16 in our survey who had children) so we can't draw too many conclusions about this group. Their children attended religious services thirty-four times per year, not much different from those whose parents were married by one member of the clergy. It is possible that children who fell into this category were more likely to attend religious services in both faiths, thereby increasing their overall attendance.

✦   ✦   ✦

Why would a couple who found faith important enough to bring their children to religious services fairly regularly have a secular official preside at their ceremony? It's possible that, for some, religion became more important to them once children entered the picture. But surely not for all. Why don't more couples use two clergy members? One explanation is the difficulty of finding clergy of different faiths who would agree to do it.

For some interfaith couples, this question of who will preside over the ceremony is not much of a question. In the Jewish community, for instance, only Reform rabbis will preside over a ceremony for an interfaith couple—Conservative and Orthodox clergy will not be involved in interfaith ceremonies at all, even as co-officiants. Imams will conduct a ceremony in which the groom is Muslim and the bride is not. But almost none will do the reverse. Different Protestant denominations take different stands on the issue of interfaith marriages, though most would perform a marriage between a Protestant and a Catholic, at the very least. Mormons have two types of marriages. Those performed in temples (known as "eternal marriages") are limited to Mormons only, and devout Mormons at that. However, Mormons also perform civil marriages, typically in an LDS meetinghouse (that is, the local church building, not a temple). These marriages are not considered eternal. Such marriages can be between a Mormon and a non-Mormon.

In some cases, members of the clergy who accept interfaith marriages will accede to co-officiating at a ceremony. Abigail and her husband Peter are among the small minority of couples who used clergy from two different denominations at their wedding. Abigail was not willing to compromise when it came to getting married in her family's Catholic Church. But Peter is the son of a Presbyterian minister. So his father participated in the ceremony as well. They didn't have a mass. "We felt really strongly that if we wanted it to be about Christ and be faith-filled, we had to decide 'This is not Catholic, this is not Protestant.'"

Their religious differences actually prevented them from getting engaged sooner. They dated seriously for two and a half years first, before Abigail finally decided, "This is silly." She concluded that God would not have brought them together only to have their religious differences keep them apart. That being said, they now have a three-year-old son and are still torn about in which church to raise him. He was baptized Presbyterian, but often attends two church services each weekend. The couple feels they will have to make a decision for one faith or the other soon. But they have managed to skirt the issue.

Many clergy who will officiate for interfaith couples simply will not do so when there is more than one religion represented. Rabbi James Gibson of

Pittsburgh tells me, "I don't co-officiate ever. Sometimes people will say, 'Well, Uncle Jack's a priest. Can he say something?'" The most Gibson will allow is for the other clergy member to offer a blessing at the meal following the ceremony.

Mark Brewer, the pastor of Bel Air Presbyterian Church in Southern California, says that his denomination doesn't prohibit him from officiating at interfaith ceremonies with other clergy. Indeed, he used to do so fairly regularly. But he says it "became strange" for him at some point. "What weirds me out," he explains, "is when I'm riding shotgun." Sometimes the couple will get him involved because one of their sets of parents "are strongly Christian and they're upset by the wedding." Brewer doesn't like to be brought in "just to please Grandma."

The Catholic Church doesn't prohibit a priest from co-officiating— Father Andrews says that "the church believes that it is not the minister or the rabbi or the priest who marries; rather it is the couple themselves who are the ministers of the sacrament or the ministers of the marriage." But a number of couples and at least one priest told me that the some Catholic clergy are not always willing to accommodate requests for co-officiation. They might say they have a scheduling conflict, but many of the couples suspect that excuses are being made. Whether it's an individual preference on the part of the priest or a sense that he is making some kind of theological compromise, many priests are simply unwilling to participate.

Thomas and Charlotte arranged to be married in a Catholic church in St. Louis, where they both grew up. Charlotte's family had a strong connection to the Catholic Church, but Thomas grew up a Southern Baptist. "If the church doors were open, we were there," Thomas says of his childhood. By the time the two got engaged in the mid-1980s, they had had extensive conversations about their religious agreements and disagreements. (Thomas eventually went on to get a degree at the Southern Baptist Theological Seminary.) They asked the priest at Charlotte's parish church if the pastor of Thomas's church could participate in the ceremony. The priest said he would permit the pastor to do a reading at the ceremony, just not a biblical one.

"I cried all the way home from that meeting," recalls Charlotte, not only because she felt Thomas was not being fully represented in the ceremony, but because she worried this would "set the stage for things later." In the end, Thomas's pastor read one of Shakespeare's sonnets and according to Charlotte, "he really captured the attention of the congregation there."

Let me not to the marriage of true minds
Admit impediments. Love is not love
Which alters when it alteration finds,
Or bends with the remover to remove:
O no! it is an ever-fixed mark
That looks on tempests and is never shaken;
It is the star to every wandering bark,
Whose worth's unknown, although his height be taken.

Not surprisingly, most of the couples I spoke with had fond memories of their wedding ceremony itself. But finding the right person to perform it was stressful. And for many, it was often the first time they confronted the difficulties that an interfaith marriage might bring them.

Until now, we have been discussing couple's preferences for their weddings, as if they are the ones making all of the decisions. But for many couples that is plainly not the case. For one thing, they may not be the ones footing the bill. According to *Brides* magazine, the average cost of a wedding in the United States in 2011 was $26,501.[3] Though couples may be older when they tie the knot these days, it is a safe bet that parents are paying for a significant slice of that wedding cake. In other words, many couples do have to "make Grandma happy."

Even if that weren't the case, though, interfaith couples must navigate some difficult waters to make sure the guests are all happy. It is rare these days to find the parents who disown their son or daughter upon learning of his or her engagement to someone of another faith (though it does happen), but if certain considerations are not granted, some key family members might decide to make a statement by staying home. That may mean ensuring that a clergy member officiates or that the wedding takes place in the appropriate religious venue or that certain words are recited at the ceremony.

Christopher, a lapsed Lutheran (who has since become a Catholic), and Rachel, a lapsed Jew (who has since become observant), met in graduate school in Washington, D.C., and decided to marry a few years later. Rachel had an almost completely secular upbringing, but when the couple announced they were going to have the wedding ceremony performed by a Methodist minister, her father was not pleased. "My mother said, 'Oh that would be lovely,'" recalls Rachel. And her father proceeded to kick her mother under the table. Clearly, "this was not cool with him." Which she found a little surprising. But since neither she nor Chris had particular religious commitments, they told her father he was welcome to find a rabbi to do the ceremony. The "rabbi for hire," as Rachel referred to him, didn't ask too many questions. He just told the couple what he usually says in a ceremony (using language that is as inclusive as possible) and asked if they would like to "edit" the words in any way.

In some parts of the United States and other parts of the world, it is still nearly impossible to find rabbis who will perform interfaith ceremonies. Beck and Elin, who emigrated to this country a few years ago, tried to find a rabbi to marry them in their native Sweden. Elin did not grow up in a terribly observant home but her mother was a Holocaust survivor and Elin's religious identity was important to her. At her request, Elin's father called a Reform rabbi in Stockholm, who told him, "You will not find a rabbi in all of Europe who will do that." Saddened, Elin agreed to a civil ceremony.

When Rev. Dr. Bob Brashear, now of the West Park Presbyterian Church, married his wife, Andrea (the daughter of a Jewish father and Catholic mother) she was working at the Stephen Wise Free Synagogue in Manhattan. The couple asked a rabbi there to perform the ceremony but she turned them down. She offered some advice, though, that Rev. Brashear took to heart. "Look, you don't really have to have a rabbi to have a Jewish part of your ceremony." Decades later, he offers the same advice to other interfaith couples: "Instead of having a rent-a-rabbi—it'll cost you big dollars just to have a symbolic presence—find people that you have a relationship with that are close to you who you to love to represent the Jewish part of the service."

It was not uncommon for clergy I spoke with to complain about the so-called rabbis or ministers for hire—people who would perform any ceremony the couple wanted for the right price. Rabbi Gibson, who has endured a great deal of criticism from his colleagues in the rabbinate for his willingness to perform interfaith ceremonies, says that he does not accept any payment for his services because he wants money out of the equation. "To take away the monetary taint is a huge, huge thing because one of the first accusations against rabbis who do interfaith weddings is they're just in it for the money." Rabbi Gibson also only performs weddings for members of his own synagogue and their children.

Often, though, the financial issue is a more subtle one. Some Reform congregations will only hire rabbis who will perform interfaith weddings. Jack Wertheimer, a professor at the Jewish Theological Seminary, which trains Conservative rabbis, says that he knows of specific instances where a candidate for a position at a Reform synagogue has been turned down because they will not perform such ceremonies. "They will interview for a job, and [the conversation] just goes dead the minute that comes out."

So even if the financial incentive is not there for one particular ceremony, some clergy are aware that they are more employable if they're willing officiate at interfaith marriages. This, by the way, is not just an issue for the Jewish community.

"Many ministers face social and employment pressure to marry couples indiscriminately," complains Russell Moore, the dean of the Southern Baptist Theological Seminary. If a minister decides not to officiate at the wedding of the daughter of the chairman of deacons when she wants to marry a non-Christian, he "will have revolt on his hands." Still, Moore insists, "If you don't have the courage to make those decisions, you shouldn't be a minister at all."

✧   ✧   ✧

For interfaith couples, approaching a member of the clergy to perform a wedding can become a sort of negotiating process, in which the couple announces what they are looking for and the cleric either agrees to proceed with premarital counseling (and, presumably if all goes according to plan, with the ceremony) or he or she begins to push back, either turning the couple away or pushing them to consider other options.

Rabbi Charles Simon, a leader in the Conservative Jewish movement, recalls the way in which one of his older colleagues would deal with requests that he perform an interfaith marriage. A groom would come to him and say: "You know, I'm Jewish, she's not, we want to have a rabbi and a minister. Would you do it? Could you participate?" The older rabbi would say, "No, but I'll tell you what. I'm a chaplain. I was in the war. So, I know the Christian liturgy. I'll do both."

Then the couple would reply, "You can't be both a rabbi and a minister." And, that, says Rabbi Simon, "would be his entrance, his segue to getting them to understand the differences" between the faiths and why they are important. And why he can't simply paper over those differences in order to perform a ceremony alongside a priest or minister.

Many of the clergy members I spoke with clearly understood the pain that an interfaith couple might feel if they did not get some kind of communal approval from a religious leader. Not only might they be personally hurt, but they might incur a great deal of anger from their families. Having a religious leader bless an interfaith ceremony can save many brides and grooms from years of familial acrimony.

Some members of interfaith couples also had meaningful personal relationships with their clergy and were hurt to find their spiritual mentors could not participate in the next major milestone in their lives. As it stands now, Conservative and Orthodox rabbis are prohibited from even *attending* an interfaith wedding.

Rabbi Simon, for one, would like to see this rule changed. "When couples come to you and say, 'Rabbi, can you come to the ceremony?' And you think, 'I named this child. I bar-mitzvahed this child.' I think a rabbi should have the right to make this a matter of conscience. There are those couples who are really serious [about their faith], and I think the rabbi should say, 'It's my honor to come as a guest and to be there. I'm not going to say anything. I'm going to sit with everybody else as a guest, but I'm coming to be supportive of your marriage and the choices you're making because I know you're going to make Jewish choices.'" Rabbi Simon feels that a rabbi can make this choice without looking like he is ignoring the differences between faiths or that he is approving of interfaith relationships generally.

Even when performing a wedding for an interfaith couple would be theologically permissible, as in the case of a Catholic marrying a Protestant or when one member of the couple is willing to convert for the sake of the marriage, many clergy still make use of premarital counseling sessions to ensure that the couple really understands their religious differences and what they might be giving up in an interfaith marriage. Some simply discourage such matches because they believe they are not likely to succeed in the long run.

Mohamed Magid is the Imam and Executive Director of All Dulles Area Muslim Society (ADAMS) Center in Sterling, Virginia. He tells me unabashedly of couples who have come to him for premarital counseling "and after I spoke to them they changed their mind" altogether about getting married. One such couple he describes included a young man, a Christian, who wanted to convert to Islam. Magid asked him: "What's wrong with Christianity?" The groom replied that there is nothing wrong with Christianity; rather he was converting for his Muslim fiancée. Magid asked, "How fair is that? That you should change your religion for someone else?" He told the young man, "Religion is between you and God and marriage is about accepting the person for who they are." He told the man that he would not perform the conversion ceremony or marry the two. At which point the young woman said that her family would not accept him. And then the groom, by Magid's account, announced, "I'm out of here."

Magid reports that he "gets yelled at by some women. They say 'you ruined my marriage.'" But he says he is simply being "practical." If it is the parents who are dictating the religious terms of the ceremony and the bride and groom to be are merely going through the motions, many clergy would prefer to be left out of it.

For most religious leaders, of course, premarital counseling is not quite as antagonistic as it might be with Imam Magid. Typically, both same-faith and interfaith couples are presented with a set of diagnostic quizzes to see in what areas they do and don't seem to agree—everything from home finances to raising children to who performs household chores.

The Catholic Church probably offers the most formalized program of any in terms of premarital counseling. Pre-Cana, as it is known, includes first a lengthy questionnaire, the kind that many secular marriage counselors make use of, to understand a couple's compatibility better. The course, often done in six weekly sessions or at a weekend-long retreat, also provides basic information about Catholic theology and principles of family life, as well as tools for conflict resolution.

Mary Ellen Hughes, former director of family life for the Catholic Archdiocese of Atlanta, says that about 47 percent of the couples in her diocese are interfaith. For those couples she would offer an additional (optional) interfaith workshop as an "addendum." Hughes has noticed that many of the couples who came through this course were thinking about what their families want from them and what their communities want from them, but they haven't figured out what they want as a couple. Building a religious foundation as a couple, she says, "has to start with a common respect for each other's faith and understanding of each other's faith."

Hughes's observations are interesting because they suggest that couples see their religious obligations as obligations to a community (not necessarily to God), and their marital obligations as to their partner. That is, they do understand that there are competing loyalties at stake. But interfaith couples before they get married officially seem to have a kind of bifurcated understanding of what they're doing. Once they are married (and certainly once they have children), it will be harder to divide up these obligations so neatly.

Hughes asks future husbands and wives to answer some open-ended questions. "What was your best experience in your religious upbringing? What did you love the most? How did it affect you?" Then she asks about their worst experience. They write down the answers and share them with each other. Hughes has found that couples rarely talk about these types of questions. "I'd say they're amazed at what's gone on in that part of the other person's life that was meaningful to them and that they loved and cherished. And what parts they didn't want to hand on to their kids."

Father Paul Kaplanis of the Greek Orthodox Cathedral of the Annunciation in Atlanta also gives engaged couples an inventory of about fifty questions about their family background and career goals as well as what marriage means to them and why they want to marry in the church. For interfaith couples, by which he means members of the Orthodox church and other "Trinitarian" Christians (he is not permitted to perform weddings of Orthodox and non-Christians or of Orthodox and Christians who don't subscribe to the doctrine of the Trinity), Father Kaplanis asks questions about how they plan to raise their children, what church they plan on attending, and how they're going to resolve future conflicts that arise.

Rabbi Gibson requires eight hours of premarital counseling for interfaith couples. He asks them to watch an old video put out by the Union of Reformed Judaism called "This Great Difference" about the ups and downs of interfaith relationships. He used to employ a survey called the Premarital Inventory, which mostly measured a couple's agreement on particular issues. But he switched a number of years ago to a program called Prepare/Enrich (one that seems, anecdotally anyway, quite popular among religious leaders), which is supposed to put couples on the road to more healthy communication.

Gibson has been a rabbi for almost three decades and has developed his own set of questions he would like couples to discuss. Even the issues that don't seem to involve religious beliefs often do. When they talk about finances, for instance, he asks couples about whether they have budgeted for *tzedakah* (charity).

✦ ✦ ✦

Even once the decision has been made about who will marry a couple, the negotiations are far from over. The ceremony itself is an area where interfaith couples often find themselves at sea. Couples and their friends and families expect to hear about religious themes things at weddings—the power of the Divine, grandparents watching us from above, the children God intends for us to have, about the meaning of marriage and its significance beyond the tax code. But finding the words that express how both bride and groom feel about such matters is challenging, to say the least. It is why some interfaith ceremonies begin to sound like top-forty love songs.

In a book called *Interfaith Wedding Ceremonies* the authors provide dozens of samples of readings and blessings (taken from actual interfaith ceremonies) that couples might use in their own. "I believe in the power of love," both the bride and groom recite. "I believe that love is the single most potent force in the universe. It is the source of all joy, the unifying strength which links spirit to spirit. . . ." Then the officiant says, "The hand offered by each of you is an extension of self, just as is your mutual love. Cherish the touch, for you touch not only your own but another life. Be ever sensitive to its pulse. Seek always to understand and respect its rhythm."[4]

Many of the words at interfaith ceremonies seem to involve detailed explanations of the promises involved in a marriage. "For richer or poorer" does not seem to suffice in these ceremonies (though certainly the same can be said for some same-faith ceremonies in which the couples insist on writing their own vows). I remember the first interfaith wedding I attended in which the bride and groom promised to be each other's "lovers." Several of the friends and family gathered concluded afterward that this might be a little too explicit for the occasion.

Here is another sample statement (to be offered first by the groom, then the bride) from *Interfaith Wedding Ceremonies*:

> I [Groom], take you, [Bride], with all my heart and soul to be my wife, my friend, my love and my lifelong companion. I promise to respect that our ideas and opinions may differ, and to remember that yours hold as much truth and value for you as mine do for me. I promise to support you in times of trouble, and celebrate with you in times of happiness; to care more about your feelings than about being right, and to listen without judging. I promise to treat you with respect, love, and loyalty through all the trials and triumphs of our lives together; and to give you, [Bride], all the love I can give my whole life long. This commitment is made in love, kept in faith, lived in hope and eternally made new.[5]

Someone who has been married for a few years might wonder about the feasibility of, say, the promise to "listen without judging." But these are vows that young men and women seem to be creating out of whole cloth. If a same-faith wedding ceremony is a way for a couple to agree to live by a religious community's rules for marriage, interfaith couples seem to be trying to make their own community and their own rules with each new ceremony they write.

Many interfaith ceremonies involving Christians and Jews aim to scrupulously avoid any mention of a Judeo-Christian notion of religion. It is then odd to see how it is also not uncommon for interfaith couples to turn to religious traditions other than their own as a means of compromise. Some wedding officiants have at the ready Eastern or Native American blessings to be used in the ceremony. Take "The Blessing of the Apaches," for instance. I thought the Justice of the Peace who married my husband and me was a little strange when she suggested it, but then I realized that it is standard fare at many interfaith ceremonies:

> Now you will feel no rain,
> For each of you will be shelter to the other.
> Now you will feel no cold,
> For each of you will be warmth to the other.
> Now there is no more loneliness for you,
> For each of you will be companion to the other.
> Now you are two bodies,
> But there is only one life before you.
> Go now to your dwelling place,
> To enter into the days of your togetherness.
> And may your days be good and long upon the earth.

This Buddhist blessing on a couple shows up on a number of websites geared toward interfaith couples:

> Do not deceive, do not despise each other anywhere. Do not be angry nor bear secret resentments; for as a mother will risk her life and watches over her child, so boundless be your love to all, so tender, kind and mild.
>
> Cherish good will right and left, early and late, and without hindrance, without stint, be free of hate and envy, while standing and walking and sitting down, what ever you have in mind, the rule of life that is always best is to be loving-kind.

Lovely sentiments, no doubt, but the decision to co-opt a third tradition instead of using readings from a religious tradition represented by the bride or the groom suggests just how delicate these negotiations over ceremonies must be.

Many couples I interviewed seemed to take an "everything but the kitchen sink" approach to the wedding ceremony. Why leave out any tradition? One couple gave me a copy of their wedding program from a dozen years ago, which included two New Testament readings, the reading of a Ketubah (a Jewish marriage contract), the Apache Wedding Prayer, a transcendentalist poem, the breaking of the glass, and much more.

✧   ✧   ✧

One advantage of having a member of the clergy perform an interfaith ceremony is that he or she brings along a traditional liturgy. It may not be the same one that he uses when marrying people of the same faith, but because it is more likely to include an emphasis on the community and the history of the institution of marriage, it also seems more likely to have an underlying gravitas.

The liturgy Rabbi Gibson uses for interfaith couples is not the same as it is when he marries two Jews. But it bears some similarities. There are three elements to a Jewish wedding, the *birkat erusin*, the blessing of engagement; the giving of a ring with a legal vow; and the *Sheva Brachot* during the ceremony itself. Gibson explains: "I don't do *birkat erusin* at all for an interfaith couple because it says 'praised are you who are permitted partners to be with each other.' But the law does not permit these partners to be with each other, so that would be, in my broad language, a lie."

Gibson also doesn't perform the *Sheva Brachot* because they "weave a narrative of how two Jewish souls have been waiting for each other since Garden of Eden. And they finally found each other in fulfillment." "It's a great story," says Gibson, "but it is not the story of interfaith couples."

Which leaves him with the ring and the legal vow. In an Orthodox ceremony, a man gives a woman a ring and says, "Behold, I'm acquiring you because a woman who had no protection is going from a protected domain of her father to the protected domain of her husband." In almost all Jewish ceremonies, though, the groom says "Behold, you are consecrated to me with this ring according to the laws of Moses and Israel." But the laws of Moses and Israel say they can't marry, explains Gibson. So he has the bride and groom in an interfaith couple say, "Behold you are consecrated to me with this ring. *B'ahavat olam*, with an enduring love." Rabbi Gibson's attempt to tweak the words of a religious ceremony, but not too much (in his own estimation) is rather unusual.

In 2008, *New York* magazine published a directory of folks willing to officiate at interfaith ceremonies. "For many interfaith and same-sex couples, finding the right officiant can be more challenging than meeting the parents. Fortunately, New York is full of ministers and rabbis willing to unite all couples. We've sought out those most willing to personalize the ceremony according to your wishes, however unorthodox."[6]

The wishes of the couples I interviewed were rarely unorthodox. They weren't trying to go out of their way to be different. Rather, they wanted the attendees to feel comfortable, while at the same time making clear that the words they were reciting reflected the deep significance they attached to the occasion.

Take Sheila and Mark, who met while working at a newspaper in Southern California. She was the product of an interfaith marriage, though her family practiced Judaism more than Christianity when she grew up in New Jersey. Mark came from a strongly Catholic household in Illinois. Sheila had only positive things to say about her experience with the priest who married them. The couple had one very specific request for him. When they were constructing the ceremony, she says, "I asked him not to use the word Jesus, just call it 'our Lord.'" The priest was "completely open to that," she reports. Catholics "love the Old Testament, as they call it, so he was very good about including" some Jewish traditions, according to Sheila. Her grandmother even lit Shabbat candles at the end of the ceremony.

Pastor Mark Brewer finds couples' desire for Jesus not to be mentioned in the ceremony to be difficult to accommodate. "I'm licensed by the state of California. I could do a Buddhist wedding if I wanted. But I use Christian vows." He tells couples, "Since this is your wedding, I don't want to put words in your mouth." The couple needs to know that when they ask Brewer to perform a wedding, they are asking a Christian minister. He "respects the choices of interfaith couples," but he can't change the words he says.

The request that clergy leave out what could be considered a religiously specific name for God is not uncommon. I can think of at least three weddings I've attended where that was the compromise explained to me. Not surprisingly, perhaps, for Jewish-Christian couples in particular, this is a decision that seems to soothe the extended families.

When Nicole, the granddaughter of a Baptist preacher from Missouri, married a Muslim man from Amsterdam whom she met in college, the two found an interfaith minister to perform their ceremony. She says it was strange not having her grandfather do the wedding, but she didn't want to put her husband in an uncomfortable position. When they met with the officiant, "we told her we wanted the ceremony to refer only to God [not Allah or Jesus]. That's what we both believe in."

✧   ✧   ✧

It is, of course, not just the words that reflect the tone of the ceremony. The symbols of a wedding are perhaps just as important.

Jim Keen, the author of *Inside Intermarriage: A Christian Partner's Perspective on Raising a Jewish Family*, recalls his early discussions with his now-wife Bonnie about their wedding ceremony. He said, "Well, you know, I always thought I'd be married in a church." She said, "Well I always thought I'd be married in a synagogue." Eventually they agreed to be married in a civil ceremony by a friend of hers who was also a cantor.[7]

They went back and forth between Jewish and Christian elements of the ceremony. Ultimately, he says it was "a Jewish-ish wedding," which included a chupah and the breaking of the glass.

The symbols may be easier to compromise on than the words, though. There is not much variety from one tradition to the next about the significance of the ring. It symbolizes a promise. It is a circle. It has no beginning and no end. Some interfaith programs include unity candles or sand ceremonies (where sand of different colors is poured into one container to symbolize the mixing of the families and traditions).

There are cases in which couples use symbols that have a particular religious meaning and make them universal. The most common explanation for the breaking of the glass at the end of a Jewish wedding ceremony is that it is meant to signify the destruction of the Temple. As the Chabad website would have it: "The broken glass represents the wreckage of our past glory, and the destruction of the ancient Temple in Jerusalem in the first century. It recalls, at the most joyous and momentous occasion of the life cycle, that there is a continuing national sadness. It is a memory of Zion that stands as a reminder that in life great joy can be cancelled by sudden grief. It enriches the quality of joy by making it more thoughtful and by inspiring gratitude for the goodness of God. It is customary to recite the following words when breaking the glass: 'If I forget Thee, O Jerusalem, may my right hand fail . . . at the height of my joy.'"

Needless to say, this is not a message that resonates much with non-Jews. And so there are many alternative explanations employed in interfaith ceremonies for the breaking of a glass. *Interfaith Wedding Ceremonies* offers a few: "One is that the loud noise . . . scares away evil spirits wishing harm to the newly married couple." Another is that the broken glass signifies "the frailty of human relationships." Another is that while this marriage signifies joy, "the world is still in turmoil" and that its breaking is an "expression of hope for a future free from all violence."[8]

The wedding ceremony is a celebration but it is also the sealing of a contract. While the ways in which the contract is sealed—with a glass breaking or an Apache prayer, whether the person putting his signature on the contract is a judge or an imam, whether the wedding is in a hotel ballroom or a Catholic church—are certainly important from a symbolic perspective, the substance of the promises made in that contract seem more significant.

There are some, like fidelity, that are the same across religious traditions. There are some, like "listening without judging," that seem like they are difficult to enforce, let alone measure. But the promises about the particulars—the question of how a couple will live out their days together—are rarely mentioned. Few interfaith ceremonies, for instance, will discuss how children will be raised.

Clergy don't want to push their luck. The Catholic Church used to require that the non-Catholic promise to raise children in the Catholic Church. The notion was offensive to some, like a child is part of a trade. In fact, as part of the reforms of Vatican II, the Catholic Church decided that it could not in good conscience make such a request. Now, as Fr. Andrews explains, "It's up to the Catholic to reaffirm his or her faith, and then promise to do all in his or her power to rear the children Catholic and baptize them Catholic." Now the non-Catholic needs only to acknowledge that his or her partner made that promise to the church. "It still doesn't guarantee that the kids will be Catholic. I always tell people, 'If it doesn't make a difference or if it's positive for your family life, we would ask you to baptize.'"

Perhaps the church is catching more flies with this honey-based approach. And other religious leaders have told me that they see the wedding and its preparations as a time to make a good impression on the person who is not a member of the same faith. There may be limits to the extent to which religious leaders will compromise on the words and rituals of the day, but most try to be as compassionate about it as possible.

Many also take the opportunity to invite the new couple to come to religious services. Rabbi Daniel Schwartz of Temple Shir Shalom in West Bloomfield, Michigan, talks to interfaith couples before their weddings about raising their kids as Jews and what it means to be part of the Jewish community. And then he offers them a free membership to the synagogue for the first year. It's "a wedding gift from the congregation," he says. It is meant to signify that both the rabbis and the congregants are "here when questions arise for you guys as you're exploring this and trying to figure out how to create this Jewish household."

The wedding ceremony and the preparations for it are the first time that many interfaith couples come into sustained contact with a religious leader. For some, it is the first time they can have their questions answered about another faith and the first time that they are questioned about their own beliefs and whether they understand what it means to enter an interfaith marriage. Increasingly, religious leaders are worried that this will also be their last contact with a couple. As we discussed earlier, young adults are falling off in their religious observance and attendance. The question for clergy remains: How can a wedding ceremony be the beginning and not the end of a couple's relationship to a religious community? As one priest told me, churches tend to see many people only when they are "they're hatched, matched and dispatched." If they don't have a good experience being "matched," then things may not look good for what happens when they decide to "hatch" their own.

CHAPTER FOUR

◆

Passing It On

THERE ARE ABOUT ONE MILLION MEMBERS OF THE DRUZE FAITH in the world and Oran is one of them. The Druze are monotheists whose faith dates back to the eleventh century and combines Jewish, Christian, Gnostic, and Neoplatonic elements. The population is mostly concentrated in the Middle East, though a significant number of Druze have moved to Europe and the United States in recent decades. Unrest in Lebanon in the 1970s resulted in one significant exodus, particularly of Druze men. Oran grew up in a small village there and came to the United States almost forty years ago for medical training.

It was then that he met Amelia, a nurse at the hospital where he worked, and decided to stay here. Amelia didn't know anything about her husband's religious background. She was a lapsed Catholic, though she had grown up in a very religious home and community in Ohio—her uncle became a member of a religious order and her grandmother, who lived down the street, prayed the rosary every night and listened to Bishop Fulton Sheen's radio address on Sundays, often with Amelia at her side.

Oran had only a basic grasp of Christianity—and American Catholicism in particular. When the time came, the two had a Catholic wedding because

Amelia said it was important to her (they asked the priest to leave the word "Jesus" out of the ceremony to make Oran and his family more comfortable). For a few years afterward, they made no effort to incorporate faith into their lives. "I respect Amelia's background and who she is, but until we had kids," Oran explains, "I didn't feel we needed a religious home or faith."

Oran's attitude is fairly typical of interfaith couples I interviewed—and of Americans in general. Most become more interested in questions of religion once they begin to have children. Even the ones who are fairly observant to begin with find that children concentrate the religious mind—they force husbands and wives to think about what it means to create a religious home. Once interfaith couples have children, going their own ways to religious services and holiday celebrations no longer seems like a workable solution.

Deciding how to raise children is probably the highest hurdle interfaith parents face. In general, American parents find it important that the children carry on in their faith—according to my survey, 42 percent say it is very important and another 27 percent say it is somewhat important. But, not surprisingly, those in interfaith couples are much less likely to say it is very important to pass along their religion to their children (32 percent vs. 56 percent).

There is also a significant amount of variation by faith. Religious traditions differ in the importance placed on intergenerational transmission of the faith. Mormons, Jews, evangelicals, and black Protestants are all more likely than Catholics and mainline Protestants to place a lot of importance on passing one's religion along to the next generation.

The decision about how to raise children is not a single discrete event. There are choices that parents have to make every year—if not every day— about how religion will be practiced in the household, what kinds of ceremonies to adopt, how strict observance should be, how to answer children's questions about important issues like death or sex. Religious practice is dynamic. Few families keep rituals exactly the same year in and year out. Not only do parents change their minds about what is important, but children start to express their own preferences at a certain age. If a child simply does not take to religious education, for instance, how much will parents push?

In addition, all sorts of outside factors affect a family's religious practice— a new minister with a different preaching style takes over at church, a grandparent who used to host holiday meals passes away, tuition for religious school goes up. Couples are often caught off guard by these changes. They feel they have achieved agreement on their religious practice and are ready to move on to other discussions. But faith keeps coming up.

For many religious leaders and parents, the question of raising children in an interfaith marriage is a question of results. How did the kids turn out? Were they confused? Do they practice any faith as adults? Did they rebel? Did our team win or lose?

According to data taken from the 2006 Faith Matters survey, there were some differences between the ways that people who were raised in interfaith and same-faith homes practiced religion as adults. Of those raised by parents who practiced different religions, 37 percent reported weekly or near-weekly attendance at religious services compared with 42 percent of those raised by parents with the same faith (table 4.1). Similarly, a higher percentage of adults who were raised in interfaith homes reported having no religious affiliation when compared with adults raised in same-faith homes—19 percent versus 15 percent. These are both statistically significant differences, but they are not as large as some religious leaders might have suspected. Additionally, there was no difference in the frequency of prayer reported by adult children of same-faith and interfaith parents and no difference on the level of importance that they placed on religion.[1]

When thinking about "results," it is important to keep in mind something every parent knows. Children are malleable—but they are also unpredictable. Raising kids is a long-term process—some mothers and fathers believe that it doesn't end even when children reach adulthood. Some religious communities are more adept than others at retaining members, but there is no foolproof formula for creating an adult with faith. Even siblings who have the same religious upbringing may turn out completely differently.

TABLE 4.1 Frequency of Religious Attendance

	Parents had same religion	Parents did not have same religion
Weekly/Nearly weekly religious attendance	42	37
No religious affiliation	15	19

I imagine that my parents have puzzled from time to time over the fact that they gave my sister and me almost identical religious upbringings (including Jewish day school, an after-school Hebrew high school program, bat-mitzvahs, etc.), and yet I am married to a non-Jew while she is married to an Orthodox rabbi. In some ways, though, it is not surprising at all. We have different personalities, different political views, different intellectual interests, and different hobbies. If our religious views were the same, they would be the exception.

✦ ✦ ✦

For some couples, like Oran and Amelia, religion doesn't seem like it has ever been a particularly contentious issue. Despite the fact that they were raised on opposite sides of the world in different cultures and different faiths, Oran says their "values are very similar." When asked about those things they hold in common, both Amelia and Oran agree that the "world religions" have the same basic tenets—"God and goodness and helping others."

When their first child was born, the couple wanted "to be able to have the children share those values." They sensed that their children would need "a push not just from home, not just from the parental examples," as Amelia puts it.

So they went church shopping in the Atlanta area, where they live. For reasons neither can explain, the local Catholic parish was the last church on their list. Perhaps Amelia didn't want to push her own faith on Oran, but hoped instead to place them on equal spiritual footing as parents. In the end, though, Oran was the one who said he liked the Catholic Church best. "I personally enjoy the Mass service and the ritual."

Though many adults tend to look for something familiar in a church, Oran had the opposite reaction. He didn't grow up with that kind of ritual. His religious upbringing was, in his telling, "whatever you want to do. We didn't have a structure. We have our saints and our sanctuaries and monasteries in the mountains and beliefs and information, but I didn't have a frame." He recalls visiting remote shrines, lighting votive candles, and giving donations, but not much else in the way of regular religious ceremony or prayer. When he encountered Catholicism for the first time, Oran liked the "guidance" it offered. In this sense, it was not simply their common values that allowed Oran and Amelia to agree on a faith. It was also their shared feelings about what kinds of rituals and day-to-day practice they were looking for.

Even now, decades after their first visit to the Catholic church, Amelia remembers how the priest was standing outside the door before mass, "welcoming people." She believes that set the tone for the couple. "As time has gone on we have become more regular participants." Oran, she says, "can walk into Mass anytime he wants. Every priest at that parish knows his name." When their kids, who are now twenty-seven and thirty, were growing up, the family generally went to mass most Sundays. The monsignor once asked Oran if he would like to convert but Oran declined. He considers himself a "non-Catholic member" of a Catholic parish.

Another reason that it was rather easy for Amelia and Oran to decide to bring up their children Catholic was that, as far as Oran is concerned, it's virtually impossible to raise children as Druze outside of, say, Lebanon, Syria, and Israel. Much of the faith is based on visits to particular holy sites. The religion does not translate well to a suburban American context. Moreover, there is basically no provision in the Druze religion for intermarriage or even for conversion. In some of the communities in the Middle East, marrying out results in total excommunication. This policy didn't fly with Druze in the United States, as one might expect. A number of years ago, Oran heard that the American Druze Society announced that children of Druze and non-Druze parents would be considered Druze (in part to address the problem of a significant gender imbalance of Druze who had come to the United States). But the organization is not invested with any theological authority, so he wasn't sure what this would mean.

Oran was surprised, then, when he returned to his village a few years ago to find the names of all his family members in the village records. He was listed as Druze, his wife as Catholic and his children as Druze.

Though he was happy to share some cultural traditions with his children—taking them once or twice to national conventions of other Druze—he and Amelia made a very conscious decision to raise their children Catholic. He attended church with the family, something that pleasantly surprised Amelia. She was prepared, she tells me, to bring the kids on her own. In fact, Amelia feels that Oran sent a stronger message in his attendance than if he were Catholic himself. "The kids knew he wasn't Catholic, but he was demonstrating to the kids, 'This is something important to do . . . the priest is up there sharing information with you that's good information.'"

Both Amelia and Oran see the Catholic faith in a vaguely utilitarian way, as a tool to help teach their children to be better people. Amelia clearly has a deeply felt attachment to the church, but she questions several of its teachings. She never worried about Oran not being baptized because "there's an awful lot of non-baptized good people in the world who probably deserve to be someplace other than purgatory." In fact, Amelia takes the church's changes in the doctrine on purgatory, as well as reforms of the Second Vatican Council, as evidence that her faith's particulars are malleable. "I think there are things that are dynamic and have a human input, and then there are components of religion that are universal to almost all religions . . . something similar to the Ten Commandments."

Neither one of their sons attend church now except when they visit their parents for holidays. The older one just married an Episcopalian. The ceremony took place in the Episcopal cathedral, but he did insist on having the wedding co-officiated by a Catholic priest. Oran and Amelia think there is a good chance their kids will return to the faith in some form or another as they form their own families, but it is not something that seems to worry them one way or the other.

Amelia and Oran may be an unusual religious match, but they are actually fairly typical in many of their decisions. To begin with, more than three-quarters (77 percent) of Americans say that "parents should provide a religious upbringing for their children." Only 23 percent said that "children should choose whether to be raised in a religion." There is a small difference between people in an interfaith versus of same-faith marriage, although majorities of both take the view that parents should provide religious guidance: 84 percent of same-faithers, compared to 75 percent of inter-faithers.

The desire to bring up children in a particular faith can come on suddenly, just when the child is born. Peggy had fallen away from her Mormon faith and was married to Bret, a follower of Christian Science, for two years before they had their first child.

As Peggy recalls, "There's a baby and then all of the sudden it's like everything, the whole world changed." She thought she was going to go back to work, but suddenly decided to stay home. And she thought she didn't care about religion, but suddenly she did. "I called the ward [a local Mormon religious community] up here and asked if I could have the baby blessed . . . It was kind of a surprise because that's how abrupt it was. It was like he's born and, well now I have to, now all of the sudden these doors started opening up everywhere. You have to think about this."

Sometimes, when faith surprisingly becomes important to one partner after having a child, it can cause serious tensions. But Bret didn't seem to mind Anne's new embrace of Mormonism.

He has found the people in their ward to be "so open and so warm and so friendly." Initially, he says he didn't understand the Book of Mormon at all. But that didn't really bother him. He was more interested in "experiencing the people and how they practiced. That was the clincher for me." Once he became more familiar with the community, he wondered, "How could this be wrong for my kids? . . . [The Mormons] were just kind, loving people. What got me the most was how service-oriented they are, and how they're not looking for any pat on the back or accolade when they perform service. It's just pure kind of thank you for letting me serve you." He remembers wondering, "Wow, are people really like this?" Looking back, he knows he made the right decision. "I have a very soft spot in my heart for all the people that have . . . helped raise our kids."

Many of the men and women I interviewed who agreed to raise their children in their spouse's faith despite their own theological misgivings praised the people in that religious community and expressed a heartfelt desire for their children to be part of such a community.

It's been almost a quarter of a century and, despite these warm feelings toward the faith, Bret has not converted to Mormonism. He listens politely, even thoughtfully, to the missionaries who come visit him. (He has a habit of tearing up when he is talking about spiritual things, and I can't help but wonder how many missionaries think they have gotten through to him when they notice him weeping during their conversations.) Interestingly, he says that one of his biggest sticking points when it comes to the LDS theology is their exclusive claim to truth:

> The one thing that has kept me back up until now has been that the Mormon religion believes that they're the one true church. So well what about my church? It was pretty good. And all these other churches that people are really getting some good and benefit out of. So I always felt like everybody that was practicing a religion, no matter what it was, if it's helping them and making them a better person, it's great.

Despite this hang-up, Peggy actually remains convinced that her husband will eventually convert. She hasn't pressured him. "I know that Bret is going to be baptized and I don't have any problem with him waiting," she tells me as he listens. Peggy herself was not very active in the church as a child and her parents were only recently "sealed," the Mormon rite that, they believe, enables a marriage to endure beyond death and is limited to devout church members. In other words, she has seen how people's religious beliefs and behavior can evolve over long periods of time.

Bret has fallen away somewhat from his own practice of Christian Science. He goes to church with his parents on holidays and attends testimony meetings sometimes, but regularly sees doctors when the need comes up. (Generally, Christian Scientists believe that adherents can heal themselves through prayer and therefore eschew medical treatment.) Bret and Peggy actually dated for a time in high school, and she ended the relationship in part because she could not imagine calling in a Christian Science practitioner instead of a doctor if anything happened to him. So Bret has made some compromises in his own religious practice as part of his relationship. Still, he says he "continues to practice what I was raised with every day. So I'm not studying it every day. But I feel like I'm implementing it every day."

Bret and Peggy now have five children between the ages of seventeen and twenty-three. The oldest, who was planning to propose to his girlfriend on the day I visited them, had recently returned from a two-year stint as a Mormon missionary in North Carolina. Throughout their childhood, Bret attended services with them on Sundays, though he only stayed for the early part. The later part, he felt, was less inclusive of religious seekers. Bret supported the kids' religious education and after-school endeavors. And when it came time for them to serve a full-time mission (which is not required but is strongly encouraged by the church, particularly for men), Bret actually pushed the kids harder than his wife did. Peggy said she had difficulty imagining her kids being off on their own like that. But she remembers that "as Bret spent time listening to adults talk about their missions as the highlight of their lives," he became convinced this was the right thing for his own kids. "It probably matured them ten years in two years," he says. "They come back a whole different person."

✦ ✦ ✦

Like Peggy, many parents feel the first pangs of wanting to raise a child in a particular faith when the time comes to discuss a birth ceremony. Baptism for Catholics and the Brit Milah, or circumcision ceremony, for Jewish boys, are the two most urgent of these rituals. The latter is supposed to take place on the eighth day after a boy is born. The Catholic baptism is supposed to take place within the first couple of months.[2]

Birth ceremonies seem, from my interviews, to be the source of significant conflict. The urgency with which some Catholic and Jewish parents feel the need to act can make some partners nervous, though others are understanding. In the case of one couple who had agreed to raise their children Jewish, the mother told the Catholic father that she would let him baptize the children anyway if it would make him feel less concerned about the state of their souls. He declined.

Obviously the circumcision issue may cause conflict for reasons other than religion, particularly if the non-Jewish member of a couple does not come from a culture where circumcision is common. As one Jewish man told me, the argument that he and his German (now ex-) wife had about circumcision was nothing less than a full-scale "war."

According to my survey, the children of interfaith marriages are less likely than same-faith couples' kids to have undergone baptism, ceremonial naming, or some other birth ceremony. But the percentages are high across the board. Just over half of same-faith parents say that their children have undergone such a ceremony. For interfaith couples, the number was 45 percent.

✦ ✦ ✦

The birth ceremony is in some ways just the opening gambit. This is simply what feels right to many adults. Having a baby can leave one bewildered, to say the least, and so it seems natural that we would try to repeat the things our own parents and grandparents did for their children.

Many couples simply cannot come to an agreement on how to raise their children religiously. I have spoken to couples with children who are six or seven years old and who might want to start some kind of religious education but they cannot agree on what kind. Even the couples who agree on a religious upbringing for children when they are dating may feel entirely different about the matter once a child actually arrives.

Julie grew up in a strongly Southern Baptist household in Alaska (her parents were originally from Oklahoma and Texas). She attended church on Wednesdays, Fridays, and twice on Sundays. But by the time she met her Catholic husband after high school, she was not deeply attached to her faith.

At first, they decided not to have children. This is actually a choice that is somewhat more common for interfaith couples. While 87 percent of same-faithers have children, 80 percent of inter-faithers do. That gap, while obviously not enormous, is statistically significant. In part, this may reflect the trend that interfaith couples are more likely to be older and also more likely to be on their second marriages. In general, though, religious people are more likely to have children and likely to have *more* children than non-religious people.

Twelve years into their marriage, Julie and her husband had a baby girl. They decided to wait until she was old enough and then let her pick a faith. Now their daughter is ten years old and the couple is at loggerheads. Julie's mother, who now lives with them, wants to take the daughter to church, and Julie is inclined to let her. But her husband is not. She says she is not surprised that they can't agree on this, but she is a little disappointed that her daughter will not have the experience she did. "I do feel that growing up, there was a closeness, and a definite feeling or belief in a direction that your life is taking, whereas now, I don't know where it's going."

If the couple does ever agree on what to do about their daughter's religious upbringing, it's not clear how it will change things. Bringing her to church for the first time as an adolescent will almost certainly not have the effect of replicating Julie's upbringing, in which she has no memories of *not* being part of a religious community. And given the attitudes of most adolescents, who don't tend to take kindly to the introduction of new forms of authority, their daughter may have no interest in church at all.

There are a lot of changes in a family's religious practice in the years after that birth ceremony. And when we asked couples whether their children had participated in an adolescent religious ceremony such as a confirmation or a bar mitzvah, the gap between same-faith and interfaith couples widened significantly. Forty percent of same-faith couples report that their child had such a ceremony compared to only 20 percent for interfaith couples. For religious leaders, this is an enormously significant change. It means that many interfaith couples have the intention of raising their children in a faith when they are young, but because of a variety of issues—including, in some cases, a lack of institutional support—the family falls away.

Adolescents, of course, have a general tendency toward rebellion; at least that's what Americans expect. And in same-faith households, there are no doubt plenty of teenagers who would prefer to sleep in on Sunday mornings while their parents go to church. As Christian Smith points out in his book *Souls in Transition*, religious parents often shirk their duties, perhaps believing the "cultural myth" that they have no influence over their children once they hit puberty. Smith has found, to the contrary, that, when it comes to religious faith and practice, "who and what parents were and are" is more likely to "stick" with emerging adults than the beliefs and habits of their teenage friends.[3]

But same-faith households can at least provide a united front when it comes to urging their children to take faith seriously. Many interfaith households do not. When they first got married, Marlys, who is Jewish (though not devout), agreed to raise her children in the Catholic faith of her husband Jack. When they were little, he often took the kids to church by himself, but they went less frequently as they got older. While no one suggested that Marlys was undermining the children's upbringing by telling them that Catholicism was wrong, it was clear that she offered them a different example. None of their kids identify as Catholics today and only one identifies as a Christian, according to Jack.

Sometimes the difference between a mother's and father's practices is even noted derisively by religious teachers or other members of the community. One Presbyterian mother in Atlanta recalled the time when her daughter's Catholic Sunday school teacher pointed out the mother's absence and said, "I see your mother is worshipping the pillow again."

Even if both parents attend religious services, the notion that one parent identifies himself as a member of a religion and the other does not is often enough to make adolescents wonder. Religion becomes more of a choice and less of an obligation. Obviously, when they get to be adults, these children of intermarried couples will recognize that they have a choice about faith, just like everyone else in this country. But that knowledge will come earlier. And it may have an effect on the likelihood that they continue to practice a particular faith as adults.

So what does the regular religious practice of interfaith families look like? The ceremonies we've discussed so far tend to take on all sorts of symbolic weight, particularly when viewed by the extended family and friends. But the day-to-day involvement in a religious community may be more significant in the long run.

Let's look first at the celebration of holidays. Religious holidays are celebrated by large majorities of people in both same-faith and interfaith couples. Eighty-two percent of respondents in interfaith marriages say they celebrate religious holidays, compared to 87 percent of those in same-faith marriages. The particulars of those rituals may differ in sub-stance (a subject we will discuss in greater detail shortly), and we have no way of distinguishing in the survey between major and minor holidays. But the numbers are remarkably similar. About 67 percent of same-faith couples say they celebrate holidays in their own home compared to about 64 percent of interfaith couples. One might expect that interfaith couples would be more likely to celebrate elsewhere because they are keeping a less religious home generally or that they are more likely to celebrate in their own home so that the spouses who do not observe the faith are not put in any awkward positions. (Is the Muslim son-in-law expected to eat the traditional Christmas ham?) But perhaps these two factors simply cancel each other out.

Frequency of religious attendance tells a similar story. Children of interfaith couples attend religious services less frequently than those with same-faith parents. However, the reported rate of religious service atten-dance is extremely high for both types of families. That high rate is pre-sumably inflated owing to social desirability bias—people want to be seen as providing a religious education for their children. But even accounting for that bias, for many American families, religion is "for the kids." For example, roughly half of parents in interfaith marriages report that their children attend religious services frequently ("several times a year" to "sev-eral times a week"). That is certainly lower than children of parents in same-faith marriages, where the rate is between 60 and 70 percent, but it is still quite high.

Even in cases where a mother and father have decided to raise kids in one faith and, as with Marlys, the parent whose faith is not being practiced has no objection to the children attending religious services, it is easy to see why religious attendance would not rise to the level of a same-faith couple. Leaving aside the question of whether the members of an interfaith couple are less religious to begin with—that is, whether self-selection accounts for some of this difference—it is also the case that religious attendance is gen-erally a family activity. One parent might feel awkward taking children to religious services without the other parent. Even logistically, it can be diffi-cult to accomplish this with young children. Who is going to sit with the five-year-old while the younger child is crying and needs to leave the room? Saturdays and Sundays are also times that families are typically together. And attending religious services without one parent would inevitably cut into that family time.

My survey also looked at whether parents pray or read scripture with their children, or have their children participate in religious education: Same-faith parents are more likely to do these things than interfaith ones, but the overall percentages are high for both groups. Roughly half (47 percent) of parents in interfaith marriages say that they pray or read scripture with their children, compared to three-fifths of same-faith parents. About a third (34 percent) of inter-faithers say that they send their children to religious education, compared to 47 of same-faithers.[4]

The gap between same-faith and interfaith couples on each of these measures is quite similar, but the measures themselves are different in one important way. One is a home-based ritual while the other involves an institution. Each presents its own challenges for interfaith couples. Performing home-based rituals in the presence of the spouse whose religion is not being passed on to the children can make that partner feel uncomfortable. Where should she or he go when you are lighting candles on Shabbat or discussing passages from the Qur'an or praying with the kids before bedtime? To what extent is it acceptable for the nonmember to participate or even to observe?

The advantage of home-based rituals for interfaith families is that they can make these decisions for themselves and adjustments can be made so that everyone is reasonably comfortable. Just as with wedding ceremonies, the wording of blessings can be altered or certain more exclusionary parts can be skipped over altogether.

Sending children for religious education means that other people will be interpreting the faith for your children or at least helping them interpret it. Outsourcing the religious education of children in interfaith families may seem like a good solution—once a decision has been made, it may produce less conflict than, say, deciding whether to go to a mosque as a family every week. And the socialization with children in the same faith will probably lead to a greater sense of religious identity over time.[5]

Members of interfaith couples who are trying to raise children in a particular faith report that religious institutions are simply invaluable in these efforts. Alissa, a Catholic woman married to a Jewish man, calls her family's involvement in their synagogue "essential." She says, "We've got a big support network there." She thinks at least 20 percent of the congregation is made up of interfaith families and she herself has been able to take adult education courses there. "I want to know what they are talking about in the religious school." Not only does she want to grasp the religious principles they are teaching but she also wants to make sure that her children are being treated as legitimate members of the community. She says she never wants a child of hers "to come home and say, 'Mommy, they don't think I'm Jewish because you're not Jewish.'" If that happens, Alissa says, "I'll lose it." I heard a similar sentiment from a woman who told me that her son's Sunday school teacher told him that his mother was going to hell because she wasn't a Catholic.

An association with religious institutions can also help families to observe some rituals that might usually be home-based. Breaking the fast of Yom Kippur or Ramadan at the synagogue or mosque surrounded by one's coreligionists is easier than doing it at home where one partner might not want to participate.

I also looked at what kinds of rituals seem to have more of an effect on a child's religious upbringing. Do some types of rituals have a bigger impact on religious socialization, or specifically on whether children remain in a faith?[6]

To find out, I relied on the question about "adolescent rituals" (confirmation, bar/bat mitzvah, etc). The decision to participate in such a ritual marks a greater commitment to a religious identity than does an infant ceremony (naming, blessing, baptism, etc). Note that these percentages exclude people who say that their religion has no such ceremony or that their child is not old enough for the ceremony (meaning that they are not counted, and thus are not artificially pushing the percentages down). I define institutional participation as parents' frequency of religious attendance, and home-based religion as whether parents report praying and/or reading scripture with their children at home.

There is some difficulty in untangling these two factors—home practice and institutional practice typically go together. While there are a reasonable number of families who have low religious attendance and still report praying or reading religious material at home, there is only a negligible number who attend services frequently but do not participate in religious activity at home.

Table 4.2 reports, for interfaith families, the incidence of adolescent religious rituals in four types of families:

1. Low/Medium Religious Attendance and Do Not Pray/Read

2. Low/Medium Religious Attendance and Do Pray/Read

3. High Religious Attendance and Do Not Pray/Read

4. High Religious Attendance and Do Pray/Read

TABLE 4.2   Religious Socialization in Interfaith Families Families with adolescents only

	Low/Medium attendance + Do Not Pray/ Read	Low/Medium attendance + Pray/Read	High attendance + Do Not Pray/ Read	High attendance + Pray/Read
Adolescent Ceremony	11 (98)	24 (50)	31 (7)	41 (37)

Parentheses indicate the number of cases in each cell.

Not surprisingly, families that participate in more religious activity—whether at home, away from home, or both—are more likely to have their children participate in religious rites of passage. The numbers are small, but it would appear that institutional participation (attending religious services) is a better predictor of adolescent rituals than is home-based religion alone.

When we test the simultaneous impact of both a parent's religious attendance and whether they pray or read religious texts at home, it is the former that offers a statistically significant predictor of adolescent rituals. One reason for this may be that institutional participation increases child's socialization with other members of the faith and that in turn strengthens their identification. Also, the adolescent ritual is itself institutional in most cases. So if you are already committed to institutional involvement, you might be more likely to participate.

There are obviously a number of other factors that influence the religious upbringing of a child of an interfaith marriage. It matters, for instance, which parent holds to which faith. While the religions themselves have rules about this—children of a Jewish mother are considered Jewish; children of a Muslim father are considered Muslim—these rules can be no match for the norms of American society. Generally, the mother's faith is a bigger factor. Roughly a third of children of interfaith marriages are being raised in the religion of their mother, while only about 15 percent are growing up in their father's faith. This gap seems to persist no matter what the age of the children.

There are a variety of explanations for this. First, women in the United States are generally more religious than men are. For decades, there has been about a 10-point gap between the percentage of women who attend church weekly and the men who do so—usually more than a third of women and around a quarter of the men. It's much more likely that a woman would bring her children to religious services without her husband than that a man would go without his wife. Second, the wife will have more of an influence over home-based rituals—like whether Hindus set up an altar for prayers or whether Jews keep a kosher kitchen. And finally, during the week, mothers are more often in charge of scheduling and ferrying children to activities. If they want the kids to be attending some form of religious education, they will make it happen themselves.

✦　✦　✦

Once a couple has agreed to raise their children in a particular faith, the project's success or failure (if one is willing to put it in such stark terms) depends on the level of commitment of the parent who shares the child's religion but also of the attitude of the nonmember. Amelia found herself in the fortunate situation of having a husband who supported personally and fully the children's Catholic upbringing, despite the fact that he wasn't Catholic.

This was true for many of the couples I interviewed. In particular, non-Jews married to Jews seemed to be very supportive of the decision to raise kids Jewish. Harvey Cox, a professor at Harvard Divinity School who is married to a Jewish woman, told me that he knew that their children would be raised Jewish because in Judaism, the mother determines the child's faith.[7] Another Catholic man married to a Jewish woman told me: "If your mother is Jewish, then by definition you are Jewish." Christianity, in his view, "is really an adult choice that you make. . . . It's not by birth."[8]

That is not, obviously, the beginning and end of it for most couples. The child of a Methodist father presumably has just as much of a claim to be Methodist. But the issue of interfaith marriage has become so important in Jewish circles in recent years that many non-Jews readily agree to raise children Jewish. We'll look more at these community attitudes in a later chapter, but in interviewing individual couples, it has been interesting to hear that many of the non-Jews are often pushing Jewish spouses toward greater observance of their Jewish faith.

Sally was definitely giving up something when she decided to raise her kids Jewish. She worried about missing Christmas, about her children not having their first communion, about not going to mass. But once David told her that he really couldn't raise kids anything but Jewish, she made a decision to compromise. And then she told him, "If we're going to do it, we're going to do it right." So while David was not a particularly involved Jew before they married, Sally has made sure the family attended services every week. In other words, Sally took the rigor of the religious Christian upbringing she had as a child and imposed it on the religion her family was going to practice.

David has been surprised by this development. His marriage "has forced me to be much more active and engaged and involved. . . . If I had married someone Jewish, I guarantee I would be coming to synagogue on the High Holidays and that's it."

When I asked people in interviews about what they felt were the biggest surprises in their interfaith marriages, many say they never would have predicted that they would be so involved in religious practice at all. Whether it is becoming more involved in their own religious community or in that of their spouse, many respondents would have predicted on the day of their wedding that they would be foregoing religious commitment. But things turned out otherwise.

CHAPTER FIVE

———◆———

The December Dilemma

ABOUT TWENTY YEARS AGO, ELISE OKREND WAS AN ARTIST working for an advertising agency in New York. She was in her early thirties, and she noticed that many of her friends and family members (including her brother) were marrying people of different faiths. It occurred to her that there was a marketing opportunity here. Interfaith couples needed interfaith holiday cards. And other people needed cards they could send to their friends in interfaith marriages without offending them.

So Okrend started to doodle. She joined a Christmas tree to a Star of David. She drew trees with menorahs on them. She sketched elves spinning dreidels. She didn't want anything "over the top" or "tacky," she tells me. When she had a few samples, she showed them to her coworkers. Before long, Okrend had launched a company called MixedBlessing and found that more and more stores were demanding her products. The business has thrived and she has added other lines of cards, some with symbols of Kwanzaa, some with peace signs. There are now cards with pictures of Santa's hat and a yarmulke and one with a Star of David and a Yin and Yang symbol.

When her business launched, some were upset by her idea. Okrend reports getting angry letters and even finding a newspaper article accusing her of inappropriately diluting religious traditions. Mind you, there is something a little ham-handed about Okrend's designs. They are perhaps typical of some of the initial attempts at happy-clappy multiculturalism that marked America in the 1980s. People still hold similar sentiments today of course—we may look different, but at bottom we all believe the same things, share the same values, etcetera—but Americans seem to have become a little more sensitive about merging different religious traditions. And the interfaith couples I've interviewed seem disinclined to water down or mix up religious messages, let alone do it for the sake of sending out cutesy greeting cards.

There are still some attempts to present holidays to children in this way—perhaps the theory is that children are not sophisticated enough to understand or cope with real differences. One popular book called *Light the Lights*, by Margaret Moorman, describes a girl named Emma first lighting the menorah and then putting lights on her Christmas tree. After warm holiday celebrations with her family on both occasions, the story ends: "She remembered the bright winter lights in the dark winter nights for a long time."[1] The notion that Hanukkah and Christmas are both ultimately celebrations of light is now common in certain settings, but it requires an extraordinary dilution of both religious occasions—the birth of the savior and a Jewish military victory over religious persecution—in order to arrive at this point.

For the most part, interfaith cards—and other paraphernalia—seem kitschy now. Chanukah bushes and Christmukkah celebrations are punchlines. Such interfaith feel-good rituals were even sent up on *Seinfeld*. Festivus, the winter holiday started by George Costanza's father on the wildly popular sitcom, is supposedly an answer to the commercialism of Christmas. (George was too cheap to buy Christmas gifts for his coworkers and when he was caught, explained that his family celebrated Festivus growing up and were persecuted for their beliefs.) Festivus ("for the rest of us") is a mock response for those who feel bad that they can't participate in the majority culture's holidays. So they make up their own. Festivus rituals include putting up a bare aluminum pole (perhaps the ultimate anti-commercialism symbol) and the "airing of grievances" around the dinner table.

There are many Jews who have simply made their peace with Christmas, getting their own Christmas tree, celebrating with Christian friends, or making a ritual out of eating Chinese food and going to the movies. But the larger culture has become increasingly sensitized to the beliefs and practices of minority religions. Public schools regularly include Chanukah songs in their "winter" concerts even if there are no Jews attending the school. Retail establishments have told workers to say only "Happy Holidays," but nothing more specific. And Americans don't want to leave out anyone's holidays, either. Someone recently forwarded me an email from an administrator at a Catholic College who worried that Ramadan was not going to coincide with the period when classes were in session for the next few years. So he sent out a note to all faculty wishing the handful of Muslims on campus a peaceful holiday several weeks in advance.

All of this has made it easier to be a non-Christian in America around the Christmas season. (Though some might argue that the lengthening of the season—it now starts around Halloween in some stores—has made matters more difficult.) But there has been another interesting development. Minority faiths seem to have grown less interested in accommodating themselves to the Christian culture. Many Jews—even somewhat observant ones—who grew up fifty years ago had no problem singing Christmas carols or going to visit the windows decorated for Christmas in New York City. But today, in some circles anyway, there seems to be much more concern about the slightest sign of accommodation to this culture.

My Jewish mother and father took me to visit those windows—on Christmas day when the crowds were smaller. My sister sang in an annual performance of *Amahl and the Night Visitors*, a one-act opera that tells the story of the Adoration of the Magi and is performed at Christmas time. We attended the Christmas parties of family friends. And none of it struck me as the least bit strange. My husband, on the other hand, never had a Christmas tree—with the exception of one year, before we were married, when I bought one for him. Indeed, he did not grow up with Christmas at all and his late mother, who was a Jehovah's Witness, was much stricter about keeping other religious influences out of his life than my parents were with me. It was only once he was an adult that he started sending out Christmas cards.

When we got married, Jason was a little surprised to find that even though we were raising our children Jewish, I had no problem with them watching a Dora the Explorer episode in which the main character meets Santa Claus. I wanted to take them to look at the Rockefeller Center Christmas tree, and I didn't mind listening to Christmas carols either. Of course, I knew all the words. I didn't mind the idea of sending out "holiday cards," but the wording of such greetings is something we continue to struggle with. Are we representing our beliefs or merely offering others good wishes in their celebrations?

Christians and Jews often like to push aside the question of whether it's okay for non-Christians to celebrate Christmas by pointing out the pagan origins of the Christmas tree or the fact that Santa was not the one sleeping in a manger. But I would not suggest that these Christmas rituals are not religious in nature. Who am I to say which parts of other people's traditions are connected to their faith? I just think that sometimes it's okay to watch and enjoy the way our fellow Americans celebrate their cultural and religious traditions.

But things get a little dicier when those "fellow Americans" are living in your house. I have heard many interfaith couples use the analogy of a birthday party to explain the celebration of holidays to children: You can help your friend celebrate his birthday by going to his party and singing and eating and giving him a present. It's not your birthday, but you can still participate. We can help dad celebrate Christmas even if it's not our holiday.

Americans are mostly reluctant to raise their children in more than one faith. Even if they make some compromises about allowing elements of other faiths to be observed, they would not call it a dual-faith home. According to my survey, about 80 percent of same-faith couples raised their kids in one faith and about 20 percent raised them in no faith. A plurality of interfaith couples, about 40 percent, agreed to raise their children in one faith. About a third are raising their kids with no faith; and another 20 percent are trying to raise them in both. Even parents of two different Christian denominations seem reluctant to raise children in both. A report from the Center for Marriage and Family at Creighton University found that more than three-quarters of parents in such "interchurch marriages," were raising children in one faith, while only 12 percent were raising them in both.[2]

Though the group of couples who report raising their kids in two faiths is smaller than many might have expected, it is worth looking at their experience in more depth. Also, we should acknowledge that it is difficult to define what it means to raise children in both faiths. There are purists who would say that any regular (even annual) exposure to a holiday like Easter would suggest that the children are being raised Christian, at least in part. Others would argue that they merely celebrate with family or that they tell their children it is not a religious holiday but merely an occasion to hunt for eggs.

When we look at the survey questions broken down by the age of the children, some interesting patterns emerge. For instance, in families with children under the age of five, 24 percent of respondents said they were raising kids in both faiths. That number dropped to 21 in couples with children age five to eleven and dropped again to 18 percent in families with kids age twelve to eighteen. Most of the interfaith couples I interviewed suggest that raising kids in both faiths is impractical or, in some cases, unfair to the children. It seems likely that as time went on and the kids got older, raising kids in two faiths seemed even more difficult or impractical.

Also, as one might expect, people who are raising children in two faiths are less likely than those raising children in their own faith to say that passing on their faith is important. For parents with children under five, for instance, only 28 percent of those who are raising their kids in both faiths said that it was very important to pass on their religion to their children. That's compared with 23 percent who are raising their kids in their spouse's religion, that is, those who have given up on passing on their own faith completely. In other words, passing on one's faith can feel important, but it is also something on which members of interfaith families often compromise. It is interesting that this compromise leads to a two-faith approach in only one out of five cases.

Religious leaders, not surprisingly, recommend against raising kids in both faiths—sometimes even if that means losing the child to another faith. Russell Moore, dean of the Southern Baptist Theological Seminary, tells me that he would rather have a couple choose another Protestant Church or even a Catholic one if they are going to go to church together as a family than have them try to raise children in two religious traditions with parents splitting duties. He won't marry a husband and wife who don't plan to be a part of the same church.

Jihad Turk of the Islamic Center of Southern California tells me that he regularly sees couples who want to bring up children in both religions or neither religion and then let the children make the decision. Turk says, "I think that's noble. I think that's great, but a three-year-old is not going to choose. You can't raise them this way because there are some real differences. Trinity or no trinity? Is Jesus the son of God, or is he not? There are some very fundamental tangible differences." Like many religious leaders and parents I spoke with, Turk cites "the psychology of the kid," as the reason to choose one faith for the family. He says, "you raise them within one tradition, and you do the ritual and the practice." He sees religion as a "discipline" in some sense. And picking and choosing among different faiths when children are young seems too loose of an approach for him. Turk himself was actually the product of a Christian mother and a Muslim father. The couple agreed to raise Turk and his siblings Muslim.

Sally told me that she and her husband never considered raising their children both in her Catholic faith and his Jewish one. They decided to raise them Jewish, and though Sally has not converted, she says, "they need to have a united front." Raising them in both "would be very confusing." Even as things stand now, she is regularly asked questions by her children about her own upbringing and beliefs. And her answers, she says, seem to befuddle them. She recalls once when her kids questioned her about Good Friday. She told them, "Jesus was this Jewish person that Christians view as the son of God. And he died and Friday is the day that he died. So when you see like a little cross, the way they killed him is they nailed him. So when you see like a dead body hanging on a cross that's what that is." She recalls that her children "were horrified."

Regardless of whether they say they are raising kids in one faith or two, most interfaith marriages seem to involve compromises. Maureen and Bob are one example of this type of arrangement. Maureen grew up Jewish in what she describes as a "Jewish-Italian neighborhood" in Brooklyn. Her father was so enamored of the actress Maureen O'Hara that he named his daughter after her, even though it wasn't a very Jewish-sounding choice. Her family attended a Reform synagogue, and she became very active in youth group activities there, particularly during her teenage years. At various points in her life, she attended Conservative and Orthodox synagogues too. For a while she dated a rabbi and says that she could have seen herself marrying him if she hadn't met Bob.

Bob grew up in what he describes as a "mixed" household in Chicago. His father was Catholic, his mother Presbyterian. He attended mass and Sunday school every week. When his parents got divorced, he and his brother lived with their mother but continued to go to Catholic mass on their own. Bob became an altar boy. As a teenager, he was also attracted to Young Life, an evangelical group at his high school. He continued his association with Young Life and then Campus Crusade for Christ in college, though he still thought of himself as a Catholic. He dated people of different faiths. The "key issue," he tells me, smiling, "was more if the girl was willing to go out with me." Toward the end of college, he began to fall away from his faith a bit. He married an Episcopalian girl he met in college. They had no kids and divorced within a couple of years.

Bob met Maureen when she showed up as a graduate student in a class he was teaching. She was twenty-six and still living with her parents. She came home from their second date and, despite the late hour, she insisted her mother guess the last name of the man she had gone out with, the man she was convinced she would marry. It was, of course, O'Hara.[3]

Bob and Maureen O'Hara agreed to raise their children Jewish. They knew they wanted to bring up their kids in one faith "because to do anything else is just to confuse kids and it's not fair to them," says Bob. But the family continued to celebrate Christmas and Easter in their home outside of Seattle. On Christmas, Bob read the kids the story of Jesus's birth from the Book of Matthew and they would watch *Amahl and the Night Visitors*. Maureen says she wanted to make sure that her kids didn't find Bob's traditions to be "alien" to them. The family attended a Reform synagogue and both of their sons were bar-mitzvahed there. The older one, who is in college, is not particularly religious today, but the younger one decided to attend a modern Orthodox high school, keeps a restricted diet (though not an entirely kosher one), and wears a yarmulke. According to his parents, he still makes out a Christmas list every year.

Bob went to church by himself when his kids were younger. And Maureen actually was happy to see that. She wanted her sons to know that "religion is not just something that mothers do." But the church's attitude toward divorce bothered him—he didn't have his first marriage annulled and so could not receive communion—and he has since stopped attending mass except on Christmas. Despite the observance of Christmas and Easter, the couple says they have a "Jewish household." That affects not only what happens inside their home, but how they present themselves to the outside world. While they do have a Christmas tree, they don't put up lights or Christmas decorations in their yard.

Inside a home, it is possible to make distinctions among the beliefs of different family members, but when it comes to putting up decorations outside the home or sending out holiday cards, the family is sending a message to others about its religious beliefs. There is not much room for nuance when there's a wreath on the door or a reindeer in the front yard. And that is an issue that many couples seem to have a hard time with. As Maureen told Bob, "That would be a line I'd be uncomfortable crossing."

✧ ✧ ✧

The issue of how holidays are celebrated is the one we focus on most often when we think about interfaith marriages. It is not just a cliché to say that the rituals surrounding holidays are among people's most cherished childhood memories. For many Christians, even the less religious ones, it is hard to imagine family life without a Christmas tree. For Jews, there is a deep attachment to the Passover Seder and even a sense of obligation to attend synagogue on the High Holidays. There are Muslims who don't find much occasion to go to a mosque during the rest of the year, but during Ramadan they feel a certain pull toward tradition.

Holidays have become like bargaining chips in many interfaith marriages. They test the limits of a couple's ability to compromise. Deborah Ross, a couples therapist who is based in the Washington, D.C., area, says that she has seen a real uptick in the number of interfaith couples who have come to her recently. She advises couples having disagreements about religion not to think about their resolution as a "compromise." Rather, she encourages them to think about how they can become "differentiated and linked." She thinks the former leads people to curtail their religious practices to avoid offending their spouse, which can result in resentment building up over time. The latter, though, allows people to "honor religious rituals by bringing them into the home." She advises couples to talk about what rituals they find meaningful and important rather than making the issue "what it says in the Bible or the Qur'an." This approach, she says, "leaves room for people to have their faith be a dynamic faith." Things that may be meaningful at one point in life may not be later and vice versa.

Some families see holidays as the best basis for forming a new religious identity, and their attitude becomes "the more the merrier." Dorit, an Israeli Jewish woman married to an Egyptian Muslim man, tells me that she takes such an approach to raising her son. She is happy to have him celebrate Muslim, Jewish, and even Christian holidays. They take him both to a mosque and to a synagogue where they live in Southern California. But they also want him to be able to observe Christmas with friends. "What I think," says Dorit, "is that we have only one God. There is not one for the Jews and one for the Muslims. This God created us all equal." She says her son doesn't need to be a "religious kid," but she wants him to understand that "we are all people born to God."

Still, attending holiday celebrations does raise questions for him, she acknowledges. And she does her best to avoid certain parts of them. When she has friends who are lighting candles for Chanukah, she calls and asks,

"Are they praying? Call me when they stop praying." In the mosque, too, she is happy to come for the celebrations after the prayers. "You can see your friends and eat the food."

Daha, a Sikh, and his wife, Haimi, a Hindu, also believe strongly that their children should be exposed not only to each other's holidays but also to those of other faiths. Haimi recalls that when she was growing up, her parents would put up a Christmas tree. "We do that for our children. We don't ever want our children to feel isolated. Those are great holidays. Why wouldn't we want to celebrate them? We have no problem. If it's a holiday, we'll celebrate it." Daha and Haimi also typically celebrate their respective holidays with their families. Indeed, they have asked both sets of grandparents to take an active role in raising the kids religiously.

The religious leaders in their faiths do not generally see any incompatibility between celebrating both Sikh and Hindu traditions. Srinivas Khedam, a priest at the Hindu Temple and Cultural Center outside of Seattle, explains that there is nothing in the scriptures to suggest that marrying outside the faith is a problem, just cultural "superstition." Khedam tells couples, "both faiths are equally important. You can raise [children] however you want to. Just look into your values and see what are most important for them."

But the Hindu-Sikh combination is uncommon in this respect. For the Abrahamic faiths, bringing up children in more than one tradition means you must get beyond the traditional meaning of the holidays or at least gloss over how the meanings of the holidays may contradict each other. Embracing holidays without acknowledging their underlying meaning does not seem like an option for most couples. When couples ask Rev. Bob Brashear of West Park Presbyterian Church in Manhattan for advice on how to navigate their holiday dilemmas, he responds, "it's what you do with the other 50 weeks of the year that matter. They make the holidays important or not important. If you don't have anything else happening the other 50 weeks, the holidays will have a giant intimidating presence. You're putting the weight of your whole religious tradition and culture on a couple of days." Rev. Brashear, who is himself married to a Jewish woman and whose own children were raised in the Jewish tradition but exposed to Christian holidays, says that "You have to work out what your ongoing weekly relationship [with your faith] is going to be. Then the other stuff will take care of itself."

✦   ✦   ✦

A number of interfaith couples I spoke with really wanted their children to understand and take seriously both religious traditions. And they did want to engage the issue in months other than December. Those couples faced an uphill battle. Many tried but decided when the kids were young that it was too difficult.

Christopher and Rachel did not have a sense of how important religion was going to become for either one of them when they got married. Rachel says she did mention to Christopher before they got married that she wanted her children to be Jewish and that she wanted him to consider conversion. But she acknowledges that it was a pretty casual suggestion, and Christopher admits he didn't give it much more consideration than a suggestion that the two have Chinese food for dinner. Christopher, who was raised in a mainline Methodist Church but whose parents were often critical of organized religion and Christianity in general, told her he might consider converting. Again, the tone of his response, they both say, jokingly, was something along the lines of, "Sure, I'll try the shrimp fried rice."

Shortly after their first son was born, Christopher's father became ill. Christopher was also doing fieldwork for a dissertation that brought him into contact with serious Christians for the first time, he says. "I was very impressed with them. They were self-sacrificing and adopted children. They weren't rapaciously pursuing their own happiness. They were admirable and I think their example in a way helped me believe." After his father passed away, Christopher started reading the Bible and trying out different churches. Finally he decided to convert to Catholicism.

Meanwhile, after their son was born, Rachel says she "started to fantasize more about Jewish education" for him. Rachel and Christopher talked about religion for their children, and for a while Christopher said "it wasn't clear what we'd become. Things were in flux." Rachel made a big Easter dinner in honor of Christopher's conversion and the family attended church together. Christopher started participating in Sabbath rituals with the family at home, including saying the Kiddush, the blessing over the wine traditionally recited by the father of the household.

Christopher and Rachel did not consciously plan to raise kids in two faiths, but it was starting to happen anyway. Until the two realized they could not keep it up. Their son started asking questions about his father's church. Rachel didn't feel comfortable with the messages they were sending.

And Christopher didn't feel inclined to practice his religion by himself. "It was hard going to church alone. Sometimes it seemed I should get more involved but the consequence always seemed to be that it created more distance between me and my family." Christopher concludes that he wanted to be "one flesh tied to [Rachel]," which is the Catholic teaching on marriage. Instead he felt like he was trying to be a "sovereign self." Christopher and Rachel eventually concluded that two religions in one household simply wasn't feasible for either of them. In fact, the lesson they have taken away from the experience is rather stark. Christopher says, "I wouldn't want my children to intermarry, despite the fact that we have a happy family. Interfaith marriage is not good for faith or for marriage."

Others have had more luck with a two-faith solution. A woman named Ruth, profiled in the book *Interfaith Families*, explains, "The way we do things in our family, everything is very equal. All of the kids have my name as a middle name. We try to do everything half and half. We have Hanukkah and Christmas. We have Easter and Passover." In a way, Ruth realizes how unique her situation is and how delicate their balance has become. She says that she and her husband cannot agree on to whom they would entrust their kids if something ever happened to them. "The logical thing is for the kids to live with someone in one of our families. But by doing that, we would really be choosing for them to have a life that is only Catholic or only Jewish. . . . This is a discussion we've had over and over, especially every time we get on an airplane. We just can't decide."[4]

There are a few couples who seem to be able to find a balance of two faiths for their kids that satisfy the family. But it is not an easy path. Even members of couples who don't set out to make everything "equal" can grow resentful if it feels like their religious beliefs and celebrations are getting short shrift. Usually, things start off well enough. A number of interfaith spouses told me they did extensive research on their partner's faith. Women often learn to cook traditional dishes for their husbands' religious holidays. Some couples take classes together about one another's faith to understand them more deeply. And early on in a relationship, as we speculated, when kids are young, parents can have a lot more control over the kinds of religious rituals and education their children participate in. Parents can attempt to make things as "equal" as possible. But as children get older and begin to ask questions or simply become more attached to one religious community or another, it can easily upset the balance.

Certainly, this two-faith approach can force parents to be more intentional about exposing kids to faith. But it can also be exhausting and difficult. Living as an interfaith family in a vacuum can mean that every religious decision is a source of argument. Many of the couples look to find support and pool their knowledge and resources with other interfaith families.

Matthew and Helen met when he was in graduate school and she had just returned from the Peace Corps. He grew up in a small Conservative Jewish congregation in North Carolina, and she had grown up Catholic on the West Coast. (Her mother was Catholic, and her father was Lutheran.) The two were married by a judge; readings in the ceremony included passages from the Old and New Testaments. Once they were married they began to try out different religious institutions. From my interviews, this seems fairly unusual. Most of the interfaith couples I spoke with didn't seem to feel it necessary to find a religious institution until there were kids in the picture. Either they just stayed home or worshipped separately. But there was something important to both Matthew and Helen about belonging to a religious community, not just holding beliefs or keeping certain observances. Matthew has a special affinity for religious services. "Whether it's a church or a synagogue, I just like the services, the prayers and the chanting."

The couple tried an Episcopal Church and then a synagogue. But Helen wasn't really comfortable with either. Helen says that she felt "very welcomed, personally," by the synagogue. And she very much liked Jewish rituals. "But for me," she explains, "the struggle was Jesus was not welcome there and I just can't separate that from my spiritual life. I couldn't bring that piece in with me so I could never really feel comfortable."

When their son was born, they joined a small, informal, interfaith family group that had launched a few years earlier. They met every other week, sometimes for holiday celebrations, sometimes as a kind of "group counseling thing," as Matthew calls it. There were about a half dozen families with about ten kids among them. According to Helen, "the group started meeting initially so that they could talk with each other about how they were going to work out their religious education and identity for their kids."

Matthew says the group has been a great help to them and now seems like an extended family with whom they can participate in religious rituals. "There is a difference," he says, "between being interfaith and being a couple that's from two different religions." He explains: "If you're interfaith, you have to engage and actually be both faiths and figure out what you're going to do. If you just happen to be different religious traditions and you get married and you don't really care, it's not interfaith." In their relationship, he says, the issue of religion has "required attention and negotiation." This distinction between being interfaith and being a couple from two different religions is an interesting one. The latter is obviously much more conceivable before kids have arrived. It's easy for two adults to go their separate ways. But it's harder with kids. Even beyond that, though, Matthew is clearly talking about something much more intentional here, not to mention time consuming. It may be something more along the lines of what the couples therapist Deborah Ross had in mind when she said the interfaith couples should strive to have faith identities that are both "differentiated and linked".

Matthew and Helen have tried other religious communities as well. And they seem to be still seeking when it comes to their spiritual identity as a family. Their son went to a "humanistic Hebrew school" for a while. And they seem open to other options should those present themselves.

In some ways, Matthew and Helen's desire to be part of a religious community has made their journey easier as a family. Some of the conflicts that might have been concentrated between husband and wife have become the subject of broader discussions in their interfaith group, which has relieved some of the tension that comes from trying to raise kids in two faiths. It's also clear that both of them see community as a vital part of their respective religious traditions and wanted to make sure that even though their children were growing up interfaith, they had a sense of belonging to a community as well.

As a college professor, Matthew says he has encountered a lot of kids who grew up in interfaith homes. "I would ask them what religion they had and they felt like they didn't know what they were. We were trying to figure out a way not to have that happen [to our kids]." They wanted them to have a sense of the spiritual. Their thirteen-year-old son, they say, identifies strongly with both Judaism and Christianity. He had a bar mitzvah and gave a speech in which he compared his situation to riding a camel, that "it's like being between the two humps." Their eight-year-old son, they see as leaning more toward Judaism, but say it's still too early to tell.

Some of these interfaith groups start small and remain that way—a group of friends who meet regularly to give their kids a religious community in which to grow up. Often after the kids are grown, the parents report needing the group less and the couples can start to drift apart a bit. But other interfaith gatherings become quite large, to the point where they could be considered religious institutions of their own.

Eileen O'Farrell Smith, a faithful Catholic, met her Jewish husband Steve through a mutual friend who served on the board of Chicago's Hull House.[5] At the time, Eileen describes herself as "very attentive to my faith life. I was singing at a local church. I was celebrating Lent and Advent. I loved it." Steve wasn't particularly observant, but he worried, according to Eileen, about the "lack of parity between them," that any kids they had would be more inclined in the Catholic direction. But Eileen was thirty-five when they got married, and they weren't even sure they would have kids. So religion was not a deal-breaker.

As it turned out, Eileen got pregnant two weeks after the wedding, and they had three children in four years. After her first two were born, Eileen continued to attend mass and sing in her church, but she left the babies home with Steve. When she was pregnant with her third, she says, "things got dicey. I was filled with grief that all my Catholic friends were going through the steps of baptism." She wondered, "What are we doing? We're not doing anything. I don't want to do nothing. It unleashed a fury in me, a huge sense of loss that this was not what I wanted." They received an invitation just around this time to go to a Catholic-Jewish group. And they started attending Shabbat on Friday nights and mass on Sunday mornings.

A small number of the couples in the group had young children and were trying to figure out how to give them a religious education. They got space in a church and began to hold classes. Their mission statement, according to Eileen, said they wanted to "explore a common moral code and instill in children a sense of belonging to a Jewish-Catholic community.'" That was in 1993. The school has since grown to about a hundred families and includes an adult education program as well. They received support several years ago from the Lilly Foundation for a five-year study to see how children's religious faith was formed.

Eileen's children have grown up—one identifies as Catholic, one as Jewish, and one she describes as a "philosophy major." Steve passed away suddenly a few years ago. Eileen has less involvement in the group now, but it has clearly brought her enormous satisfaction. The group was actually meant to be supplemental, meaning that most of the families would attend religious services of one sort or another as well. Like other interfaith couples who are trying to raise kids in two faiths, Eileen and Steve acknowledged that the process required not only a great deal of attention but also a lot of their time. "I think our philosophy about this," Eileen tells me, "was that we are going to dedicate ourselves to creating a family where God was God. We didn't want sports to be God or money to be God or sleepovers to be God." With all of their attendance at religious services and interfaith events, she says, it took up a lot of hours. "It didn't hurt that our kids weren't athletic."

The past two decades have seen a rise in the number of such interfaith family groups. It's hard to quantify, but almost every major city in the United States and plenty of smaller ones seem to have them.

The Interfaith Families Project of Greater Washington began in 1995. It was also not supposed to be a substitute for belonging to religious congregations, but for a number of the families that I interviewed when I visited on a Sunday shortly before Christmas, it had become just that.

Lila and Glenn were married in 1997 and they had talked about trying to raise children in both faiths but hadn't arrived at any firm plans. They were concerned that raising a child in two faiths would lead her to have no religious identity at all. A friend recommended they look into IFFP, and after their daughter, who is now nine, was born, they decided to visit. They began attending adult group discussions and for a while found it helpful to listen to other couples air their frustrations. But after a few years, they stopped going and instead simply began to attend religious services with the group and enrolled both their daughters in the Sunday school. The religious services are generally organized around a particular holiday or set of holidays. And Lila believes IFFP does a good job of "finding commonalities between Christianity and Judaism" and "integrating the two traditions."

She is unsure how her daughters would respond if they were asked about their religious identities. "They assume everyone is both," she says, half-jokingly. Glenn says he "wants them to be at peace in terms of where they're from. Our job is to give them a spiritual base, to teach them religious tolerance, to have respect for others. Our kids are seeing that at an early age, whatever they decide in the future."

A big part of imparting those lessons, as Lila and Glenn see it, is performing community service. They have volunteered at homeless shelters. They have provided Thanksgiving dinners to struggling single mothers. Their kids visit a retirement home to lift the spirits of elderly residents. They have helped plant a community garden and distribute its harvest to people in need.

Lila and Glenn have largely worked out the compromises of being an interfaith family, but there are about fifty people participating in a "December Dilemma" discussion that I attend, and many of them are either new to the group or new to interfaith marriage or both. Rabbi Harold White, who leads the discussion, is something of a legend in interfaith circles. He is a chaplain at Georgetown University, a warm grandfatherly type that many of the younger couples seem happy to open up to. But he also seems a bit of a throwback. He talks about the ways in which Chanukah and Christmas are similar for a while, pointing out that they come at the equinox, and "come to dispel the darkness and cold of winter." He tells a story of going to sit on Santa's lap as a child. When White told Santa Claus he was Jewish, the old man replied, "Blessings upon your head," an old Yiddish aphorism.

Religiously, White suggests that Jews celebrating Chanukah must not emphasize the military victory of the Maccabees over their oppressors, so much as the miracle of the oil lamp burning for eight days after the Temple was desecrated. Of both holidays and both religions he says, "the values are more important than anything else." He says the holiday season is a time to remember that "we live in affluence" but we must care for the poor.

White listens patiently as the couples explain all of their deep-seated childhood memories of holiday celebrations and how difficult it will be to break with any of these traditions. "Having a Christmas tree was always indicative to me of being a bad Jew," one woman recalls. "You're living in a post–Vatican II era," Rabbi White responds. Though "it's hard to let go of ancient ideals and historic persecution," he advises the woman to worry less about acceding to the requests of her Catholic husband.

Rabbi White notes that Christmas is really more like Passover in the Jewish tradition because so many of the rituals are performed in the home rather than in a religious institution. And it is that conflict over what objects and rituals make their way into the home that can be very difficult for couples. No one wants to be made uncomfortable in their own home.

At one point during the discussion, White pauses to remind the couples that the "December Dilemma" really isn't (or shouldn't be) the greatest source of tension for interfaith couples. "Easter and Passover are more of a dilemma," he points out half-jokingly. You have to decide: "Was Jesus the messiah? And who crucified him?"

Or maybe they don't have to decide. During the course of my interviews and my visits to two interfaith congregations, it became clear that few mixed families feel the need to make such theological distinctions. Take, for instance, the Passover/Easter celebration hosted by the Interfaith Community of Westchester. Like most of their meetings and events, this one took place at St. John's Episcopal Church in Larchmont, New York. The leaders of the group (which began in New York City but has subsequently expanded into the suburbs) regularly make clear that they do not want to create any form of "syncretism." Christianity and Judaism are supposed to remain distinct. Following that directive to its literal conclusion, the model Passover Seder took place in one room and the Easter vigil was conducted elsewhere.

The Seder took place in the parish hall with families seated at four long tables. Places were set with matzah, horseradish, grape juice, and haroset (the apple-nut mixture that is supposed to resemble the mortar used to build the pyramids). One of the leaders explains that it was not really the Red Sea that was parted—"It's not the Charlton Heston story." Rather the words have been mistranslated. It was the "reed sea not the Red Sea." In other words, the Jews just found a path through "a swampy area in the Nile," not a dry path through the middle of the river. We also learn that Elijah was not really a prophet, but rather a "man of God." The kids go open the door for him (a traditional Seder ritual) anyway.[6]

Before the Easter vigil begins, the participants snack on a buffet of chopped liver and Easter candy. If food is going to help kids decide which faith to choose, it's easy to see who wins this contest. When we enter the church basement, there is a large wooden cross with tealights surrounding it. The Sunday school teachers leading this part of the event explain that there are times in life "when things start off one way and then they turn into something else," an oblique reference, apparently, to the resurrection. "Jesus," one of the leaders explains, "was like the very hungry caterpillar." Just as the caterpillar becomes a butterfly, so Jesus becomes . . . well, we are never quite told what. The children march around the room holding butterflies that they pin to a clothesline stretching from the cross to a couple of posts in the room. As they do, they sing the hymn, "Lord of the Dance."

> I came down from Heaven & I danced on Earth
> At Bethlehem I had my birth:
> Dance then, wherever you may be
> I am the Lord of the Dance, said He!

Perhaps the strangest omission in the whole ecumenical afternoon is that there is no mention of the traditional belief that the Last Supper was actually a Passover Seder. Rather it seems as if these are two religious celebrations, both stripped of some of their theological meaning, taking place at the same time, almost coincidentally.

Charlie and his wife had heard about the Interfaith Community while they were still living in New York City, before they had children. They had agreed to raise kids in two faiths, but it was more difficult than they expected. "When it's actually there and happening, you know, it's a whole different conversation. It's real as opposed to theoretical." They tried to talk to their children about Christianity and Judaism, but they found that IFC "was a way to sort of broaden it and deepen it with a real program behind it." What appealed to them, says Charlie, was not just the IFC "curriculum," but also "the community being created. It's not just about you and your own family."

These are the two themes that I heard repeated by the dozen or so parents I spoke with at IFC. They liked the fact that the group could provide them with a sense of community for their families and that it could equip the children, and even the adults, with enough education to make them feel comfortable in both faiths—giving them a "passport to two religions," as one woman put it.

✦　✦　✦

The group certainly had the feel of a large extended family. Parents, kids, and teachers at the Sunday school seemed warm. But the interfaith education component was the more regular and unique part of IFC. Religious classes for children usually take place every other week. At each meeting, the teachers typically focus on one holiday and one religious tradition. Again, they are wary of seeming to combine the two religious traditions, and understandably so. Despite these efforts, it does seem as though the kids are having trouble sorting some things out.

Crouched on a low-to-the-ground sofa in the back of the room, I listened one Sunday afternoon as a group of six- and seven-year-olds learned about Passover. At this age, of course, there was bound to be some confusion in terms of the two faiths. The teacher began by asking what the kids knew about Passover and the story of the Exodus. One mentioned matzah and the next said something about dipping something green in salt water. He couldn't remember what we dip in salt water, though. The answer was supposed to be parsley. But, this being a wealthy suburb of New York, of course, the first guess was "cilantro."

The teacher quickly moved on to the story of Joseph being sold into slavery by his brothers and coming to the land of Egypt. "His brothers told their father they did something bad to Joseph," the teacher said, mentioning neither the brothers' feelings of jealousy toward Joseph, nor their throwing him into a ditch, let alone the notion of slavery.

The students nodded together until one little boy asked: "But where was Joseph's son? You know, Jesus?"

"Different Joseph, ok?" the teacher replied.

The class picked up the story next with a baby being born and put into a basket on the river Nile so nothing bad would happen to him. "Who was that baby?" the teacher asked. Three kids yelled out "Jesus." And the woman standing by as that baby was plucked out of the water was, according to two boys in the class, "Mary."

The teacher, frustrated but still determined to get through the lesson, moved on then to the rise of "a bad Pharaoh who did mean things to the Jews." "Is he still alive?" one student asked. "No, he's been dead for a long time." "Is he in heaven?" asked one of the students. Another child recalled from the previous session the story of Lazarus and was concerned that Pharaoh would rise again.

Patiently, the teacher encouraged the students to return to the point of the story. He told them that Pharaoh did mean things to the Jews "because he didn't like people who were different from him." "Do you know anyone different from you?" he asked.

And then, the students understood. This was a conversation they had had before. Almost every hand in the room shot up. "I have a friend who has darker skin," one student offered. "He's cool." Another one brought up Martin Luther King, Jr. And the teacher approved. "Pharaoh," he told them, "didn't realize how awesome it is to have friends who are different."

As a purely educational matter, one has to wonder how much these children eventually understand about the Bible. But as a spiritual matter, it seems, there is something else missing. These stories are not simply stories. They are also supposed to present the great themes of human nature and the ideas behind faith.

Instead of a story about jealousy and forgiveness (in the case of Joseph) or a story about freedom and God's love and anger (in the case of the Exodus) or about responsibility and leadership (in the case of Moses), students are left with a banal notion of embracing differences—a lesson they can get almost every day in their elementary schools anyway. Maybe "tolerance" is what interfaith couples have in mind when they say that they share common values and that is what is most important. But surely many couples would be willing to dig a little deeper for common spiritual and theological themes in their religious traditions.

Despite what may strike some as the shallowness of this religious education, it is true that the Interfaith Community is working well as a community—it is providing children with an identity and a place where they feel comfortable. I asked a number of the mothers and fathers which faith they thought their children might choose when they grew up. Two parents from different families told me that their children say they want to be "interfaith." One child even reportedly told his mother that whatever religion he decided to be he would seek out a wife who was a different one so that his children could grow up interfaith.

As I said earlier, these consciously interfaith congregations are still a relatively small phenomenon, but it will be interesting to see whether, in a decade or two, there will be adults who grew up in these communities who see their religious identity as "interfaith."

There is another option that some interfaith couples pursue when they want to join a religious community but do not want to join one of the ones from which they hail. Recall from our survey that there was a group of same-faith couples who were from different faiths before they married. Of the quarter of same-faith couples for whom this was true, we found that in 19 percent of the cases both husband and wife converted to a new religion.

These couples had every option open to them, of course. But it is unlikely that a Jew and Catholic both happened to become evangelicals or that a Muslim and a Baptist picked Mormonism. Any data collected on these kinds of conversions would really be too small to draw any conclusions from. But, anecdotally, there seem to be at least two "compromise faiths"—Unitarian Universalism and Messianic Judaism. Though neither one likes to be thought of in that particular way—as we will see—and the two religious groups are miles apart in their beliefs and practices, it is nonetheless worth examining briefly what these groups have to offer interfaith couples and why they have become a plausible, if not popular, option for these husbands and wives.

Unitarian Universalism, or UU as it is sometimes called, has attracted interfaith families for as long as Rev. Tom Goldsmith can remember. Goldsmith, who pastors a UU congregation of about four hundred families in Salt Lake City, recalls a cousin of his who was Jewish and met her Southern Baptist husband at the University of Georgia in the 1950s. They decided to attend a Unitarian Universalist church together.

Interfaith couples typically learn about UU when they are looking for an officiant to marry them. They could go with a justice of the peace but decide that they want something a little more spiritual. Goldsmith performs between twenty and thirty such weddings a year.

"What is the attraction?," I ask him. Goldsmith, who has written a number of pamphlets for interfaith couples on behalf of the denomination, says, "It helps that UU are not dogmatic." "Since we don't have a corner on the truth market we are able to concentrate on being a celebrant for couple. We are there to serve the couple rather than getting our particular ideology across." He provides examples of all sorts of different rituals couples have asked to be used in their weddings, from "Japanese tea ceremonies" to "Latino traditions." He explains, "I don't have to use any particular language or tradition. I am free to celebrate the couple."

Of these twenty to thirty interfaith couples whom Goldsmith marries, only two or three end up joining his congregation. He acknowledges that many of the couples are using a minister at their wedding simply to please their families. Still, sometimes they become more interested in learning about UU once they get a foot in the door. A number of them, according to Goldsmith, come back after they have children. In part because Goldsmith's congregation is in the midst of such a highly religious city, he thinks, people feel a real pressure to choose some faith institution "as a kind of defensive measure."

The Unitarian Universalist Church does not try to proselytize, and while it realizes that there is a certain attraction for interfaith couples to the faith, the church has not targeted them in any particular way. The pamphlets Goldsmith wrote are decades old, and there are no plans to issue new ones. "The church leadership is pleased this happens [with interfaith couples], but we don't want to be seen as a compromise religion. As liberals, it is so difficult to forge one's own identity because one is open and democratic. It is tough to find consensus on what it is we're about. That undermines a UU identity."

Instead of suggesting that Unitarianism is some kind of middle ground among different faiths, Goldsmith prefers to think of it as "leaving aside" some of the most contentious theological issues. "We are a historically Christian faith. We have grown increasingly humanistic. We're looking for a more earth-based spirituality that is really leaving aside the traditional gods and rituals. We are not ignoring them, but looking instead at the spiritual challenges we face in the world today." The kids in Sunday school read the

Bible and other religious texts. But the community is also very focused on "social justice." And tolerance. Many of the families in the congregation include same-sex couples who, he says, would not be accepted elsewhere. "So much of our Sunday school is about making kids feel at home in a religious community."

✦ ✦ ✦

In 2009, Rabbi Stuart Dauermann published a pamphlet called "Keeping the Faith in Interfaith Relationships." In it, Dauermann, who is the leader of a Messianic Jewish congregation in Los Angeles, presents a fictional conversation between himself and an interfaith couple thinking of tying the knot. The woman, Cindy, is a Christian and the man, Jake, is Jewish. "Both came from large and loving families: hers Los Angeles evangelicals and his, Reform Jews from Las Vegas." According to Dauermann's description, "The families loved Jake and Cindy, but Jesus, or Yeshua as we call him, had become an obstacle between Cindy and Jake, and a big issue for their families. Cindy felt she couldn't entertain the possibility of marriage unless Jake and she were of one mind on Yeshua, and Jake knew he couldn't and wouldn't make room in their marriage for Yeshua if it meant betraying his Jewishness and his family."

In the twenty-five pages that follow, Dauermann tries to explain to the couple, particularly Jake, why it is that he needn't leave his Jewish traditions and rituals behind in order to accept that Jesus is the messiah. In fact, as Dauermann has it, Jake has an obligation to keep the laws of the Torah even if he does become a believer in Yeshua.

Messianic Judaism is probably on the opposite end of the religious spectrum from Unitarian Universalism. Its leaders are decidedly not trying to leave theological issues aside. In fact, it is theological issues that usually bring people into Messianic Judaism's fold. Dauermann's pamphlet, and the other material one can find from the Jews for Jesus, is generally littered with references to the Old and New Testaments.

But there is some anecdotal evidence, at least, that when an interfaith couple converts to a new religion, Messianic Judaism is one that they consider. Messianic Jews are very clear that they don't want Jewish-Christian couples to somehow combine their theologies into one. As David Sedaca, the president of the Union of Messianic Jewish Believers of America, tells me, "Messianic Judaism is not half and half. It's not a compromise. It's a new identity for the couple." While Sedaca does acknowledge that some interfaith couples explore Messianic Judaism for this reason, the faith "is not a remedy for mixed marriages. It is a commitment."[7]

And the level of commitment is very high. Messianic Jews often take the rituals of Judaism as seriously as Orthodox Jews do—keeping kosher and observing the Sabbath, for instance—while their fervor and proselytization efforts resemble those of evangelical Christians. Dauermann makes clear to his interlocutors, Cindy and Jake, that he is offering Messianic Judaism as an alternative to a watered-down compromise of their faiths.

"So if you follow this 'two religions under one roof' idea, and your first child says to you, 'Mommy! Daddy! What am I?' What do you say? 'Well Mommy is a Christian and Daddy is a Jew, and when you grow up you can decide what you want to be?' Doesn't that sound a little like passing the buck? . . . I mean the kid is looking to you two to tell him or her what he or she is, and you are saying, 'Beats me! You'll have to figure that one out yourself when you get older!'"

Religious leaders of every stripe, in other words, want families (and especially children) to have one identity. They acknowledge that sometimes this is not possible and sometimes parents will arrive at the only compromise they can. But no parent or rabbi or minister wants to have his or her faith seem like a safe middle ground. Though we may not always practice it that way, Americans see faith as a conviction, an unshakable foundation. Even though they may have to compromise sometimes, men and women in interfaith marriages want to find a way to teach their children something true, something unified. Sometimes, though, because of the dynamics of a marriage or the tenets of a faith, this is simply not feasible.

CHAPTER SIX

—◆—

Interfaith Divorce

WHEN JOSEPH REYES AND REBECCA SHAPIRO GOT MARRIED IN 2004, they had a Jewish ceremony. He was Catholic but converted to Judaism after they married, and they agreed to raise any children in the Jewish faith. However, after their daughter Ela was born, Reyes began to worry about the fact that she had not been baptized. "If, God forbid, something happened to her, she wouldn't be in heaven," he told me.

Two years after the Illinois couple's bitter divorce battle began, the fight over Ela's religious upbringing involved criminal charges. Things escalated in November 2009, when Reyes had Ela baptized in a Catholic church and emailed his estranged wife a photo. She filed a complaint, and a judge barred Reyes from exposing his daughter to "any other religion other than the Jewish religion." In January 2010, Reyes violated the judge's order and brought Ela to church again, this time with a camera crew in tow.

The divorce was settled in April of that year, and Reyes was finally allowed to take his daughter to church. But he could have gone to jail for up to six months for his original violation.

The Reyes-Shapiro divorce is about as ugly as the end of a marriage can get. Of course, people often behave badly when a union unravels. But the fight over Ela's religion illustrates the particular hardships and poor track record of interfaith marriages: In certain combinations, they fail significantly more often than same-faith marriages.

I didn't follow couples over time in my survey, and therefore I cannot calculate a "rate" of divorce. However I did ask respondents about their previous marriages and can compare the likelihood that someone in an interfaith marriage has been divorced versus someone in a same-faith marriage.[1]

We compared two groups of respondents:

1. People who are currently married and have never previously been married (currently married).

2. People who, regardless of their current marital status, are divorced (divorced).

Roughly speaking, I asked what happened in someone's first marriage. I say "roughly speaking" because some people may have been divorced more than once and are only reporting on their most recent divorce.[2] Some of the people classified as divorced have remarried. I opted to include remarried respondents in the analysis, since to exclude them would probably bias our sample of divorced respondents.

When we make a simple comparison between the currently married and the divorced, we see that there is no difference in the proportion who are in same-faith and interfaith marriages. Of those who are currently married, 60.5 percent are in same-faith relationships while 39.5 percent are in interfaith ones. Of those who are divorced, 48.2 percent were in same-faith relationships, while another 12.3 percent were in relationships where neither couple professed a religion. In total, that would be 60.5 percent in "same-faith" relationships and 39.5 percent in interfaith ones. Even when we compare the likelihood that a Christian married to a non-Christian will be divorced to the likelihood that two Christians will be divorced, there is no discernible difference.

However, these comparisons obscure the fact that some religious combinations are significantly more likely to end in divorce than others. To calculate the numbers below, I look at the religion of one's current spouse if married and never divorced and the religion of one's former spouse if divorced.

In each case, the first religion listed is that of the respondent. The second one is either the religion of the current spouse (for currently married respondents) or the previous spouse (for divorced respondents). So Catholic–non-Catholic refers to a Catholic respondent married to anyone who is not Catholic (table 6.1).

Following that, I report the percentage of specific interreligious combinations that end up in divorce (table 6.2). I am unable to report on every possible combination because some are too rare for reliable analysis.

In general, Catholics are no more likely to divorce when married to someone of the same faith than when married to a non-Catholic. However,

TABLE 6.1 Percentage of divorced respondents who were from same-faith and interfaith marriages

Catholic–Catholic	29%
Catholic–non-Catholic	29%
Evangelical–Evangelical	32%
Evangelical–non-Evangelical	48%
Jew–Jew	16%
Jew–non-Jew	34%
Mainline–Mainline	42%
Mainline–non-Mainline	45%
None–None	44%
None–non-None	30%

TABLE 6.2 Percentage of divorced respondents who were from certain interfaith combinations

Catholic–Evangelical	40%
Catholic–Mainline	24%
Catholic–None	26%
Evangelical–None	61%
Mainline–None	63%

divorce is roughly 10 percentage points more common among Catholics who marry evangelicals.

Indeed, evangelicals are more likely to divorce when married to someone of almost any other religion. While roughly a third (32 percent) of all evangelicals' marriages end up in divorce, that climbs to nearly half (48 percent) for marriages between evangelicals and non-evangelicals. It is especially high for evangelicals married to someone with no religion (a "None")—61 percent.

Mainline Protestants look a lot like Catholics in that their frequency of divorce is about the same for same-faith as interfaith marriages. However, the frequency is substantially higher for mainline Protestants married to Nones (63 percent). There are very few cases of mainline Protestants married to evangelicals, which is likely because, in the eyes of most Protestants, such intra-Protestant marriages are same-faith rather than interfaith.

With a relatively small number of Jews in the sample (44), their inclusion here is tenuous. With the caveat that these numbers are based on a very small sample, it is nonetheless striking that the frequency of divorce more than doubles for marriages between a Jew and a non-Jew (35 percent vs. 16 percent).

People with no religious affiliation are outliers, as there is a greater frequency of divorce among Nones married to Nones than Nones married to religious people. Before making too much of this surprising finding, however, it is important to note that we do not know much about former spouses from our survey. We do not know whether these "non-None" spouses are actually "Nones-in-disguise." In other words, some proportion of spouses who are described as having a religious affiliation might not be religious in practice, meaning that they are essentially Nones.

None of these findings is particularly new. In a 1964 book called *Intermarriage: Interfaith, Interracial, Interethnic*, sociologist Albert I. Gordon estimated the likelihood of divorce among interfaith couples as three times that of same-faith ones. Based on his own survey conducted at forty colleges and universities, as well as other studies and his own anecdotal experience, he concludes: "Whether or not religious difference in these cases is only one of the factors that has resulted in the ultimate dissolution of the marriage," he writes, "the fact is that interfaith marriages fail in far greater numbers that intrafaith marriages." He concludes, "If I were a betting man, I would certainly not wager against such odds."[3]

In a paper published in 1993, Evelyn Lehrer, a professor of economics at the University of Illinois at Chicago, found that if members of two mainline

Christian denominations marry, they have a one in five chance of being divorced in five years. A Catholic and a member of an evangelical denomination have a one in three chance. And a Jew and a Christian who marry have a greater than 40 percent chance of being divorced in five years.[4]

According to calculations based on the 2001 American Religious Identification Survey, a survey of more than thirty-five thousand respondents, people who had been in mixed-religion marriages were three times more likely to be divorced or separated than those who were in same-faith marriages.[5]

Because the methodology behind these surveys differs significantly, it is hard to calculate how the likelihood that an interfaith couple is divorced has changed over time. But these studies do demonstrate the persistence of the problem. In order to understand what is behind these divorce statistics, we can look at two sets of factors. The first are macro-level changes in society that affect the significance of faith as a factor in the end of marriages. For instance, distinctions between Christian denominations have faded somewhat during the past half century and so marriage among people from, say, a Methodist church and a Baptist church is not unusual. Nor is it likely the cause of great tension for the couple.

Meanwhile, other factors, such as the greater number of women in the workplace, have altered the way that couples view marriage and the satisfaction they derive from it. The division of household chores when both spouses work full time has become more important to marital happiness, for instance. So there is some evidence that having the same religion as a spouse matters relatively less than it used to for family stability.

Finally, as our society becomes more tolerant, interfaith families are no longer outcasts in their communities and thus will probably feel less outward pressure to split up. In the 1960s, when Albert Gordon was writing, he described interfaith families who were unwelcome by the families and religious groups from which they came and the heavy toll this took not only on the couple, but on their children. He cites a paper by a young man named Philip M. Rosten called "The Mischling: Child of the Jewish-Gentile Marriage."[6] Rosten, who was himself the product of such a match, describes the difficulties of these "mixed" children: "Fate has been both kind and cruel to the mischling; kind because it offers him an opportunity to move within two cultures, unshackled by predetermined customs of an anonymous past; cruel because it has not given him a secure ethnic place in life, but has left him in a limbo between two larger cultures which will never completely accept him as one of their own."

As we will discuss in a later chapter, the environment for intermarried families has changed significantly over the almost half century since Gordon was writing, and the kind of isolation caused by intermarriage is not nearly the factor it once was in breaking up marriages. Religious institutions are on the whole more welcoming of interfaith families. And as we saw in the last chapter, there are new options for them as well—communities that are specifically devoted to serving interfaith families and making them feel welcome without even having to pick one faith or the other as the dominant one.

In general, most Americans report having happy marriages. Or, as sociologists put it, they have high levels of marital satisfaction—roughly eight on a scale of one to ten. (Given how easy it is to get a divorce, it would be odd if too many people reported being in miserable marriages.) Even with that high "floor," though, we found that same-faith couples are more satisfied than interfaith ones: 8.4 versus 7.9, a statistically significant gap. The difference is real, but modest.[7]

Marriage counselors and social scientists have long known that the most harmonious marriages are the ones in which the husband and wife have the most in common. The notion that opposites attract may be a good way of explaining that oddball couple who live next door or why your straightlaced daughter just ran off with a delinquent on a motorcycle, but there's not a lot of sociological evidence to back it up. Moreover, even if those couples attract, they are not as likely to stay together in the long term.

It is interesting to compare marriages that cross religious boundaries with those that cross other sorts of lines. Interracial marriages, while on the rise, are still far less common than interfaith marriages. About one in seven marriages in the United States include members of different races or ethnicities.[8] These relationships, on the whole, have a higher likelihood of divorce than marriages between people of the same race.[9]

Inter–political party marriages are far less common than interfaith marriages and slightly more common than interracial ones: Only 18 percent of married Americans have a spouse who claims a different political affiliation, compared with at least a third of Americans who are in interfaith marriages.

According to my survey, the difference in marital satisfaction between same-party and interparty marriages is comparable to the difference for same-faith versus interfaith marriages—roughly 0.5 on the 10-point scale.

Which raises the question: Why do Americans seem so much more reluctant to marry outside of their political affiliation than their faith when the gap in marital satisfaction produced by both is comparable? One possibility is that they are unaware or unwilling to acknowledge that religion can be a serious dividing line in a marriage. But shouldn't political differences seem less important? Are varying views on tax rates or foreign policy really as significant as varying views on where we will go when we die?

Of course, political views can encompass more serious disagreements about the permissibility of abortion or how wealth should be distributed in society. Indeed, the point is not that serious political differences can or should be ignored. It's that religious differences often are.

But there is another explanation for the fact that interparty marriages are less common than interfaith ones. Political differences seem to be more frequently discussed by couples than religious ones and therefore seem to be more of an initial barrier to the formation of a relationship. Or we are more likely to live near, go to school with, or work with people of a similar political bent. (The famous red-state/blue-state election map certainly leads one to this conclusion.) And therefore we're more likely to date them and marry them.[10]

As with the likelihood of divorce, the difference in marital satisfaction between same-faith and interfaith marriages varies across religious traditions (table 6.3). While it is nearly always the case that people in same-faith marriages report a happier relationship than those in interfaith marriages, that gap is bigger for some groups than others. There are certainly interfaith couples whose marital satisfaction seems very much like that of same-faith couples. For instance, there is only a 0.1 point difference for Catholics in same-faith and interfaith marriages. And those who profess no religious beliefs did not experience any difference in marital satisfaction whether they were in same-(non)faith or interfaith marriages.

These findings are mostly not surprising. Catholics and mainline Protestants tend to have less exclusivist understandings of God and faith and can probably more easily assimilate the idea of a partner who does not share their views. The "Nones" might not agree with the ideas or practices of a

TABLE 6.3 Marital Satisfaction by Religious Tradition of Respondent (%)

Religious Tradition of Respondent	Same-faith	Interfaith	Satisfaction Gap
None	7.9	7.8	−0.1
Evangelical Protestant (incl. "Other Christian")	8.9	7.7	1.2
Mainline	8.5	8.2	0.3
Black Protestant	8.3	7.1	1.2
Catholic	8.2	8.1	0.1
Jewish	8.2	9.1	−0.9
Mormon	9.3	8.8	0.5

religiously affiliated partner but apparently such differences don't seem to affect the nonreligious partner to a great extent.

When we look at the religious tradition of the respondent, we find the biggest gap in marital satisfaction for evangelicals married to non-evangelicals: 8.9 versus 7.7 (a 1.2-point gap) and Black Protestants who are in interfaith marriages: 8.4 versus 7.3 (a 1.1-point gap).

What is it about being an evangelical or a Black Protestant married to someone outside of the church that makes a relationship less satisfying? For one thing, both of these groups tend to have more exclusivist views of faith. They are more likely to believe that there is a single path to salvation and that nonbelievers cannot achieve it. According to the Pew Religious Landscape Survey in 2008, "fewer than half of evangelicals (47 percent) say many religions can lead to eternal life . . . while 49 percent say theirs is the one, true faith." The survey also found that "among black Protestants, 49 percent take the view that many religions lead to everlasting life, while 45 percent see theirs as the one, true faith."[11]

Evangelicals and Black Protestants married to people outside of their faiths might be disappointed both in the beliefs and actions of their spouses. Generally speaking, they may be concerned that their spouses do not follow their church's dictates and perhaps that it might affect their spouses' ultimate fates. But it is not simply such abstract matters that will affect marital happiness. As Evelyn Lehrer points out, a strong or even moderate religious faith will influence "many activities that husband and wife perform jointly."[12]

Religion isn't just church on Sunday, Lehrer notes, but also ideas about raising children, how to spend time and money, friendships, professional networks—it can even influence where to live. The disagreements between husband and wife start to add up.

Let's be clear here. It is not that interfaith couples spend some significant part of their lives arguing about abstract doctrinal ideas. In my survey, interfaith couples did not report disagreeing with their spouse about religion very often. Half of respondents in same-faith couples and 46 percent of interfaith couples report never disagreeing about faith. Which makes sense. Do Jewish wives and Christian husbands argue about whether Jesus Christ was the son of God? Do Mormons and Catholics argue about Joseph Smith's inspiration for the Book of Mormon? Realistically speaking, of course, few couples argue about these things or even discuss them much in the course of daily life. And really, once you have had that argument a few times, what's the point in having it again?

It is not the doctrines of religion, but its practices and rituals that are more likely to affect our day-to-day lives, and therefore our marriages. The latter may ultimately lead to more disagreements and eventually to divorce.

Issues surrounding raising children seem to provide some of the greatest sources of tension in these marriages. Figuring out how to bring up the kids in a mixed-faith household is difficult, as we saw in the previous chapter. Religions, if taken seriously, are often mutually exclusive—notwithstanding the argument of Joseph Reyes's lawyer, who told me that taking Ela to church was not a violation of the court order because Jesus was a rabbi and "there is no sharp line between Judaism and Christianity." Frequent disagreements about what to tell children and what sorts of practices to expect of them will likely take a toll on a marriage.

Black Protestants and evangelicals also tend to be more religiously involved, attending church more often on average than members of other faiths. According to the Pew Forum, 58 percent of evangelicals attend church at least once a week, as do 59 percent of Black Protestants. Having to either leave a spouse at home or drag a reluctant spouse along seems likely to produce more marital tension, a point we will return to momentarily.

The finding on Mormon marital satisfaction rates might raise some eyebrows since, as a group, members of the LDS church tend, like evangelicals and Black Protestants, both to have a more exclusive view of faith and a high level of involvement in their religious communities. Why is there only a 0.5-point disparity between Mormons in same-faith and interfaith marriages?

The best explanation I found was contained in the attitudes of those Mormons I interviewed toward their non-Mormon partners. The Mormons I was able to find who are in interfaith marriages seemed to have a sense that God would ultimately take care of their partners. Even though Maria was married to a Muslim, she told me, her family would be allowed to live together in eternity, a fate theologically reserved for two Mormons who have been sealed together in the temple. She seemed convinced that God would make an exception for her family. In the meantime, her husband was attending religious services with her regularly.

Peggy, meanwhile, was confident that her longtime husband would one day convert. Anecdotally, such a result actually isn't that uncommon. Sometimes decades into a marriage, a spouse will finally convert. Mormon communities seem generally to be very accepting of nonmembers in their midst. And local bishops are generally made aware of the "part-member" families in the congregations. These Mormon spouses might be less "unsatisfied" in their interfaith marriages than we would predict because they might see their spouse's lack of interest in or commitment to Mormonism as a temporary state. And they may see it as less of a personal burden to alter—but rather something that God and the whole community are responsible for ultimately.

Finally, when it comes to marital satisfaction in interfaith couples, Jews seem to be the exception. Jews in interfaith marriages actually report a higher level of satisfaction than those in same-faith marriages: 9.1 (interfaith) versus 8.2 (same-faith). This difference, however, is not statistically significant because of the small sample size.

Most American Jews do no tend to have an exclusivist view of faith in the traditional sense. They don't tend to worry about the path to salvation for non-Jews, and they don't engage in evangelization efforts toward non-Jews. All of that perhaps eliminates some of the tensions. But given that Judaism is by its nature an exclusivist faith—its laws and traditions are meant only for Jews—it's somewhat surprising that there is not less marital satisfaction. And since we do see an increased likelihood of divorce among Jews and non-Jews, one wonders about the cause if it is not due to a decreased level of marital satisfaction. Again, of course, these samples are very small and so it may not be possible to draw too many conclusions.

✦   ✦   ✦

Another way to compare the marital satisfaction gap is by looking at the frequency of religious attendance (table 6.4).[13] When we split married respondents according to their religious service attendance, we find that the highest rate of satisfaction is among the high-attendance same-faith couples.

This echoes much previous research suggesting that couples who attend church together often are more likely to have happy and long-lasting marriages. Not only is it beneficial for couples to spend time together regularly, praying together also seems to help spouses forgive each other more easily, another significant factor in marital happiness.[14] One study found that a couple's religious involvement together was likely to produce a higher degree of marital fidelity: "We found that religious involvement helped to sanctify marriage by helping couples set aside sacred time to spend together, share a holy vision and purpose, enhance interpersonal virtues, find spiritual help in conflict resolution, and receive divine relational assistance."[15] It is interesting to note, though, that the benefits of attending religious services together do not seem to accrue to interfaith couples. There is almost no difference in marital satisfaction for these interfaith respondents depending on how frequently they attend. One can imagine that these respondents do not share with their spouses "a holy vision" that will "sanctify marriage."

Another way to think about religion and marital satisfaction is to compare the religious attendance of both spouses. The graph below (figure 6.1) uses the three-part measure of religious attendance, subtracting the spouse's frequency of attendance from the attendance of the respondent. Thus, a negative number means that the spouse attends more, while a positive number means the respondent attends more. A zero means that they attend with the same frequency. Marital satisfaction is lowest in those marriages where the respondent attends more than the spouse (positive numbers), rather than where the spouse attends more (negative numbers).[16]

TABLE 6.4   Religious Attendance and Marital Satisfaction (1–10)

	Low attendance	Medium attendance	High attendance
Same-faith marriage	8.0	8.2	8.6
Interfaith marriage	7.95	7.8	7.9
Gap	0.05	0.4	0.7

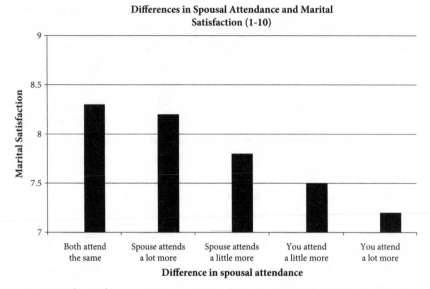

FIGURE 6.1 Differences in Spousal Attendance and Marital Satisfaction (1–10)

People who attend church seem more bothered by spouses who don't attend than the reverse. A husband (we may imagine, since it is women who more frequently attend services) is perfectly happy to stay home and watch football while his wife is at church. But the wife may be stewing about it the whole morning.

Other research concludes that differing degrees of religious belief and observance can cause trouble in marriages. For instance, in a 2009 paper, scholars Margaret Vaaler, Christopher Ellison, and Daniel Powers found higher rates of divorce when a husband attends religious services more frequently than his wife, as well as when a wife is more theologically conservative than her husband.[17]

✦   ✦   ✦

Divorce is obviously complex. Few of the divorced people I spoke with who had been in interfaith marriages would say that religious differences alone were the reason for the end of the marriage. Nonetheless, it is possible to see in some descriptions of these relationships how religion was a contributing factor.

Take Nathan, for example. He married his girlfriend in graduate school when she became pregnant with their daughter. Nathan grew up in a fairly secular Jewish home. His wife was raised in Germany in an irreligious home. Nathan hadn't given a lot of thought to raising children before getting married, but he knew that he wanted them to have some kind of Jewish upbringing. After their fight over circumcising their son, Nathan realized that his wife's entire approach to Judaism was going to be a problem. "I realized over time," he says, "that her approach was it was fine for them to have some Jewish education, just as long as they don't believe it. She made it clear to them that 'this is not to be taken seriously.'"

While there were other, personality-driven factors contributing to his divorce, Nathan easily sees the problems that arose from religion now that he is married to a Jewish woman. He says he feels more comfortable now engaging in religious rituals and teaching his children about the faith, that it is not "an uphill battle." If his children (who are teenagers) ever asked his advice about whom they should marry, he would advise them to marry inside the faith. Still, he knows, "you love who you love and that's just a compelling reality." Indeed, a number of people I interviewed who felt tension in their marriage as a result of a difference between the faith of the spouses would not go so far as to say that their children should stay away from interfaith matches. Just as there were overriding factors for the parents—"you love who you love"—so there may be for the children.

Parents of these tension-laden matches may try to warn their children about the potential pitfalls of interfaith marriages, but entering interfaith marriage with eyes wide open may not be enough to avoid problems down the road.

Even among those who have tough conversations and agree about faith before they get married, says Joshua Coleman, a psychologist and cochair of the Council on Contemporary Families, religion can become a serious point of contention later. One parent may agree to raise the children in the other's faith, he says, but then that faith "becomes repellent" to him or her. Coleman doesn't think that people get married with the intention of deceiving their spouse; "they just have no idea how powerfully unconscious religion can be."

Bridget Jack Meyers, an evangelical Christian who lives outside Chicago, married her husband, Paul, a Mormon, only after a lot of counseling and a lot of research.[18] Meyers, a student at the Trinity Evangelical Divinity School, jokes that there aren't a lot of books on evangelical-Mormon marriages. So she looked at ones on Christian-Jewish relationships. "A lot of the advice was to pick a religion and raise [the kids] in one. But neither one of us wanted to give up ours," she said. So the couple agreed to raise their children in both faiths, letting them choose their own at some point.

Shortly before their first anniversary, her husband walked out. Meyers, who writes about her interfaith family at ClobberBlog.com, explained in one posting: "He claimed that I had been a perfect wife and he had no complaints about me, but he was having second thoughts about a lifetime of interfaith marriage. He had decided that he wanted to get married in the temple and have his children be sealed to him, and he wanted to raise his children in the church, so he thought it would be best if we went our separate ways before any children entered into the union."

The two reconciled and, according to Meyers, religion wasn't the only issue. Still, it's clear to her that these questions are lurking. "We didn't account for all the ways that the different religions will affect our children," she told me. Mormons typically baptize children around age eight. But Meyers believes that is too young. Since her daughter is only three, she says, "I'm not getting worked up over it yet." But she worries that if they wait too long, her child will be ostracized in the Mormon Church. As for the long term, she tries not to "religiously manipulate" her daughter. But she knows she will be disappointed if her daughter chooses her husband's church.

✧   ✧   ✧

Even in interviews, it was possible to see among certain interfaith pairs the kinds of tension that might cause lower marital satisfaction and even perhaps divorce eventually.

Cathleen grew up in Southern California, and recalls going to a Catholic church every Sunday until her parents divorced when she was fifteen. Every serious boyfriend she dated before her husband, Jake, was Catholic. When she shared that with me at her kitchen table in a Detroit suburb, Jake seemed surprised, even taken aback. From the next room, he interjected: "I didn't know that."

Over the course of our interview, it became clear that there was a lot about Cathleen's religious life that Jake didn't know, or didn't want to know. Cathleen said she hadn't picked Catholic men on purpose, but in retrospect she thought they shared with her a "common understanding."

When I ask Jake about his religious background, he says he was "adopted into a Jewish family" as an infant. It's not clear whether he is telling me about the adoption in order to make clear he has no strict "blood connection" to the Jewish people, but he certainly doesn't seem to mind if that's the impression I got. He grew up in what he would characterize as a Conservative household, though at some point his family switched to a Reform temple. His father served as president and his mother became the head of the sisterhood organization. He had a bar mitzvah as well as a confirmation.

But then he proudly recounts the tale of his rebellion. "I kind of developed a reputation in the temple for asking a lot of uncomfortable questions." Among those, Jake recalls, were questions about "the separation of religion and politics with regard to Israel." He favored a greater separation and still does. He wanted to know why the Jews in his community and in the United States were not interested in greater interfaith dialogue on the issue of peace in Israel.

By the time Jake got to college, he says, he "wasn't interested in organized religion." He still had some Jewish friends during his freshman and sophomore years but after that, he had fewer and fewer, to the point that today he doesn't think he has any. He remembers dating one Jewish girl in high school. He and his parents were often at odds over his girlfriends. They made clear that they wanted him to raise his own children Jewish, but Jake had no interest in doing so.

When Jake and Cathleen met, she was in medical school and he was working in software development. She identified herself as Catholic right away and spoke about being raised Catholic. Jake recalls telling her that he had been raised Jewish but was very uncomfortable with organized religion. "I have no problem with having a spiritual life," he told her. It was just religious institutions that bothered him.

When the two talked about having kids, he says, he would "worry about the idea of picking a team." He didn't want to "impose" religion on his children. That was a sticking point when the couple went looking for an officiant for the wedding. The priests they spoke with turned them down, according to Cathleen, because Jake wouldn't agree to consider raising the kids Catholic. There was only one religious element in the service—one of Jake's aunts read a passage from the Song of Songs. Jake can hardly resist reiterating that he finds this "ironic" since he doesn't "self-identify" as Jewish. But Cathleen adds, "Well, you're so touchy about having Catholicism imposed on you," that's all they could agree on.

When their first son was born ten years ago, Cathleen wanted him to be baptized, but she says, "Jake freaked out. . . . I had to keep the roof from coming off the house." When I ask Cathleen why she wanted the baptism for both of her sons, she says, smiling, "So that if they died then their souls would be permitted into heaven." Jake and Cathleen laugh—she sort of nervously. Cathleen acknowledges that she doesn't literally believe that. "To me, Catholicism is so totally ludicrous that there's nothing logical in there at all. It's not something you can really think about, like how many angels can dance on the head of a pin." She becomes quieter, staring into her cup of tea. "Nevertheless, it's still a part of me . . . There are some core things about it that I just think are beautiful."

Cathleen hasn't been to church in many years, despite the fact, she says, that "there have been plenty of times where I'd like to go." She feels it would offer her a sense of "external stability." But there are two barriers. First, she hasn't identified a church where she thinks she'll feel comfortable. But she also doesn't want to go alone. Jake leaves the room briefly during our conversation and Cathleen confides, "To keep the peace in our marriage, I wouldn't take the kids to church with me."

Are there any circumstances under which Jake would allow the children to be exposed to some kind of religion? Does Jake worry, I ask him, about Cathleen's compromising too much on this issue?

"I am so firm about the idea of not indoctrinating children," says Jake, that "if we were to do this, there would have to be an entire program of them being exposed to many religions. That would require Cathleen actually organizing it because she's the person who wants them to be exposed to one." Because of their busy lives, Jake acknowledges, this plan is completely impractical. But he is not budging.

My conversation with Jake and Cathleen was very uncomfortable. It was hard to watch two people I had just met talk so openly about something that is a source of tremendous tension in their marriage. Why had they agreed to this interview?

It is tempting to wonder: How can Jake seem so blind to Cathleen's pain? But Jake would say he has been open with his wife from the beginning. By his own account and his wife's, Jake's virulent anti-organized-religion views did not arise overnight. And before they were married, Cathleen essentially agreed to Jake's conditions for raising kids.

It's perfectly possible that Jake and Cathleen's marriage will last for decades to come and that their children will never sense their parents' deep disagreement. It's possible that religion is only an issue for them when some reporter comes to the door and asks them about it. Or it's possible there are other problems in their marriage that are being expressed in their disagreements about faith. After spending less than an hour with this couple, I can say that Cathleen seems profoundly lonely, and her longing to be able to go to church with her family seems sincere. Jake has turned a blind eye to this, and the results are not pretty.

✧ ✧ ✧

Jake and Cathleen were among many people I interviewed who would not characterize themselves as particularly committed to a faith. And yet they have still found religious differences much more problematic than they predicted. For couples where one or both members do feel a stronger attachment to religion or who develop one over time, the tensions in the marriage can grow worse.

Mark was raised Catholic, and Sheila was raised in an interfaith home but as an adult identified as a nonpracticing Jew. After the couple adopted a daughter, the three would sometimes go to mass together. When their daughter began attending a Jewish preschool, Sheila began to explore her own Jewish beliefs more thoroughly. Mark went to her synagogue several times and liked it, but he continued attending his church weekly.

The two don't recall any explicit arguments over their own religious practice or the way they were raising their daughter. But Mark was nonetheless concerned about where things were heading. He remembers driving to an event together one day and saying to Sheila, "Look, the most important thing for me is that we stay together. So long as we can keep our focus on that, I think we'll be okay."

"Stay together religiously?" I inquired. Going to church or synagogue together?

"No, meaning that we remain married" Mark replied. Mark and Sheila had this talk many years ago, and they seem like a very happy couple today. So the idea that going to different religious services even brought up questions in his mind about the security of their marriage seemed to come out of the blue. It's not clear why this arrangement raised red flags for him. But he was very clear. He said, "What I didn't want to happen was for her to feel such a strong pull to her Judaism, that I would dig in and say, 'Sorry, I'm staying Catholic' and we go our separate ways."

So Sheila stopped coming to mass with Mark. And eventually their daughter stopped too. For a while he continued to attend by himself. But then he went out to dinner with his priest and told him that he had to stop, that it was too difficult. The priest was very understanding, and Mark started occasionally participating in Jewish rituals with his family. Over the years, he became increasingly supportive of the family having a Jewish identity. He didn't convert, though, until just before their daughter's bat mitzvah almost a decade later. Though Mark and Sheila were able to resolve their religious differences amicably, it was not easy for their marriage. "Being in an interfaith marriage can be very lonely," says Sheila, with Mark nodding in agreement. "Sitting in church with him was a lonely experience." Before Mark converted, Sheila says, "going to synagogue without him was a lonely experience."

But Sheila and Mark are among the lucky ones. Neither one "dug their heels in," as Mark put it. Their family's faith was clearly more important than they had imagined when they were first married. But settling into a set of rituals and beliefs was a project they undertook together, openly and cooperatively.

For other couples, a change in one spouse's faith can prove devastating. Luke and Marybeth were introduced by Marybeth's sister, who knew Luke in graduate school. Marybeth had grown up in a strong Catholic home. Luke had been raised initially in the Plymouth Brethren church,[19] and then he bounced around in a variety of Bible churches, like the Assemblies of God, a Pentecostal denomination. Before his second date with Marybeth, she had taken him to Sunday mass. It was not what he expected. He characterizes his own family as "anti-Catholic." But he was "intrigued" by the experience. Marybeth said she never pressured him to join the church but made clear that's what she did on Sundays. She was a lector. She taught Sunday school. She sang in the choir.

Luke says he decided to convert to Catholicism independent of his relationship with Marybeth—that it was "not a condition of their relationship progressing." He says he was mostly "self-catechized," that is, he learned all he could about Catholicism independently. He says that this was very consistent with the way he was brought up.

"It was a very knowledge-oriented approach to religious belief. There was a process of thinking through things. I have always held that if someone else presents something right, I have no problem dropping what I thought was right." This sounds like a good idea but this attitude has prevented Luke from achieving a certain kind of spiritual stability, as we shall see.

Marybeth wanted a Catholic wedding, and Luke was in the military about to go overseas. So once they were engaged, the conversion happened fairly quickly, immediately followed by the wedding.

Things were going smoothly until the birth of their first child. Marybeth had assumed that their daughter would be baptized as an infant, as is Catholic custom. But Luke wanted the child to be "of an age of reason," a policy more consistent with his Bible-church upbringing.

As Marybeth recalls, "We spent three months researching scripture and trying to work through our differences in terms of when child could be baptized. It was very difficult. I had many tears about that. He's very good at presenting his case." In the end, Luke had a conversation with a Catholic priest who had formerly been an Anglican. As Luke recalls, "He told me there are some things you may find hard to accept but which you also can't find grounds to reject. And in those circumstances we have to let the church accept those and believe those for us." The child was baptized at four months. But then the couple's religious paths truly started to diverge.

Luke began attending a discussion group at a local religious bookstore. Many of the other participants belonged to an Eastern Orthodox Church, and over time he became quite attracted to their theology. A year into his participation in this group, he told Marybeth that he was considering leaving the Catholic Church to become Orthodox. The couple was expecting their second child at the time, and Marybeth didn't feel she could deal with this issue. "Let's talk about it after our child's born," she told him. Once that happened, though, Luke announced that he could not take communion anymore and would not attend a Catholic church. In fact, he announced it on the way home from the hospital after the birth.

The way he talked to her about his decision, she says, made her take the matter very personally. He would ask, "How can you believe in that?" While she thinks he may have just been trying to think through the issue, she was devastated. "We were involved in our parish. It was my dream unfolding: A happy couple with beautiful children. We have friends in the church. We would have our priest over for dinner and that was all changing." When Luke made his announcement, Marybeth said it felt to her as if he were committing "adultery."

In retrospect, Luke says he was not very "mature" about the whole thing. He thinks he was overbearing and simply "expected her to convert along with me . . . because I was right." His process of religious discovery was all-consuming, and he took little time to think about how this was affecting his wife.

Today the couple have two daughters, ages fourteen and seven, and a son who is eleven. Marybeth homeschools them all. They attend both Orthodox and Catholic churches on most weekends (a total of more than three hours of services, in case you're counting), and they are familiar with both the eastern and the western saints. They are probably more Catholic than Orthodox, though. Marybeth says that Luke has "held fast" to his commitment to raising them Catholic. But during our conversation, Luke interjects: "The whole issue needs to be rethought."

She suspects that the kids will make their own decision soon, but (like Judy, the mother of three from Pittsburgh whom we met in the introduction), Marybeth is worried about how her side will fare. She can't really control which way the kids will go, but she doesn't want to end up the only Catholic in her family either. Unlike her husband, she says she is the one who tries to avoid conflict and does not want to get into a debating match over religion. "I am not the one that's going to read 150 books on the papacy. I'm the doer." She has gotten her kids involved in volunteering through the church and acknowledges that she has probably skirted over some of the more difficult theological issues in their family. "But you can only do that for so long before the children will say, 'Why did dad leave Catholic Church?' I'm not sure I have the answers and that's probably part of the dilemma. I don't feel as prepared as I should be. I have a lot of fear and trembling."

Faith is extraordinarily important to both Luke and Marybeth, and it feels, to an outside observer anyway, as if there is a ticking time bomb in their marriage. Marybeth fears the day when she has to defend her own faith to her children against the criticisms of her husband. Her dream of having a family strengthened and enveloped by a church community has come crashing down. She is probably too devout to consider actually getting a divorce. And given her desire for religious unity in her family, divorce would hardly help accomplish her goal.

For many husbands, wives, and children, interfaith marriage is a painful reality, a reminder that the family is not together in some ultimate sense. Divorce may not be the solution for these families, but a separation is already in place.

In a moving essay called "Faith in the Flesh," writer R. R. Reno, now the editor of the magazine *First Things*, recalls the pain his daughter felt as her bat mitzvah approached. Reno, who is Catholic, and his wife, who is Jewish, raised their children Jewish. But nothing in his past seemed to quite prepare him for this event.

"My daughter loves me very much but she is very conscious that this day of her bat mitzvah is as a hating of her father. She was bitter about the fact that I could not be with her mother at her side as she entered into an intimate fellowship with God—to be his voice to his people through the reading of the Torah. She was angry and she cried about it in the months of preparation prior to the bat mitzvah, but neither the rabbi, nor her mother, nor I could give her what she wanted."

But Reno too can feel her pain. "And now she is before me. She is being ravished by the concentration necessary to chant the ancient Hebrew. She is being drawn nearer to God. I can only witness. I cannot be by her side to hold onto the hems of her garments as she rises upward with each flourish of the canticle of recitation." He concludes: "My daughter is feeling the full blow of intermarriage. Why can't we all go together?"[20]

Most religious leaders I have spoken with advise marrying within the faith, of course, both for the preservation of the faith and for the long-term stability of the marriage. But the cases like Luke and Marybeth's are becoming increasingly common. As American religion becomes more fluid and people feel more comfortable exploring faith on their own and even adopting a new faith once they are already married, conflicts within families will inevitably arise.

Perhaps one of the most heartbreaking stories I heard was from a man named Joel. He married his wife Christina in 1989 when they had just graduated from college. He attended a Conservative synagogue growing up and dated both Jews and non-Jews in high school and college. His parents made clear they wanted him to marry in the faith. But he fell for Christina. He understood her to be some kind of lapsed Christian, but she had never during their courtship or during the first eight years of their marriage expressed an interest in attending church. Joel had made clear that any children they had should be raised Jewish and Christina readily agreed.

Then, about fifteen years ago, Christina's father fell ill. She recalls going to visit him in the hospital. Her father had recently started attending an Episcopal church, and several members came to see him during his illness. Christina remembers that the "minister spent the night on the floor in the hospital." She says the "amazing people" she met then "opened my eyes to something I hadn't seen before, something they had that I didn't have." She says, "I had a distinct experience on the night he passed away. I just sensed God was there and I wasn't sure what to do with that."

When she returned home to Florida, she decided to go to a local Anglican church. Joel was sympathetic at first. "It was a natural reaction for her to want to go to church. I thought she was seeking comfort." Even when she told her husband that she wanted to have their two-year-old son baptized,

Joel didn't object. As Christina recalls, "he didn't think it made much difference about whether we dumped water on his head."

Today, the couple has three sons, ages seventeen, twelve, and ten. Christina has continued to attend church every Sunday. She has joined the choir. She has taken classes at a local seminary and even considered becoming a priest, until Joel suggested that it would be hard to find a congregation to hire her "with a Jewish anchor dragging her down." He has tried to better understand her newfound faith, even attending a Bible study at her church for a year and a half.

The fights the couple have are almost entirely about their children. Joel will not allow Christina to take them to church. And Christina argues with Joel every time he wants them to participate in some Jewish activity. The arguments about their second son's bar mitzvah began two years ago. The children have asked their parents questions about their religious differences, beginning, of course, when they were younger with "Where does Mommy go on Sundays?"

Christina seems to think that her faith is stronger and therefore should trump her husband's when it comes to raising the kids. Joel acknowledges that he seems less religious than his wife. But being Jewish, he says, is still a core part of his identity. "I want to raise my three boys to grow up to be men who have the right values and understand right and wrong. And the only way I know how to do that is from a Jewish background. I don't know how to splice that on to the Christian experience." He continues: Judaism provides the "framework of why you live a good life, how God wants you to behave." "Why," he asks, "should I stop and help someone change a tire on the side of the road? It's a mitzvah. It's part of who I am." Maybe, Joel wonders, it would have been different if they had a daughter. But he thinks boys look to their fathers for instruction on these things.

When asked about interfaith marriage, Christina says, "I would recommend against it. Marriage is hard enough to not add the added dimension of such a fundamental disagreement. Faith is an integral part of marriage and raising children together in faith is essential. Both faiths warn against marrying outside the faith for good reasons."

So why haven't Christina and Joel split yet? Joel believes it is important for the two to stay together for the children. Christina cites First Corinthians, Jesus's admonitions to those Christians who find themselves married to nonbelievers:

If any believer has a wife who is an unbeliever, and she consents to live with him, he should not divorce her. And if any woman has a husband who is an unbeliever, and he consents to live with her, she should not divorce him. For the unbelieving husband is made holy through his wife, and the unbelieving wife is made holy through her husband. Otherwise, your children would be unclean, but as it is, they are holy. But if the unbelieving partner separates, let it be so; in such a case the brother or sister is not bound. It is to peace that God has called you. Wife, for all you know, you might save your husband. Husband, for all you know, you might save your wife. (1 Corinthians 7:12–16)

Counseling those who have found a new faith after marriage may be one of the most difficult sorts of marital negotiations that religious leaders undertake. Russell Moore of the Southern Baptist Theological Seminary reminds the Christian in the relationship that "this is a real marriage and you owe your spouse everything you owed him before—love, fidelity and understanding. Your marriage is a sanctified union before God." He also reminds them, tempting as it may be, that proselytizing to your spouse is not necessarily the best course of action. "I've never seen someone convert because of ongoing harassment," he says, "but I have seen many husbands who have converted through the examples of their wives—without a word ever being said."

The difficulties created by these same-faith marriages that become interfaith ones are such that some clergy want to discourage them. Rabbi James Gibson tells me that he has twice performed conversion ceremonies that made only one member of the couple Jewish. And he regretted it both times. In both cases, the person converting "saw Judaism only as a religion, a faith stance, as opposed to a way of life in a community." But religion generally and Judaism in particular cannot exist in a vacuum. People who want to convert but think it will only affect them individually are in for a surprise.

✦ ✦ ✦

For those interfaith marriages that do end in divorce, the conflict over raising children may become even more difficult. The Reyes case mentioned at the beginning of the chapter is not unique. Beverly W. Boorstein, a former Family and Probate Court Justice in Massachusetts, said "religion frequently came up" in her courtroom. She found that many couples "decided one thing when they got married and when they had children they decided something else." She can't say whether disagreement over religion "was always the cause of the differences in the marriage or merely a symptom." But she has seen how these conflicts evolve. "I imagine when you're young and starting out, maybe you don't care about religion," she says, but it certainly can become important later.

"Among my colleagues," she recalls, "we were all wrestling with these problems." From medical treatment issues where one parent is a Christian Scientist to disputes over whether a child should be circumcised, Boorstein believes that judges were often asked to intervene in cases where they had no expertise. She recalls one instance in which a judge was asked to decide whether a kid should have to go to Hebrew school. On a number of occasions, one of the parents would agree to something and then not follow through. "They would come back and be charged with contempt of court."

Given these hot-button questions, it is little surprise that interfaith divorce cases occasionally attract national attention. Brenda Voydatch and her husband Martin Kurowski split up shortly after their daughter Amanda was born fifteen years ago. At the time, they were both evangelical Christians and wanted to raise their daughter as such. But the two became locked in a battle that went all the way to the New Hampshire Supreme Court in 2011. Voydatch had been homeschooling their daughter using the curriculum from Bob Jones University, a fundamentalist college. Kurowski said that he wanted Amanda "exposed to the broader culture at large," according to his lawyer, Elizabeth Donovan.

Donovan insisted that her client didn't have any problem with the religious content of his daughter's schooling. But Douglas Napier, the senior legal counsel for the Alliance Defense Fund, which represented Voydatch, says that the conflict began when Kurowski (who, Napier says, fell away from the faith) remarried and Amanda started "witnessing" to his new wife. Napier says that Amanda told her new stepmother "I believe you need to believe in Jesus in order to go to heaven. I want you to be in heaven some day."

It is easy to imagine the kind of tension this might create. As Napier notes, when it comes to raising children, "Faiths are things that are mutually exclusive. There are a lot of things that can be compromised and accommodated. But faith is not one of them." As we have seen in previous chapters, this is not always true. Parents in interfaith marriages do regularly make compromises when it comes to faith. But there are cases when it becomes impossible.

A lower court judge ruled in Martin Kurowski's favor, mandating that Amanda attend the local public school. The court's reasoning suggested that it was important for children to be exposed to diverse viewpoints, not just a Christian one. Christian groups as well as the Homeschool Legal Defense Fund rightly worried that this set a precedent for favoring public schools over religious ones or homeschooling.

The New Hampshire Supreme Court upheld the decision but scaled back the reasoning to suggest that it was the specific facts of the case rather than any general principle about religious or secular education that was at stake. As Justice Robert Lynn wrote for the court: "Both parents enjoy the fundamental liberty interest to direct the upbringing and education of their children. Each parent was equally entitled to the presumption that his or her respective decision was consonant with [the] daughter's best interests."

Generally, the courts are loath to enter into such disputes. Not only do most child advocates believe it is better for such matters to be worked out by the parents outside of a courtroom setting but, as a constitutional matter, judges do not want to be seen as favoring one faith over another. And as Boorstein notes, they often have little basis on which to judge such matters.

Ideally, these issues would never be resolved by our legal system. Families, marriage counselors, and even religious leaders seem to have a better sense of what is necessary for family stability than the courts. But, given rising rates of interfaith marriage and the lack of forethought that many couples seem to give to faith before getting married, it seems likely that this problem will get worse before it gets better.

CHAPTER SEVEN

———◆———

Muslims in the Melting Pot

WHEN THE SHOW *ALL-AMERICAN MUSLIM* LAUNCHED IN THE fall of 2011, it seemed at first like a nonevent. TLC, the cable channel on which it was airing, had made a name for itself presenting reality shows about small subcultures of American life—from the toddler beauty pageant circuit to families of "little people." Trying to represent the life of millions of Muslims in the United States was going to be a slightly broader project. But the producers seemed to do a reasonable job at least of showing some of the different strains of Muslim life. The families on the program represented a cross section of classes and levels of religious observance. Some of the women wore hijabs, while others were more provocatively dressed. One was even trying to open a nightclub.

But a few weeks after the show's premiere, a group called the Florida Family Association began pressuring companies that were sponsoring the program to withdraw their support, and a few big ones, like the home-improvement store Lowes, actually agreed. The association, a group that says its "thousands of supporters" share the "goal of improving America's moral environment," released this statement: "The show profiles only Muslims that appear to be ordinary folks while excluding many Islamic believers whose agenda poses a clear and present danger to liberties and traditional values that the majority of Americans cherish."

The association cited an article from the magazine *Human Events* to drive home the point: The characters look like they're leading normal American lives, but some of them "acknowledge that they are not all that religious. And that is the problem at the heart of 'All-American Muslim.' The Muslims it depicts are for the most part undoubtedly harmless, completely uninterested in jihad and Islamic supremacism."[1]

In that sense, *All-American Muslim* is representative of American Muslims. As a group, they *are* uninterested in jihad and Islamic supremacism. They are by and large much less radicalized than their European, let alone their Middle Eastern, counterparts. And certainly secularization has been one factor in their attitudes. In fact, a number of Muslim leaders have expressed concern to me that the Muslim population is becoming dramatically less religious as each decade passes, with only a fraction of Muslims in many American communities attending mosque even once a year.

Jihad Turk, the director of religious affairs at the Islamic Center of Southern California, offers me his hard-headed assessment: "Currently, it's my estimation that the assimilation rate of Muslims who immigrated to this country—and the attrition rate in terms of their identifying and practicing and becoming a part of an organized community—is 90 percent." That's the proportion, he says, who are "no longer affiliating themselves with the community." Of the million or so Muslims in California, he has calculated that between 7 and 15 percent attend services at a mosque on a semiregular basis. As time goes on, he expects that number to decline further.

Interfaith marriage has no doubt been a cause and an effect of this assimilation. Muslims who do not feel themselves attached to the community will be more likely to marry out, and those who marry out will be more likely to raise families that do not feel connected to the community. According to a 2007 Pew Study, levels of religiosity had a dramatic impact on Muslim views of intermarriage. While 84 percent of those who described themselves as "not very religious" regarded interfaith marriage as acceptable, less than half of "devout" respondents did.[2]

Interestingly, the first major plot on "All-American Muslim" was about an interfaith couple about to get married. An Irish Catholic Chicago man named Jeff wanted to wed Shadia, a Lebanese Muslim woman from Detroit with a ten-year-old son from a previous marriage. But she felt that her family would "never let her hear the end of it" unless Jeff converted to Islam.

And so on the day before the wedding, he underwent a conversion in front of Shadia's family. In her parents' living room, he said, "I bear witness that there is no god but God. I bear witness that Mohammad is his messenger." Speaking into the camera afterward, Jeff remarks that it was very easy to convert, an observation to which we will return shortly.

Jeff's mother was upset by this turn of events and could not bring herself to attend the conversion ceremony. Explaining her objection, she told him, "It's the continuity of tradition that has been in our family. And this is a big break." Nonetheless, she tells him she still loves him and that she will learn to deal with it. "Society evolves," she says. "It doesn't stay the same. Sometimes we would like it to stay the same. But you and Shadi have worked this through." Though it was clearly an emotional moment for her, his mother said in an interview at the end of the episode that that wedding day itself was one of the happiest of her life.

The reception combined cultural traditions in a way that one might be hard-pressed to find elsewhere in the world. The five hundred people gathered in a Michigan banquet hall saw both a traditional belly dance and an Irish step dance. There was no alcohol at the party, but one of Jeff's cousins reported that he had plenty of fun in spite of that fact. Indeed, to the extent that the camera captured the reactions of those at the event, most people seemed to find it downright heartwarming.

Contrast this with the "combined cultural traditions" that a friend of mine reported from a wedding he attended in Southern France a couple of years ago. The bride, an Iranian Muslim, had lived in France since she was a toddler, and she was marrying a man from a well-established French family. As part of the evening's entertainment, the groomsmen blindfolded and tied up the groom and then turned out the lights, while they used sound and lighting effects to make it seem as though semi-automatic weapons were being shot off. Because, the audience was supposed to understand, this is the Muslim culture he was marrying into—wink, wink. In a speech, one of the groomsmen made a joke about how the groom couldn't find a "real French girl" who was pretty enough for him. And to top it all off, the groom's father offered a kind of benighted "welcome" of the family to France, even though they had lived there for decades. Intermarriage may be happening elsewhere in the world but it is not always the wacky "Big Fat Greek Wedding" blending of cultures that Americans generally experience.

Jeff and Shadia's marriage was not ultimately an interfaith one, but if this working-class, Catholic guy is willing to marry a Muslim and even convert, it does tell us something about the social acceptability in America of a Christian marrying a Muslim. Jeff says early on that he thinks converting to Islam is what was best for his wife and his new family. His mother was happy about the wedding, even if she wasn't thrilled with the conversion. And her family welcomed him as one of their own—at least, once he converted.

I found this dynamic in a number of Muslim/non-Muslim couples I interviewed. That is, there was an initial objection on the part of one family or the other to either the couple dating or to their wedding. But over the long term, there is general acceptance and even a kind of embrace.

With Amy and Farid, whom we met in the introduction, the objection seemed to come mostly from his Muslim family, who all but forbade him to marry Amy, a Christian. Farid decided not to listen to them, and they ultimately welcomed her into their family. The couple and their toddler son live near his family and see them often. Amy even helped out in their family business for a time.

When Nicole, who grew up in a black Baptist church, began dating a Muslim in college, her parents didn't say much. But once her mother realized Nicole was getting serious about the relationship, she started to become "concerned." "She is very conservative in her beliefs," says Nicole. "For her this was a crack in God's faith for me to want to marry someone who doesn't believe Jesus Christ was our lord and savior. Also she was terrified I would convert." Nicole did not convert but before she married (and since) her husband and her mother have had some long conversations about faith. Now, Nicole says, "My family has accepted him with open arms. All of our views of Islam have changed because we've taken the time to educate ourselves. My mom finds herself defending his religion to others."

Natalie had a similar experience when she started dating Hamid. She said her parents sat her down and told her she should date someone from her own faith. But after they met him, Natalie recalls, they "apologized. They said he was an amazing man. That he brought so much into their lives and that he opened their horizons." She was particularly moved that they realized "God's love is for everyone, not just for your religion."

This idea that God is universally accessible (regardless of one's faith) is actually an increasingly common belief among Americans. A majority of Americans, according to research from the Pew Forum on Religion and

Public Life, believe that people from other religions can go to heaven. And interfaith marriage seems to encourage families to come to that conclusion. As Nicole explains, "None of us chose what family we were born into. I could have been born Jewish in Israel. I didn't pick to be Christian in America. Just because someone is a religion and they don't believe in what I believe, doesn't mean they will go to hell." Nicole and her husband are raising their children Muslim, and she says, "I don't think my kids are going to hell because they're not going to be Christian. His belief system will be great for our kids."

In their book, *American Grace*, Robert Putnam and David Campbell describe something called the "Aunt Susan Principle." They write: "We all have an Aunt Susan in our lives, the sort of person who epitomizes what it means to be a saint, but whose religious background is different from our own . . . Whatever her religious background (or lack thereof), you know that Aunt Susan is destined for heaven. And if she is going to heaven, what does that say about other people who share her religion or lack of religion? Maybe they can go to heaven too."[3]

In interfaith marriages, it seems that first one person begins to fall for someone of another faith. If a Christian woman likes a Muslim man enough to marry him, she will often reach the "Aunt Susan" conclusion. If he is such a great guy, there can't be something terribly wrong with his belief system. Maybe other Muslims are great, too. The family of the Christian girl will often go through the same process.

Campbell and Putnam used data they collected to measure this dynamic. Their "feeling thermometer" effectively puts a number on how a person views another faith. There is a clear correlation between being married to a spouse of another religion and one's feeling thermometer (FT) score toward that religion. The scale goes from 1–100, and a higher number means a more positive perception.

The FT scores below (table 7.1) for each religion exclude the self-perception of those who are of that faith. In other words, the score for Catholics excludes how Catholics feel about Catholics, and so on. The column named "Not married to spouse of this religion" is the FT score for that religion for people who do not have a spouse with that religion. So, non-Catholics who are not married to a Catholic give them a score of 58. But non-Catholics married to a Catholic give them a score of 61.

In each case, the FT scores are higher when someone has a spouse of that religion. In some cases (Catholics, for example) the difference is not

TABLE 7.1   Score on Feeling Thermometer Toward Other Faiths

	Not married to spouse of this religion	Married to spouse of this religion	Significant?
Catholics	58	61	On the cusp
Evangelicals	53	56	Yes
Mainline Protestants	59	68	Yes
Nones	51	54	On the cusp
Jews	59	68	Yes (but very few cases)
Mormons	48	62	Yes (but very few cases)

huge, but in others the gap is substantial. Note that, as usual, the total number of Jews and Mormons is really small, but the gap is so large as to be statistically significant.

Perhaps these results do not seem surprising. Of course, people who marry someone from another faith will eventually come to like that faith better. But it is easy to imagine how greater familiarity with a particular faith might just as well breed suspicion. A more intimate look at a particular religion might reveal some problematic tenets—or actors—that are hidden from outsiders. A member of a particular faith might present his religion as something liberal or moderate, but what is a spouse to make of it when a radical preacher shows up one day at a mosque? Religious leaders are not always sensitive to the presence of outsiders and may make remarks or even demands on others that do not fit with the way one member of a couple has presented the faith.

More broadly speaking, Campbell and Putnam found that any kind of contact Americans have with someone of another faith is likely to lead to greater positive feelings toward that faith. And so the contact that occurs through an extended family connection is also likely to have this effect. As the authors write, "Knowing someone within a particular religious group means a more positive assessment of that group in general—whether you have known that someone for a long time or not."

✧   ✧   ✧

The interfaith marriage rate among Muslims is roughly the same as for other Americans. According to data taken from the Pew Religious Landscape Survey of 2007, in round numbers, about one in five American Muslims have married outside their religion.

This is a particularly high percentage considering that 63 percent of Muslims are actually foreign-born.[4] Even among the foreign-born, though, 12 percent are intermarried.[5] Given that they were probably unlikely to marry outside the faith in their home countries—Muslim countries mostly take a dim view of such intermixing—this is a remarkable record of inter-marriage. Compare Muslims, for instance, with Hindus, the vast majority of whom are also immigrants. Only 6% of foreign-born Hindus report having a spouse of another faith.[6] One might assume that Hindus would have an easier time assimilating than Muslims because of the association many Americans make between Islam with radicalism, but this does not appear to be the case.

If Muslim attitudes are any indication, that percentage in this group who intermarry seems likely to go up. According to another 2007 Pew survey, only 30 percent of Muslim men and 46 percent of Muslim women said they oppose interfaith marriage.[7] It is not an apples-to-apples comparison, but in my survey, we asked all participants how important it was to them that their children marry someone of the same faith. A little more than 35 percent said it was either very important or somewhat important. Assuming that people might be more inclined to oppose their own children's intermarriage than the idea of intermarriage in principle, it seems as though Muslims' views are not much different from those of the general American population.

And that seems to be part of a larger trend of Muslims integrating them-selves into the broader American culture. A Pew report released shortly before the tenth anniversary of 9/11 found that "Muslim Americans are overwhelmingly satisfied with the way things are going in their lives (82 percent) and continue to rate their communities very positively as places to live (79 percent excellent or good)." The report also found that "strikingly, Muslim Americans are far more satisfied with the way things are going in the U.S. (56 percent) than is the general public (23 percent)."[8] A Gallup poll released a few weeks earlier found that Muslims were more optimistic about their futures than any other religious group in the United States.

Given that American Muslims seem relatively happy about life here, it is not surprising that they are assimilating quickly. Again, though, the reverse also seems true. Fast assimilation may be making them more satisfied with their lives in America. According to the Pew report, "A majority of Muslim Americans (56 percent) say that most Muslims who come to the U.S. want to adopt American customs and ways of life." Also, when asked to choose, the report continues "nearly half of Muslims in the U.S. (49 percent) say they think of themselves first as a Muslim, 26 percent say they think of themselves first as an American, and 18 percent say they are both. Among U.S. Christians, 46 percent say they identify as Christian first, while the same number identify as American first." Again, if self-identification is any measure, it seems as though Muslims are not so different from other Americans.[9]

We don't have survey data from the waves of Jews who came here from Russia in the early part of the twentieth century or the Irish who arrived here during the Potato Famine, but the comparison is worth making. How were Catholics and Jews received then as compared to Muslims today? And how did each group adjust to life in America? As Campbell and Putnam wrote in a 2011 *Wall Street Journal* article, "There was once a time when Jews and Catholics faced greater hostility than Muslims . . . do today, even including mob violence. The accusations commonly leveled against Jews and Catholics—all the way up to the 1960s—should sound familiar. Among other things, their religions were said to be incompatible with America's democratic system of government, their adherents beholden to foreign influences."[10]

Campbell and Putnam explain, "While anti-Semitism and anti-Catholicism have not been completely extinguished, today examples of such bigotry are the exception and not the rule. Jews and Catholics have firmly secured a place in America's kaleidoscope of religions."[11]

Still, there are those who worry that Muslims are different, that they will be more likely than other American religious groups to stick to their own people and to their orthodox beliefs and behaviors. They also worry that America's assimilation process has been broken, that multiculturalism has led each religious and ethnic group to embrace their uniqueness while making their members increasingly resistant to identifying as Americans. They wonder whether Muslims will in fact go through the same process that Catholics and Jews did before them—whether they will be subsumed by the melting pot.

The phrase "melting pot," actually comes from a play of that name by Israel Zangwill, first staged in 1908. In it, the protagonist, David, immigrates to the United States from Russia after his family has been killed in a pogrom. He composes an "American Symphony," which he says "finds inspiration . . . in the seething of the Crucible." America, he explains, "is God's Crucible, the great Melting-Pot where all the races of Europe are melting and reform-ing."[12] David happily sheds his past and his Jewish identity in an effort to jump into this pot. He falls in love with a Christian woman from Russia, whose father was apparently responsible for the deaths of David's family. The father apologizes, David forgives, and the two live happily ever after.

Of course, it is unlikely that the melting pot ever worked the way *The Melting Pot* did. Nor do most Americans want it to. And modern ideas about multiculturalism have no doubt had their effect. But there are also forces making the assimilation process move more quickly than it has his-torically. Among them are increasing geographic mobility, modern tech-nology, the omnipresence of media, and higher levels of tolerance for all minorities. In other words, religious groups can no longer isolate themselves to the same extent they used to. And while efforts to keep the faithful from mixing with outsiders were often aided by outsiders' suspicions (or worse) of the faithful, such attitudes are less common today.

The ways in which religious differences are accepted in America often go unnoticed by Americans. But when people come here from other parts of the world, the tolerance and freedom to intermingle are immediately obvious to them. And it is something that all of the members of interfaith couples from other countries remarked upon to me, often unprompted. The contrast is probably most stark for Muslims, who are used to being marginalized in many European countries or who are used to living in majority-Muslim countries where they have little to no contact with people of other faiths.

Abbas, an Egyptian Muslim, met his wife, Dorit, an Israeli Jew, while she was working as a travel agent booking tour groups in the Sinai desert and he was employed at a hotel there. They talked regularly on the phone because he was one of the few hotel employees who spoke Hebrew—he had learned it in college—and Dorit and her colleagues did not speak Arabic.

Dorit was not the first Israeli he had encountered. Abbas had worked with a multinational military force in the Sinai a few years earlier, which he found eye-opening, to say the least. Growing up, he explained, "We don't make a difference between Israeli and Jews. Israelis are just murderers. I grew up with . . . the image that Israelis walk around with guns and if they don't like you they'll shoot you." He was surprised, he recalled, "when I met first an Israeli person in military that they are just regular person. Some are good some are bad, but they are regular people. They are 18 or 19 and they didn't care much about conflict . . . they wanted to do military service for three years and go home. It's not like they are dedicating themselves to killing."

After many phone conversations, Abbas and Dorit decided to meet. They would rent a car and leave the resort together. But they weren't being careful enough, Abbas recalls. After a few meetings like this, his friends at the hotel warned him that the Egyptian police were starting to talk about him, suspicious, apparently, that he was consorting with an Israeli. He didn't tell his family about the relationship. "I knew they would be against it. They would lock me at home if they knew." The couple could not live permanently in Israel or in Egypt, they knew. So Dorit suggested they go to America. In 1997, they managed to get tourist visas to the United States.

It was not easy coming to this country together. They had no jobs and nowhere to stay. Abbas didn't really plan for this, he acknowledges, because he had friends who told him that "if he had a Jewish girlfriend he would be able to get a green card after a week." He laughs now, but his friends told him in all seriousness, "It's a Jewish country. The Jews are very powerful there." Abbas says he was naïve enough to believe this, "but then I came here and no one cared if my girlfriend was Jewish."

Abbas and Dorit lived in New York for a few months, trying to make ends meet. He returned to Egypt briefly because he wasn't sure if their relationship was going to last. But he quickly realized that was a mistake. "I felt like I went back 100 years." He could no longer tolerate the bigoted attitudes of his friends and family. So he moved back to the United States and married Dorit at New York's City Hall shortly thereafter.

As heartwarming as some may find this story, and as nice as it is that Abbas thinks of America as being enlightened with regard to religious and ethnic differences, many Muslim and Jewish communal leaders would not be particularly pleased about the way that Abbas and Dorit are raising their nine-year-old son today. The boy is growing up celebrating holidays in both Judaism and in Islam, but he is not being offered any religious instruction per se. And just as in other religious communities, Muslims are worried that the offspring of interfaith marriages will not feel themselves connected to Islam in any particularly strong way.

Steve Mustapha Elturk, an imam in Troy, Michigan, tells me that his first marriage was to a Catholic Filipina woman. The couple sent one of their children to Catholic school, while Elturk taught him the Qur'an at home. Looking back, Elturk doesn't think this was wise. When he married her, he says, "I really didn't think much about how the children would be raised." One of his sons started dating a Christian woman in college. She converted before the two married, but Elturk believes that he did not place enough emphasis on the Muslim faith for his children when they were young and that impacted their decisions as adults. He believes that things went much more smoothly with his second wife, a Muslim, and their children because he was more religious by then and more concerned with shaping his family's faith.

Now he sees all around him that children of interfaith couples are having difficulties. Husbands and wives, he says, have not agreed on "how to plan for the children. . . . If the Christian or the Jewish sister is a practicing one and if the Muslim is a practicing one, there is going to be a clash because she wants the children to be like her and he wants them to be in his faith. And it becomes a clash that leads at times to divorces and confusion among the kids."

Jihad Turk of the Islamic Center of Southern California remembers getting a call from a father whose eighteen-year-old daughter was dating a Christian. He wanted Turk to talk her out of the relationship. Turk asked the girl about her own beliefs. It turned out that her mother was Catholic. She told Turk, "Growing up, my mom would [be] trying to influence me to become a Christian, and I'm closer to my mom. So, I'm Christian."

Turk observes, "You'll see some of that confusion play itself out, and sometimes if the relationship isn't as strong, or parents aren't on the same page about how to raise the children, then that split between the parents will inevitably manifest itself in the children. That applies to parenting in general," he observes, and to the area of religion in particular.

There are a few Muslim leaders who say that the issue of interfaith marriage is not a big one in their communities. Either they don't see it becoming more common or they don't see much conflict once such marriages occur. Victor Begg, the chairman emeritus of the Council of Islamic Organizations of Michigan, came to the United States from India in 1969. He married a Hindu woman who converted to Islam just before the wedding. He told her, "I'm a Muslim. I can't marry someone who worships idols and stuff." Even so, he was not at the time a particularly religious person. Over time he and his wife became more religious—he calls her a "pious lady" today. When I visited Victor, his wife was actually in India looking for a bride for one of their sons.

His own experience notwithstanding, Begg claims to have seen no uptick in the number of interfaith marriages in the Muslim community and seems a little puzzled about why I am asking questions about it. He does, however, see a lot of interethnic marriages among Muslim men and women.

Interestingly, these arrangements have provoked objections from families who come to him with their complaints.

He's a regular reader of the local Muslim press and observes that people will place personal ads that don't mention religion at all. They will just say they want an "Egyptian wife." He has noticed more Shia/Sunni and Arab/non-Arab matches. "It's not so much with African Americans, you know. . . . If an African comes and wants to get their son married to your daughter. Nobody wants that." He says that there is nothing in Islamic law to prevent such interethnic or interracial marriages, "but culture is culture."

Jihad Turk says that he has encountered a similar dilemma. Where he is focused on encouraging Muslims to marry other Muslims in order to carry on the religious traditions he values, he finds that many of the parents of the young people at the Islamic Center are demanding that their children find mates of the same ethnicity. "We have at our center something like sixty different nationalities, and so we try our best to bring them together and say, 'Yes, you like Pakistan. You like being Egyptian, or whatever, but your children are not that. They're American, and so let's come together. We're a faith community. We're not an Egyptian community or a Pakistani community.'" He tries to persuade parents that passing on an ethnicity is going to be difficult in this country, but that they can still pass on their faith. "The kids are American. There are no two ways about it, and so the idea is at least have the Islamic faith, to be faithful in believing in God. . . . Families need to be able to separate between the culture and the religion."

Turk himself is the product of an interfaith marriage, albeit one that is sanctioned in Islam. His father is a Muslim from Jerusalem and his mother is a Christian American. Before the two got married, though, they agreed that Turk and his siblings would be raised Muslim.

Turk says he was not confused about his religious identity as a child. His mother took the children to the mosque on Fridays. She did not teach them about Islam or have them pray regularly at home, but she also did not in any way undermine their Muslim upbringing by teaching them about Christianity. The family did not celebrate Christmas, though Turk recalls his grandmother sending him Christmas presents. "We didn't know a whole lot about Islam, but we were told we were Muslim, and yeah, we knew that we were kind of different [from Christians], but we really didn't have enough of a basis to know what that difference was, other than we didn't believe in the

Trinity." Turk's parents divorced when he was seventeen, but he attributes their differences more to culture than to religion.

Nonetheless, Turk does believe that discussing the terms of a marriage beforehand, including—and perhaps especially—how to raise the children, is vital to producing a happy marriage and a family that lives in accordance with the tenets of Islam. Turk has worked on putting together a premarital course that he encourages couples to take before they tie the knot. It's called "Before You Say 'I Do': Preparing for the Marriage of a Lifetime," and it "draws on guidelines provided by the Qur'an and Sunnah, as well as best practices in the marriage/family counseling field to address various dimensions of the marriage process."

Munira Ezzeldine, a marriage counselor in Irvine, California, who is one of the other instructors for the course, tells me that Islam in America is at a "kind of crossroads now." She explains, "We don't have something called dating in the Western context, you know with pre-marital sex and all the stuff that comes with it." But young Muslims are also not interested in having arranged marriages as their parents and grandparents did. "They actually want to get to know the person for a certain amount of time, but also within the boundaries."

This has led, among other things, to the launch of Muslim "speed-dating," in which Muslim families bring their sons and daughters to meet each other in a hotel ballroom for brief interviews to see if there is a potential match. There is also an accompanying Muslim dating website modeled on the Jewish dating website JDate. Interestingly, the man who started the Muslim speed-dating events and the website, a Pakistani immigrant by the name of Jamal Mohsin, actually married a woman from an Orthodox Jewish family. (Her family cut all ties with her, but after three decades of marriage, she told the *New York Times*, they have begun to patch things up.) He does not comment on his own marriage, but he says that the speed-dating environment is a nice mix of the Old World and the New World. "Love marriages break after one or two years. But arranged marriages aren't easy either."[13]

✦   ✦   ✦

If a young Muslim is aiming for this kind of compromise, there are other resources too. Ezzeldine, who wrote a short book called *Before the Wedding: Questions for Muslims to Ask Before Getting Married*, tries to offer her coreligionists a way of getting to know each other without violating the standards of the faith. Ezzeldine wants Muslims to have "the conversations to get to know somebody for marriage in a way" that is more than superficial. Right now they often just say, "Oh I think we get along," but they don't know "what you need to know about a person" before you marry him or her. She also notes that families in the Muslim community have wildly different expectations of religious life and marriage so it is important for everyone to be on the same page.[14]

In fact, if you want to get an idea of just how different those "pages" can be, it is instructive to look at the "premarital questionnaire" put out by the All Dulles Area Muslim Society in Virginia. It includes questions like "Do you want to practice polygamy?" Most in the Muslim community would find such a question beyond the pale, but apparently some don't. The answers to some of the other questions will be revealing as well, like "What are you expecting from your spouse when your friends come to the house?" or "What is the role of the husband?" and "What is the role of a wife?" It is easy to see how the answers to these questions will indeed reveal a community at a "crossroads." As useful as the answers might be for a same-faith Muslim couple, the answers for a Muslim man marrying a non-Muslim woman might suggest deeper divisions.

Interestingly, the lack of communication between Muslim men and women before marriage noted by many Muslim leaders is actually part of a larger problem that Ezzeldine believes is resulting in more interfaith matches. Ezzeldine suggests that the Muslim community's standards for interacting with members of the opposite sex are actually having a deleterious effect on marriage in the community. It is often easier for a Muslim to meet a non-Muslim of the opposite sex—in school for instance—than for a Muslim to meet another Muslim in a religiously sanctioned setting because Muslim prayer and religious education are all segregated by sex.

Ezzeldine says that the high interfaith marriage rates should be a "wakeup call" for the community. She thinks Muslims are "making it so hard for our young people to get to know each other at the mosque or any youth groups or Muslim Student Associations, and then you end up tying their hands and then they end up getting to know [a non-Muslim] really well and befriend somebody in a class or at work. Then of course they are going to make a connection and get married."

Even though such marriages are religiously sanctioned when they involve a Muslim man and a Jewish or Christian woman, Ezzeldine still thinks these interfaith marriages are creating problems for the community.

She believes that the theological justification for allowing men to marry non-Muslim women has been rendered moot by the sociological realities of life in America. "The way it is presented is that the Muslim man is the one who is supposed to keep the faith in that family . . . He's responsible for the children to get educated within the faith. . . ." Ezzeldine says that's not what she witnesses in her community and others she has visited. "The reality is, the woman is the one who is teaching the children, and you know, influencing that family and the faith that they follow."

In addition to the fact that the children of such marriages are not being raised in the Muslim faith, there are other difficulties that have been generated by the double religious standards for men and women. The number of men marrying out has actually created a severe gender imbalance, leaving many Muslim women without partners. In other words, the religiously sanctioned intermarriages are forcing more religiously forbidden intermarriages.

In a 2011 article in the *Guardian*, Syma Mohammed reported on the imbalance at the Muslim matchmaking events she attends in England, where there are sometimes as many as five women for every man. She writes, "Nearly all Muslim singles events are female-dominated, unless organisers artificially construct a level playing field by selling equal numbers of male and female tickets."[15]

Shortly after Mohammed's piece appeared, the American Muslim physician Qanta Ahmed made similar observations in a *USA Today* op-ed: "Muslim women living in non-Muslim majority nations frequently lack intellectually and professionally equal Muslim partners. Instead we are eschewed by our male Muslim counterparts for younger, less career-advanced Muslim women, often from countries of parental heritage. These forces drive Muslim women to either select suitable marriage partners from outside the faith or face unremitting spinsterhood."[16]

As we discussed earlier, there are two potential solutions to this crisis; the first is to allow Muslim women to marry out as well, something that Ahmed advocates in the name of gender equality. She says women should be able to make their own decisions in this regard, that they should be guided by the principles of *ijtihad*, which allows Muslims to interpret religious texts according to their own judgments. This view has been presented most forcefully by Imam Khaleel Mohammed, a professor of religion at San Diego State University. He says that the only reason that the Qur'an does not allow Muslim women to marry non-Muslim men is the concern that a man's religion would always become the dominant one. But in twenty-first-century America, with our sense of sexual equality, this should not be a problem.[17]

Even religious leaders who are sympathetic to this argument and are willing to support a less literal interpretation of the Qur'an may not find themselves in agreement with Imam Mohammed or Qanta Ahmed. Rather, they may see the strong religious influence that mothers have over their children in America as a reason to prohibit interfaith marriage across the board. If women here are so "equal" that the child of an interfaith marriage is more than twice as likely to adopt his mother's faith as his father's, then why should religious authorities trust that a Muslim man married to a Christian woman will end up with Muslim children?

Imam Magid of the All Dulles Area Muslim Society tells me that there are many imams who will not perform the wedding of a Muslim man marrying a non-Muslim woman if they are living in a country where the majority of the population is of the same faith as the woman. "If a Muslim lives in Israel and marries a Jew, they would say it would be hard to raise a child as a Muslim because Judaism is the dominant culture." He says the same would be true of a Muslim trying to marry a Catholic in Italy or a Hindu in some parts of India. "The couple has to exist in a culture where there are other factors that would help the children grow up Muslim." That simply may not be true in America.

The happy wedding reception on *All-American Muslim* did have a telling follow-up. In a later episode, Shadia's brother learns that Jeff, the new convert to Islam, is not fasting for Ramadan. Shadia defends her new husband to her sibling, saying that he has tried, but not eating from sunrise to sundown is a problem for him and not something he is used to. She also blurts out that Jeff really converted in order to marry her.

Her brother is surprised by this admission and decides to have a talk with Jeff. "You don't convert to a religion because of someone. You do it for God," he tells his brother-in-law. "I'm proud to say I'm a Muslim. Here's the question: Do you think you're ready for it? Are you going to be reflecting on billions of Muslims around the world?" Jeff assures him: "I'm very serious about my conversion. The biggest thing was that I wasn't forced into any kind of decision."

It turns out that the conversion of non-Muslim men who are marrying Muslim women is not uncommon. And whatever his wife said, Jeff seemed to take the matter seriously. He does spend a couple of days trying to fast for

Ramadan, and he even abstains from drinking after his conversion. That said, a number of Muslim community leaders have complained to me that conversion to Islam is something that is often undertaken too lightly.

Ezzeldine says she has seen numerous cases in which a non-Muslim will become a "token Muslim." "They'll say the shahada, the declaration of faith." But since often the Muslim member of the couple is not very observant, the non-Muslim is merely doing the conversion "for the sake of having a Muslim marriage." Ezzeldine observes, "So it is kind of funny because it's almost a charade where it's kind of like, 'I'm going to say I'm a Muslim,' and you know, of course," that they're not. She acknowledges that she doesn't "know what's in people's hearts and if they are really Muslim."

Part of the problem, observes Ezzeldine, is that conversion to Islam is not a lengthy or even slightly arduous process—it's easier than the conversion process in, say, a Catholic church or a synagogue. There is no curriculum to master, no test of knowledge by religious authorities. Rather, Islam is a little bit like some strains of evangelical Protestantism in which people can say they were moved by the Spirit and they are instantly "born again."

Salma Elkadi Abugideiri, a marriage counselor in northern Virginia who works with interfaith couples, says that she has seen a number of cases in which people convert "just so they can get married." In fact, she tells me, "I often think of a marriage to a convert as interfaith. If it's a new convert, this person is still not internalized the new faith" and so some of the same issues can still arise. In fact, some of them never internalize the new faith at all.

No Muslim leader I know of is suggesting that the requirements for conversion could or should be made steeper. Ezzeldine explains, "If a person says they want to be Muslim, okay, there is nothing that we can say beyond, 'Are you sure you want to be a Muslim?'" An imam "may counsel them and say, 'Make sure you understand the faith and understand what you are doing. And we're not trying to do fly-by-night Shahaadas.'" But that's about it. Imam Magid probably goes the furthest to deter these superficial conversions by conducting friendly interrogations in his premarital counseling sessions. He inquires about the rationale of the person who wants to convert. He has on a number of occasions talked the less serious men out of converting and, as a result, out of marriage. Still, Magid does not see any theological route to changing the requirements for conversion to ensure that converts are acting in good faith.

✧   ✧   ✧

The combination of these issues does not bode well for Muslim continuity in the United States. Muslims are marrying out at the same rate as other Americans now, and there seem to be a number of factors that will hasten this trend. If men continue to marry out at such high rates (with the support of their religious leaders), the women left behind will be more inclined to marry out because there are fewer available Muslim partners. Indeed, Muslim women's professional and social circumstances may dictate that it is easier to meet and get to know non-Muslim men than Muslim ones. Meanwhile, assuming they follow the patterns of other American families, the children of Muslim men married to non-Muslim women will more than likely be raised in the faith of the non-Muslim mother.

In marriages where the mother is Muslim and the father is not, it is easy to see how the family might begin to move away from the Muslim community since technically their marriage is forbidden. Even in marriages where both members are nominally Muslim because the husband has converted, the man may not adopt any sort of Muslim beliefs or practices. The conversion may effectively be, in Ezzeldine's words, "a charade" performed in order to have a Muslim wedding. All of these circumstances are unlikely to result in a significant number of children being raised homes that identify singly or even strongly as Muslim.

Obviously Muslims in America represent only a small portion of the 1.57 billion Muslims in the world.[18] So the strength of the faith in America is not as integral to the continuity of Islam as, say, the survival of Jews in America is to the continuation of the Jewish people as a whole.[19] Nevertheless, America can be viewed as a kind of experiment for Muslims in the West. As we saw from the various Pew and Gallup surveys, Muslims seem to be assimilating well into American society, but if they find that their community is slowly but steadily losing a connection to the faith, their attitudes of optimism about life here may change. Or they may change for a certain segment of the population. It is easy to see how Muslims and Jews will begin to follow the same trajectory demographically.

Many Jewish communal leaders have observed that intermarriage has effectively grown the total population of Jews with some connection to the faith. But that connection, according to scholars like Jack Wertheimer at the Jewish Theological Seminary, is becoming ever weaker. Meanwhile, Orthodox Jews, who have a much stronger connection to the faith and who are marrying each other and having more children on average than Conservative and Reform Jews will end up becoming a much larger proportion of the population here.

It is certainly possible that Muslims will end up following a similar pattern. The number of religiously nonobservant Muslims may continue to grow thanks to intermarriage. Their children will also marry out, perhaps making their connection to Islam even more tenuous. Meanwhile, a small number of more orthodox Muslims will grow in prominence. They will determine the future of Muslim institutions from mosques to religious schools because they are the ones who will remain involved in them. Whether these Muslims will be "radicalized" is a separate question, but they will certainly appear less assimilated to American life than their more secular peers.

✦   ✦   ✦

A number of American Muslim leaders I spoke with saw interfaith marriage as a pivotal one for their community. But they had not yet resorted to consulting with members of other faiths about the issue. In fact, it may simply be too counterintuitive to expect clergy of any religion to ask other clergy about the way they deal with this sensitive question. It would be like asking the coach of another team for advice on strategy.

Nonetheless, a few of the Jewish leaders to whom I spoke were willing to speculate about the road that Muslims were headed down. Jonathan Sarna has written extensively about how interfaith marriage is not just a Jewish issue. He says it is American attitudes toward religious intermixing that have changed, not Jewish ones. So he does see the Muslim community's trajectory as necessarily looking very similar to the Jewish one, as Muslims come face-to-face with America's extraordinary level of tolerance.

While Muslims are in no way facing the kind of population crisis that Jews are, he does say, "if the Muslim community wants to see endogamy they want to do a few things. First, the ideal is to create plenty of opportunities for Muslims to meet other Muslims in the natural course of events, and that entails schools and camps and certain kinds of colleges, all sorts of experiences . . . Throwing people together in intensive kinds of activities is so wonderful because on the one hand people are making free choice, the ultimate American value, and on the other hand people they can choose from conveniently all have the same faith background."

But there are other less concrete ideas, says Sarna, that Muslim leaders might consider. He believes that they need to "find ways to articulate arguments that could be sold to young people and their parents as to why they should marry among themselves even as their friends are free to marry anybody." He explains, "even as we celebrate America for making the melting pot possible—and I at least celebrate the America that has allowed people of different races to marry—nevertheless they need to articulate a rhetoric that they want to preserve Islam in America." And that can only happen, he says, "if Muslims marry other Muslims."

CHAPTER EIGHT

—◆—

The Welcome Mat

"HOW WELCOMING ARE WE?" THIS IS THE QUESTION THAT seems to consume most religious congregations in the United States. Do we have a good-looking website? Do we have a committee to greet new members? Do strangers feel out of place at our services? Do we offer enough programs for singles? For families with small children? Why don't more parents in the nursery school become involved in the rest of the congregation? Do we advertise our programs enough? Do people visit our Facebook page? Can we offer more activities during the week? More on the weekend? Are we accommodating the schedules of working mothers? Do we have enough activities geared toward men or is it all women's groups?

Whether a particular faith is actively trying to gain converts or is trying to connect with believers who grew up in the faith but have fallen away, American churches and synagogues and mosques have become very engaged in the pursuit of new members. According to a 2008 Pew Survey, 16 percent of Americans claimed no religious affiliation. If headlines are to be believed, this is the New Atheist movement at work. But only 10 percent of those who were unaffiliated identified themselves as atheists and 15 percent as agnostics. In fact, most of the unaffiliated not only believe in God, many of them are not averse to finding a religion and/or a religious institution to join. About four out of ten of the currently unaffiliated said religion is at least somewhat important in their life. Among those who were raised Catholic or Protestant, according to Pew, "1 in 3 say they just have not found the right religion yet."

Leaders of religious institutions (both clergy and laypeople) have been trying hard to lure these people off the fence and through their doors. As James Twitchell put it in his 2007 book, *Shopping for God*, this has led to quite a bit of innovation in how congregations cater to the needs of their current and potential members. "In a highly competitive market, suppliers have to stay on their toes. . . . Coke sells more going up against Pepsi. McDonald's needs Burger King. When markets are supplying interchangeable products, selling can become frantic. Brand war! The complacent get killed." The formulation is perhaps a little overwrought but it is true that in our current spiritual marketplace few congregations can afford to rest on their laurels.[1]

Interfaith families present both a special opportunity and a formidable challenge for many congregations. As we have seen, most interfaith families seem to have relatively traditional views about the importance of religion, particularly in raising children. The husbands and wives often grew up in affiliated households themselves. In fact, as we saw earlier, they were just as likely to go to church when they were young, just as likely to receive religious education, and just as likely to consider their families "very religious."

But now that they are in interfaith relationships, they are not sure how to make affiliation with a religious institution work for their own family. And yet, whether they know it now or not, the presence of a church or synagogue in their lives may be the very thing they need to raise their children successfully—at least by their own standards.

While a few of the couples I interviewed suggested that they wanted to craft their own religious program for their children, exposing them to both (or even all) religious traditions, most couples who wanted to expose their children to religion wanted to raise them in *one faith*. But they needed help. The member spouse often feels underequipped to teach the tenets of the faith alone or to bring religious traditions into the household. The non-member spouse is often lacking the most basic kind of knowledge necessary for supporting the family's participation, let alone raising children in the faith. Indeed, even when the nonmember spouse is the more enthusiastic one, he or she may not know where to start. Congregations can provide programs, classes, and support groups to aid both members of the couple in their religious pursuits. But some kind of concerted effort is often needed. The question is: What kind? And how should congregations approach these families?

As a starting point for this discussion, I asked people how welcoming they feel their religious congregation is toward interfaith couples. Of those who have a regular place of worship (roughly 50 percent in this survey), 66 percent say that their congregation is "very welcoming to interfaith couples." This percentage is nearly identical whether or not respondents are in interfaith marriages (67 percent for those in same-faith marriages, 68 percent for those who are in interfaith marriages). That statistic is good news for religious congregations. Interfaith couples generally feel comfortable in houses of worship.

Across religious traditions, there is not much difference in the extent to which interfaith couples are welcomed—with one exception. Between 69 and 71 percent of evangelicals, mainlines, Black Protestants, Jews, and Mormons say that their congregation is very welcoming toward interfaith couples.

Yet, oddly, only 54 percent of Catholics say the same. As we discussed in the previous chapter, Catholic clergy seem very open to the idea of performing interfaith weddings. And the Catholic Church has removed many of the restrictions that were once placed on such ceremonies. So why do many feel that Catholic parishes are not welcoming toward such couples? One possibility, I suppose, is that people who are not Catholic may find the mass or other rituals to be foreign. Or they may be put off by the idea that only Catholics may take communion in Catholic Churches, leaving those of other faiths sitting in the pews as the rest of their row proceeds down the church aisle. Other Christian denominations may take a similar view of communion, but Catholics tend to be more vocal about it and communion tends more to be the center of a Catholic service than it might at other churches.

In that case, though, one might expect many Jewish congregations to seem even less welcoming. Not only is much of the service often in another language, but non-Jews are not permitted to read Torah or (in most cases) to lead prayers of any sort.

There are other, less formal factors that may enter into someone's assessment of how welcoming a particular religious institution may be. Do others come up to you after services to chat? Is there a coffee hour afterward? In some sense, one might expect that any religion that proselytizes would be seen as more welcoming because the members have a kind of mandate to seek out new faces. Maybe Catholics are less inclined to engage in this kind of direct evangelization than their Protestant counterparts.

It is true that, anecdotally speaking, the interfaith couples I interviewed that included Catholics often seemed inclined to raise children in a faith other than Catholicism, though this seemed more out of a desire to be sensitive to, say, the Jewish spouse, than out of any feeling that the Catholic Church was not welcoming to interfaith couples. A couple of veteran reporters on Catholic issues suggested that many parishes simply were not as welcoming as the congregations of other faiths in general. They can seem large and impersonal and the roles for the laity are few in number.

One proxy for a congregation's attitudes toward interfaith couples might be their willingness to participate in ecumenical activities. Obviously, there are many congregations that would make a distinction between participating in a joint event with an institution of another faith and allowing members of their own flock to marry out. But the most theologically conservative congregations would probably steer clear of such activities altogether and the most liberal ones would have no problem with interfaith marriage or with ecumenical events.

Of those Americans who have a regular place of worship, roughly a third (35 percent) said that their congregation "never" engages in ecumenical events—leaving two-thirds of congregations that do. Fifty-seven percent said that their congregation does this "occasionally," compared to 8 percent that do it "frequently." Reports of ecumenical activities in a congregation do not seem to vary much by whether the respondent was in an interfaith or same-faith marriage. Thirty-three percent of same-faithers say that their congregation never does this, compared to 36 percent of inter-faithers—a statistically meaningless difference. One implication of this is that interfaith couples are not necessarily seeking out congregations that are eager to participate in ecumenical activities—at least no more than same-faith couples do. Interfaith families that choose to attend a religious congregation seem, in a real sense, to be choosing a faith. They are not looking for ways to participate in two faiths. Or if they are, it's not something they expect to be supported by their congregation.

So what are interfaith couples looking for in a congregation? Religious institutions face a litany of questions about how to present themselves to interfaith couples. It is not merely an issue of how strictly to follow the theological dictates that their own faith tradition has established. As Rabbi Charles Simon has noted, synagogue policy is not the same thing as Jewish law. In his booklet, "The Role of the Supportive Non-Jewish Spouse in the Conservative/Masorti Movement," Simon explores such questions as whether public congratulations are to be bestowed upon a member of the synagogue who marries a non-Jew, whether an intermarried Jew should be employed by a synagogue or Jewish school, whether non-Jews may become actual members of a synagogue and, if they do, whether they may serve in leadership positions. Often, synagogues go against the strict letter of Jewish law.[2]

Currently, it seems as though the bulk of programs for interfaith couples are based in Jewish congregations. Leaders of other religious communities, while they may offer individual counseling for members of interfaith couples, have either not detected or not acknowledged a need to address interfaith families in a more formal way. Though synagogues only make up a small percentage of religious institutions in the country, it seems likely that some of their struggles will become relevant to lay and clerical leaders in other institutions—if not now, then in the future. Jews are ahead of the curve. Or, if you prefer, they are the canaries in the coalmine. So much of our discussion here will center on synagogues.

Temple Sinai in Atlanta, a Reform temple, has gained a reputation for being very friendly toward interfaith couples. According to Rabbi Brad Levenberg, non-Jews are allowed to participate in every aspect of synagogue life except reading the Torah. He believes that many interfaith couples are turned off right away by other synagogues. A couple will call to inquire about whether a rabbi will perform their wedding and, they report to Levenberg, that the entire conversation will proceed without the rabbi uttering a "mazel tov." Levenberg says he doesn't always agree to perform such a wedding, but he does offer his congratulations regardless. He doesn't require that an interfaith couple promise to raise kids Jewish, but in order to enroll in the synagogue's Hebrew School program, parents must confirm that the children are being raised in the Jewish religion alone. He acknowledges, though, that "the reality for many families is different." He knows from the Hebrew School teachers and others that some children are celebrating the holidays of other faiths, but he does not make it his business to check up on these families or scold them.

Between 20 percent and 30 percent of Temple Sinai is made up of interfaith couples. Levenberg believes that he is fighting against the larger trend of disaffiliation. Only 15 percent of Jews in the Atlanta belong to a synagogue, so he wants to make as many as possible feel welcome. In fact, he tells me that recently the congregation worried that there was not very high attendance at some events they were having for interfaith families. It turned out, happily from his perspective, that the interfaith families felt comfortable enough at the regular events that they didn't feel the need to attend these separate ones.

At Herzl-Ner Tamid, a Conservative synagogue on Mercer Island outside of Seattle, senior rabbi Jay Rosenbaum takes a much different approach. He sees his job as "to preserve whatever Jewishness I can for this particular family within the bounds of what a conservative rabbi can do." Rosenbaum cannot perform an interfaith ceremony. He does explore the topic of conversion (an issue to which we will return shortly) with a couple. And if that's not an option, he says, "the next best thing is for the non-Jewish partner to learn as much as possible about Judaism and to be supportive of raising Jewish children." Rosenbaum's attitude toward intermarriage has not changed significantly during his career. He doesn't publicly congratulate congregants on interfaith marriage, though he may do so privately. But he also doesn't preach against interfaith marriage from the pulpit.

His congregation includes relatively few interfaith couples—in part, he believes, because they think they will feel more comfortable in a Reform setting. But he does say there are a significant number of couples with extended non-Jewish families because one member has converted. So the question of how these non-Jewish family members may participate in life-cycle celebrations like bar mitzvahs has come up. He has no problem mentioning these family members or congratulating them from the bimah. But it was not until recently that Rabbi Rosenbaum decided to allow non-Jews to recite a prayer. He chose the "Prayer for Peace," which is a part of the Conservative liturgy but not one that is mandated by Jewish law, like, for instance the Sh'ma. "I have to admit there's a little bit of discomfort," he says about his feelings on this new policy.

He explains: "The Jewish prayer service is meant to be recited by Jews . . . The blessings say 'Thank you, God, for making me a Jew and I am committing myself to the commandments of the Torah.' It makes no sense for a non-Jew to say that. To me, it's a presumption. It's imposing something on a non-Jew that they have not accepted and they do not wish to accept. And therefore the words become meaningless."

Harry and Deborah joined Rabbi Rosenbaum's congregation a few years ago. Deborah had been raised in a Unitarian Universalist church in Connecticut and Harry had a Conservative Jewish upbringing in Maine before deciding that he wanted to study at an Orthodox yeshiva. He was not particularly observant, though, as an adult. When he discussed marriage with Deborah, he told her he wanted his kids to be raised Jewish. She eventually agreed. And they decided to join a synagogue in Seattle. Deborah said she didn't have any preference about which one as long as it was Reform. She worried she wouldn't feel comfortable with a Conservative one. "It needed to be accessible for me," she recalls. The services at the temple they joined were short, largely in English, and there was even a choir, so Deborah said it didn't feel foreign to her; it was more like what she was used to in a religious service. The two kept a Jewish home for many years, celebrating Shabbat and going to synagogue. They continue to discuss the possibility of keeping kosher but are simply not there yet. Just before their older daughter's bat mitzvah, after almost twenty years of marriage, Deborah decided to convert.

The family was happy at the Reform synagogue for a number of years. They liked the services, the cantor, and the community. But after 9/11, Harry said he detected "very left wing" and even "un-American" messages from the pulpit. And he decided it was time for them to leave. Harry has been much happier with Herzl-Ner Tamid, but Deborah feels less comfortable. There's a lot of Hebrew, and the service is longer. And she is becoming a little less involved. Harry says that when he attends services on Shabbat, he wishes she were there with him more often. But he understands why she feels less comfortable there. For the two decades they were an interfaith couple and for the several years since, Harry and Deborah have had to work out a compromise in terms of the kind of institutional affiliation their family would embrace. But raising an interfaith family, as I mentioned earlier, is rarely one fixed set of decisions that can simply be left in place. Even if the couple doesn't change, or the kids don't change, the institution itself might. A change in religious leadership or in the tone of religious messages can force an interfaith family to have to renegotiate some arrangements.

✧　✧　✧

The question of how to draw a community's boundaries—to suggest that same-faith marriage may be preferable to interfaith marriage while at the same time not shunning those who marry out—is fraught. And many interfaith couples have complained to me about what they see as the hypocrisy of rabbis who will not perform their interfaith ceremonies but then encourage them to send their kids to nursery school at their synagogue.

Some synagogues have formed support groups for intermarried couples to talk about the issues they face. Rabbi James Gibson of Pittsburgh says he knows that the tendency is for the issues of interfaith marriage to heat up around the December holidays, which is why he recommends such discussions take place "over mint juleps in July" when people can take a calmer approach. Most of the couples I spoke with who have participated in such groups seem to graduate out of them rather quickly. They are welcome to stay, but once they have hashed out their own family's approach to religion, they don't feel the need to keep returning and would rather spend their time with the full congregation.

But there are other issues that arise for interfaith couples that they may not foresee. And they may come up long after they join a congregation. Gibson says he hosts seminars several times a year on issues like death and burial, bar mitzvahs, and so on. As these life-cycle issues come up, some congregations try to keep interfaith couples engaged. That non-Jews may not be buried in a Jewish cemetery is not an issue that usually arises on the first few dates or even in the first few years of marriage. But when it does, things can quickly go south.

One organization that seems to have become particularly popular nationally is called the "Mother's Circle," a learning and support group for non-Jewish women who are raising their children Jewish. Elizabeth grew up evangelical but married a Jewish man. She wanted to raise her daughter, Emma, with a religious faith and was moving away from Christianity. Her husband was not particularly knowledgeable about his faith and didn't express much interest. Elizabeth found a Mother's Circle group and first took a twenty-week course in Torah and Jewish tradition. "It was for Emma," she says. "Without an extended family here, I wanted to expose her to [religious traditions.]" This is another important factor that several couples mentioned to me regarding their desire to become part of a religious institution. For people who are living far from their families especially, the importance of some kind of religious community that will help pass along religious traditions becomes even more important. One woman suggested that synagogues have some kind of "bubbe" program, in which the elderly Jewish women in the congregation could "adopt" younger Jewish and non-Jewish women in a kind of grandmotherly role.

Another woman, Erin, who participated in one of the first Mother's Circles in her Atlanta synagogue, now makes a regular Shabbat dinner for her family, often including homemade Challah. Her husband, Jonah, says he and his Jewish parents never could have predicted that his wife would become so involved in Jewish life and in their synagogue. Few in the Jewish community are critical of such efforts, though there are those who suggest they have a limited appeal.

✧   ✧   ✧

One question that eventually arises when nonmember spouses become active in religious communities, concerns money: Specifically, how much do interfaith families contribute to these communities? Whether it's synagogue dues or tithing to the church or contributing to other kinds of religious philanthropies, religious leaders struggle with the question of how much such families are obligated to give.

Lillian says she has been grateful that her husband Maderu, who was raised Hindu, does not give her a hard time about her contributions to her church. "I give Maderu a lot of credit because he's never once said, you know this is ridiculous, this is silly, I'm not comfortable making a contribution. And that could have been a big point of confrontation. And it's never been and so I am really appreciative of that." Another woman I interviewed, Vanessa, said she was also appreciative that even before her husband Michael became a Catholic he was willing for their family to tithe to the church. She emphasizes that these contributions were "sacrificial,"—it's not like they had a lot of extra money lying around.

But money can be a source of great conflict in any marriage. And interfaith couples often face a serious negotiation when it comes to how they give to religious institutions and religious charities. Husbands and wives question each other's judgments: Do we really need to belong to a synagogue? Can we afford Catholic school tuition? Wouldn't the money be better spent elsewhere? Ten percent of our income to the church—doesn't that seem a little much? A trip to Mecca seems extravagant. Do the kids really need Jewish summer camp?

Anecdotally speaking, many non-Jews seem taken aback by the idea of synagogue membership dues. Such payments are not generally required at churches and seems off-putting, at least at first. Many synagogues have instituted an "interfaith rate" for membership dues. Since only the Jewish spouse can officially be a member of some temples, he or she is charged as a single adult—more if there are children but still not as much as a same-faith family.

In order to determine whether and how disagreements in interfaith couples end up affecting the actual amounts of money given to various causes, I asked people about charitable giving. In terms of who gives any amount to charity, members of same-faith couples and interfaith couples do not differ. Seventy-five percent of respondents in same-faith couples reported giving to a charity in the previous year, compared to 72 percent of inter-faithers. Where we see a difference is in where that money goes. Using a very approximate metric, members of interfaith couples report giving roughly half as much to religious charities than same-faithers.

I have assigned estimated dollar amounts to the categorical ranges provided on the survey:

None = $0

Less than $100 = 50

$100 to less than $500 = 300

$500 to less than $1,000 = 750

$1,000 to less than $5,000 = 3000

More than $5,000 = 5000

On average, same-faith respondents give $1,500 to religious charities annually, compared to $627 for interfaith ones. Same-faithers also give more to nonreligious charities, but the difference is much smaller: $671 versus $557. These results are completely consistent with the general finding that highly observant people give away more money than their less observant counterparts—both to religious and nonreligious causes. It is important to note that these differences in giving cannot be explained away by income differences between same-faith and interfaith couples because, on average, there are none.

Studies done by the Jewish community certainly back up these results. In the 1997 American Jewish Yearbook, Jack Wertheimer, former dean of the Jewish Theological Seminary, writes:

Data from the 1990 [National Jewish Population Survey] indicate that "while the propensity to donate to secular charities does not vary between endogamous and exogamous couples, the likelihood of giving to a Jewish charity declines from 62 percent to 28 percent of households annually." Contributions to [United Jewish Appeal]-Federation campaigns plummet even further: whereas 45 percent of entirely Jewish households contributed in 1989, only 12 percent of interfaith households gave to federated campaigns. Only a small minority of intermarried families are prepared to donate to Jewish causes, a sobering finding when we consider how many Jews are now in such marriages.[3]

Indeed, whether or not religious institutions are prepared to make official provisions for members of interfaith couples when it comes to their financial contributions, it seems that the end result is they should probably count on less support from interfaith families.

Outreach to interfaith couples or any nonmembers of a religious institution goes well beyond finance, but congregations and communities do need to consider the fact that resources spent to encourage interfaith couples to become more involved are resources not spent on other causes, both inside and outside the community. For instance, a project supported by the Marcus Foundation called Israel Encounter offers a heavily subsidized twelve-day trip to Israel for interfaith couples. According to Jewish leaders, Israel tends to be one of the issues that many non-Jewish partners do not understand and which divides Jewish and non-Jewish partners. As a result, interfaith couples are less likely to support it both politically and financially. Israel Encounter, which is similar to the Birthright Israel program for young adult Jews, is supposed to educate interfaith couples about the issue. Couples who have gone on the trips rave about the program and talk about how it has opened their eyes to Israel, but so far no other Jewish philanthropists have stepped forward to help support the program. Obviously, the issue of interfaith marriage is such a hot-button one that some donors may not want to get involved. But they may also feel there are better uses for their money.

It is difficult to determine how well any particular outreach program is working. But some communities that have adopted such programs point to recent demographic surveys to suggest the success of their efforts. The 2005 Boston Community Survey, for example, reported that, thanks in part to intermarriage, the Jewish population in Boston was actually growing, with 60 percent of children in mixed households being raised Jewish. The lead researcher for the study, Leonard Saxe, called the figure "exceptional."[4] By comparison, the National Jewish Population Study 2000–2001 reported that between 33 percent and 39 percent of children in interfaith households were being raised as Jews.[5] A study of the New York area suggested the number was only 30 percent.

Paula Brody, outreach director of the Northeast Council of the Union for Reform Judaism, told a San Francisco–based Jewish newspaper: "Boston has sent a particular message of welcome, and the data shows that families are responding . . . If you put resources in this area, you will get results. You will get affiliation." But Saxe and his fellow researchers went to great pains to explain that there was no evidence for "causality" in the study. That is, there was no direct evidence that this growth was the result of any outreach efforts.[6]

A similar study in Chicago said that as many as half of children in interfaith households were being raised Jewish.[7] Peter Friedman, executive vice president of the area's Federation said that the study "reinforces the importance of JUF/Federation's multi-faceted 'Joyfully Jewish' outreach programs for families with young children."

Many Jewish scholars and leaders are skeptical of such claims. Wertheimer says that he hears from many community leaders that these programs cost a lot of money but tend not to yield great results. More important, he notes, is the question of what it means when a respondent says he is raising children Jewish. Are there other non-Jewish elements mixed in? How much of a priority is it in the household? Many say the proof will be in the next generation. And, so far, the results do not seem promising. Even Rabbi James Gibson in Pittsburgh, who is a big proponent of outreach programs, notes that nationally "75 percent of the grandkids of the interfaith couples are not going to be Jewish. . . . That's very difficult to swallow. It causes me to hold myself a little short and ask myself every now and then, 'Am I doing the right thing?'"

One interesting finding from both the Chicago and the Boston surveys is the relatively high rates of institutional affiliation. In Chicago, 36 percent of households are affiliated with a congregation. In Boston, 25 percent are affiliated. When other Jewish organizations, such as Jewish community centers, are added into the equation, 60 percent of households in Boston and 48 percent of households in Chicago claim affiliation. Traditionally, the Northeast and the Midwest seem to have higher rates of affiliation with Jewish institutions.[8] So the question is whether intermarried Jews are more likely to affiliate because of these outreach efforts or because it's simply more common in these areas to do so. That being said, synagogue affiliation is a real commitment. It's often a serious financial obligation. So when intermarried Jews do decide to affiliate, it is probably a sign, though not a guarantee, that they are taking their Jewish faith seriously.

In December 2011, the leadership of the New York UJA–Federation announced that they would be supplying additional funding for Jewish education directed at intermarried couples and training for clergy and laypeople who are engaged in outreach to these couples. Hoping to replicate what they see as the success of the Boston model, the Taskforce on Welcoming Interfaith Families concluded that interfaith families in New York weren't feeling welcome enough. Wertheimer disputes this claim and notes that at many Reform synagogues, there are high rates of affiliation by intermarried couples. The reasons they are not participating more fully in Jewish life, he suggests, are much more complicated.

And he is right, to some extent. According to my survey, Jewish institutions fare no worse than those of other faiths at welcoming interfaith couples. Moreover, of the Jewish/non-Jewish couples I interviewed who were not involved in Jewish life, many said more pressing issues of family dynamics or sheer indifference were preventing them from getting involved. That said, many did describe to me long struggles to find a religious institution and religious leaders who would welcome them and help them in their spiritual journeys.

While there is a great deal of disagreement over the effectiveness of outreach policies, one thing that many communal leaders seem to agree on is the need to be a little more forthright in encouraging conversion. It is one of the most commonly understood notions about Judaism that its adherents do not proselytize. And yet in 2005, the *Boston Globe* ran the headline: "Conservative Jews Set a Conversion Campaign." What was going on?

As it happened, Rabbi Jerome M. Epstein, the head of the United Synagogue of Conservative Judaism, had set a somewhat limited target. At the group's convention he had urged: "We must begin aggressively to encourage conversions of potential Jews who have chosen a Jewish spouse."[9]

A month before that, Rabbi Eric Yoffie, the president of the Union of Reform Judaism, offered a similar sentiment. "It is a mitzvah [a kindness] to help a potential Jew become a Jew-by-choice," he told the Union's General Assembly.[10] There is nothing new about such a policy, he noted, but it has been forgotten in recent years. "By making non-Jews feel comfortable and accepted in our congregations," he observed, "we have sent the message that we do not care if they convert."

Rabbi Yoffie's statement points toward the delicacy of this matter. Many Christians, Buddhists, and atheists may have agreed to raise their children as Jews with the understanding that no one would try to change their own religious beliefs. They may now feel as if an implicit contract has been broken. Ed Case, the president of Interfaithfamily.com, a website for interfaith families exploring Jewish life, worries about this: "We think it's a real mistake for Jewish organizations to convey an attitude toward intermarried couples that conversion is a preferred option."

Case, whose own wife converted to Judaism after thirty years of marriage, believes that families in which only one parent is Jewish are perfectly capable of raising a Jewish child. Perhaps, but it is interesting to note that many intermarried families, while feeling welcome and accepted in Jewish settings, may be looking for something more. As Brandeis professor Sylvia Barack Fishman reports, while "mixed married couples experienced these congregations as 'warm and gracious,' they were puzzled at the lack of encouragement toward achieving 'greater ritual and spiritual engagement.'" Her study also found that most "senior rabbis did not, as a rule, actively invite non-Jewish members to consider conversion. . . . [e]ven when the rabbi suspected that a member might be considering conversion or when they had observed their growing engagement with Judaism."[11]

Finally, she notes, "even when non-Jews converted to Judaism, most 'synagogues do not provide mentoring after conversion.'" "Pre-occupied with welcoming non-Jewish spouses," Fishman suggests that they ignore the fact that conversion is not the end of tensions for most interfaith couples. They still have to navigate the questions that arise with non-Jewish extended family members, particularly around the holidays.[12]

Jewish leaders have long been sensitive about pushing their faith on others. Not only is there no mandate, Jewish law actually says you must turn away someone three times before agreeing to help them convert. But Jews are historically used to being on the receiving end of such proselytizing. And, frankly, often conversion was not presented as a choice. But non-Jews in America, and Christians in particular, often take this lack of interest in their spiritual development on the part of Jewish congregations as a little off-putting.

My own husband Jason has marveled to our friends on occasion that when he attends Jewish services no one makes any attempts to educate him about what's going on, let alone try to bring him into the fold. He is not interested in converting, and he certainly wouldn't appreciate the hard sell—

something he has been on the giving and receiving end of himself when it comes to other faiths—but he is simply struck by how Jews (for both theological and sociological reasons) simply operate in a vacuum.

In an episode of *Seinfeld* that lays bare the characters' secular sensibilities, Elaine is shocked to learn that her on-again, off-again boyfriend, Puddy, is a believing Christian. "So is it a problem that I'm not really religious?" she asks him upon realizing their differing worldviews. "Not for me," he answers. "I'm not the one going to hell." Though Elaine herself acknowledges that she doesn't believe in an afterlife, she becomes increasingly angry with Puddy for not caring more about her eternal damnation. Finally, she explodes: "You should be trying to save me!"

The implication is that if someone really cares about you, they should be trying to shape your religious beliefs too. Particularly in twenty-first-century America where the religious "market" seems to be thriving, non-Jews may puzzle at the Jewish lack of interest in gaining more "customers."

Rabbi Epstein argues for at least giving people a choice. "If I see two products on a shelf, one may not be better than another, but one may meet my needs more or my desires more." He thinks that Jews should at least offer people "the values and beauty of Judaism." As Rabbi Yoffie noted in his speech: "Most non-Jews . . . come from a background where asking for this kind of commitment is natural and normal, and they are more than a little perplexed when we fail to do so."

Laura was more than perplexed with the leaders she encountered in the Jewish community. Raised by parents who were "disdainful of organized religion," she married a Jewish man and readily agreed to raise her kids Jewish. She had a close Jewish friend growing up and spent a year in Germany during high school, which had a great emotional impact on her. She studied the Holocaust in college and told me that if she could raise her children Jewish she felt she would be doing her part to help Jews rebuild from that great tragedy. It's hard to think of a statement that would more quickly bring tears to a Jewish grandmother's eyes. But Jewish leaders didn't seem interested in Laura's spiritual journey.

When Laura's daughter was born she approached a few rabbis about a baby-naming, but none wanted to help her. The Reform rabbi told her to call his secretary, which Laura did, but she never heard back. When her daughter was two, the family moved to a new town, and this time she expressed interest to the rabbi there in converting. He never called her back, either. Even once she started attending a conversion class, she felt like she was put off for asking too many questions. "One thing after another led me to feel like I could not gain entry to this tradition." Finally, when her family moved to the Atlanta area, someone recommended to her a program called "Pathways," a network of interfaith families who want to celebrate Jewish traditions. There she took a class and eventually converted. But if Laura had not been so persistent, it is easy to imagine how this story would have turned out differently.

Still, conversion is a touchy subject for interfaith couples. And one could easily see how that high percentage of Americans who say their religious institution is welcoming to interfaith families might quickly plummet if too many of those couples were given the hard sell.

In determining their approach to converting nonmember spouses, it may be useful to get a sense of just how common it is for one member of an interfaith couple actually to convert to the other's religion. While we generally define an interfaith couple as two people practicing different faiths who are currently married to each other, in our survey we also asked about the religious status of the respondent and his or her spouse *before the wedding*.

The survey thus asked people in same-faith marriages (including two spouses with no religious affiliation): "Before you were married, did you and your spouse have the same religion?" Interestingly, 25 percent of people who are currently in same-faith marriages say that they and their spouse did not have the same religion when they married. This is a strikingly large number. This demonstrates not just the fluidity of American attitudes toward religion, but it also suggests that a spouse can have a very significant influence on one's religious choices.

It is common, and probably good, advice to tell young men and women that they should not plan on their significant other changing—stereotypically speaking, women who expect their husbands to become more neat, organized, or affectionate after twenty years of marriage are often disappointed, as are men who think women will be less demanding, more interested in professional sports, or bigger fans of lingerie.

Lee Strobel, formerly a teaching pastor at Saddleback Church in Southern California and the author of *Surviving a Spiritual Mismatch in Marriage*, told me in an interview that "conjugal evangelism" doesn't work. "If you're feeling like if I just marry this person, I'll be able to influence him toward God, it's self-deception." He notes that "the nonbeliever is more likely to pull the Christian away from his faith." This is a contention, by the way, that sociologists, like Brad Wilcox at the University of Virginia, generally support.

Wilcox explains: "Evangelicals who marry nonevangelicals are typically less likely to remain as or become as devout as those who marry within the fold."

But in the case of religion, there actually seems to be some reason to hold out hope that changing a spouse is possible. Not only do a significant percentage of spouses in interfaith marriages seem to convert, but many seem to do so long after tying the knot.

One might wonder which spouse was more likely to be the persuasive one. Because women tend to be more religiously observant, I expected that women would be more successful at converting men. In fact, the split was almost even. Forty-nine percent of all spousal conversions are wives switching to the husbands' religion. It is possible that women are more concerned that their children be brought up in one faith than that it is *their* faith, and so they are willing to compromise. It's also possible that women's religiosity actually contributes to their willingness to convert—they may be more likely to be religious seekers. And it's conceivable that many men go along with their wives' religious practice, but do not wish to engage in a formal conversion process because they're not interested enough or not fervent enough in their belief.

So how did those interfaith couples become same-faith couples? The results are displayed in table 8.1 below. Remember that this is a relatively small slice of the population. Roughly a quarter (24 percent) say that their spouse changed to their religion after marriage, while 18 percent say that both husband and wife changed to a new religion.

Note that 27 percent of these folks say that "neither one of us has changed religions," which may seem impossible since these are supposed to be people currently in same-faith marriages. But given the slippery boundaries of religious traditions, coupled with the vagaries of survey responses, it is not surprising that such an apparent discrepancy would appear. Recall that this is 27 percent of a small group, so it is actually a total of only thirty-two people. And, of those, seventeen are "Nones," which suggests that what this really means is that these are couples who are "same-faith" by default, as neither spouse is religious.

The most common type of conversion is to evangelical Protestantism. When you combine conversion of either the respondent or the spouse, you get the following: 38 percent are evangelicals, 21 percent who are Catholics, and 24 percent who are mainline Protestants.

There are any number of factors that might have prompted these conversions. Maybe someone has been a longtime part of a community and

TABLE 8.1   Religious Change in Marriage (Asked of Those Who Had a
Different Religion Than Their Spouse at Marriage) (%)

I changed to my spouse's religion.	18
My spouse changed to my religion.	24
We both changed to the same new religion.	19
We both changed, but to different religions.	2
We both stopped belonging to a religion.	12
Neither of us have changed religions.	27

decided to formalize it, though this seems less likely for evangelicals whose conversion process tends to be shorter and more casual. In my interviews, I came across a number of parents who converted just before a major life ceremony for one of the children—a bar mitzvah or a baptism, for instance. But there are occasions when a spouse can try to influence matters more directly.

Relatively few respondents who are currently in interfaith marriages report either trying to convert their spouses to their religion (10 percent), or that their spouses tried to convert them (also 10 percent). Remember that this was asked of people who are currently in interfaith marriages (not the same-faith ones that started out as interfaith mentioned above), and so undoubtedly undercounts the frequency by which conversion attempts are made within marriages because it does not reflect marriages in which conversion was successful.

But this varies across religious traditions. Not surprisingly, evangelicals are much more likely than the norm to try to convert their spouses: 19 percent report doing so. Twenty percent of Mormons say so as well, but the total number of Mormons in interfaith marriages is so low (14) as to make any estimates unreliable.[13] By contrast, only 9 percent of mainline Protestants in interfaith marriages report attempting conversion, the same as Catholics. Three percent of Jews report trying to convert their spouse, about the same as Nones (4 percent).[14]

When we look at the religion of the spouse in an interfaith marriage, we find similar results. For example, 13 percent of people married to evangelicals report that their spouse has attempted to convert them, although this is a little less than the rate of evangelicals' own attempt at spousal conversion. A slightly higher percentage of people married to Catholics (15 percent) report receiving a conversion attempt than Catholics report making one (9 percent). Obviously, attempting to convert someone can mean different things to different respondents. A stray suggestion, years of subtle hints, or having a member of the clergy suggest it might all qualify.

✧ ✧ ✧

Indeed, as a strategic matter, there are reasons for leaving any real proselytizing to the professionals. Trying to convert a spouse can be a very delicate matter, and it can make all sorts of other marital issues more fraught. If a husband or wife feels as if he or she has converted *for* the spouse, resentments can build over time. One interfaith couple told me a story about another now-same-faith couple they knew. Every time they fought, he would bring up the fact that he had become Jewish for her. So when he wanted a ceiling fan in the bedroom, for instance, and she didn't, he played the conversion card and he won. Obviously, this is not the norm, but it is easy to see how too much pressure on the issue by one spouse can cause tensions in a marriage. Also, there are times when the proselytizing spouse can turn into the religious authority in the relationship. There can be a temptation to either overemphasize or paper over some aspects of the faith in order to make it seem more attractive to the spouse. In the long run, this can cause problems.

Melissa, a computer programmer in Los Angeles, recalls that there was no pressure from her now-husband Adam to become Jewish when the two were dating. In college, Melissa, who was raised with no religion, sometimes accompanied him to Shabbat dinners at school. And she would celebrate some Jewish holidays with his family. His mother, she recalls, would make comments about why she should become Jewish.

When the couple arrived in Los Angeles, they started by attending some services at the USC Hillel. They were engaged before Melissa really began thinking seriously about conversion. She was worried that she didn't believe strongly enough to convert, that they would "kick her out" of the introductory Judaism class for asking too many questions, but she actually found it quite welcoming. There were a number of rabbis involved in the class she liked. Ultimately it was a rabbi from another synagogue who performed her conversion. The two go to synagogue almost every week. They don't keep Shabbat strictly in their home, but they try not to do any work on Friday nights. Melissa tells me, "I would say that I am Jewish now, in spite of his mother, not because of his mother. I'm sure she wouldn't like to hear that but I'm being honest." Adam is clearly pleased that his wife is now Jewish, but he is also glad that she got their on her own, with her questions answered by Jewish authorities rather than himself.

And perhaps that is the ideal role for a religious institution. Not that every nonmember spouse will end up converting. But more than simply being welcoming (which they mostly are), congregations can offer substantive information as well as the occasional push that will actively move an interfaith family further along on their spiritual journey.

CHAPTER NINE

———◆———

Jews, Mormons, and the Future of Interfaith Marriage

IN NOVEMBER 2011, GARY ROSENBLATT, EDITOR OF NEW YORK'S *Jewish Week*, penned a column called "Romney or Not, We Can Learn from the Mormons." The point was that no matter what Jews may think of Mitt Romney's political views—and the majority are surely not in agreement with them—the way that the LDS Church has handled the glare of the spotlight resulting from his run for president has been admirable. Rosenblatt praised the church for not becoming defensive despite the fact that Christian leaders have referred to the group as a "cult" and secular leaders have said worse. Instead, the church launched an ad campaign called "I am a Mormon," "depicting Mormons as normal and reflecting the diversity of the country."

Similarly, when the musical *The Book of Mormon* hit Broadway, church leaders offered this statement in a press release: "The production may attempt to entertain audiences for an evening, but the Book of Mormon as a volume of scripture will change people's lives forever by bringing them closer to Christ." Rosenblatt encourages readers to imagine the reaction from Jews if the hottest ticket on Broadway were called *The Five Books of Moses* and contained the kind of bawdy humor included in *The Book of Mormon*. He wrote: "I can picture the angry pickets and calls for boycotts, charges of anti-Semitism and worse, with the attendant splash of national media coverage."

Rosenblatt's comparison of Jews and Mormons may strike some observers as a little dissonant. What does this liberal, cosmopolitan group of immigrant grandchildren have in common with this American-born collection of conservative Christians?

It is actually a comparison that I have found to be welcomed by Mormons but rejected out of hand by Jews. The members of the LDS Church I have met over the years generally do not, upon finding that I am Jewish, try to convert me.[1] Rather, they often tell me about how they feel a special kinship with the Jewish people.[2] Mormons feel that their tradition and their history very much parallels that of Jews. After being forced to leave their place of origin in upstate New York (where Joseph Smith was said to have received his revelation), they were driven from a number of communities before coming to the western United States and Salt Lake City, which they came to see literally as Zion. Their "exodus" story combined with the persecution they experienced caused them to view themselves as very similar to Jews.

But there are more significant reasons to make a comparison between Jews and Mormons. For one thing, they make up a similar percentage of the U.S. population (about 6 million people), with larger concentrations in a few places—Jews in major metropolitan areas, Mormons in Utah and other western states. Mormons, on average, do not match Jews in terms of their wealth or education levels, but the former have been gaining and now seem to occupy a disproportionate number of elite positions in government, business, and academia.[3]

But one way in which they differ dramatically is that Jews are America's most intermarrying people and Mormons its least. According to the American Religious Identification Survey, 27 percent of Jews were married to someone of a different faith, compared with 12 percent of Mormons.[4]

I am offering this comparison between Judaism and the LDS Church not merely as a provocative way to suggest, as Rosenblatt puts it, that Jews "can learn from Mormons"—though Jewish leaders may indeed wish to take note—but to explore in community-wide terms some of the broader trends we have already discussed. It is also useful to separate out some of the factors that lead to intermarriage. Many of the causes of interfaith marriage cited by Jewish leaders should, in principle, lead to higher intermarriage rates for Mormons too, but they don't. What gives?

Since we know that it is not simply a factor of "religiosity" in one's up-bringing, it is worth looking at other trends. How these groups perceive themselves and present themselves to others affects not only whether their members marry out but also how the nonmembers of interfaith couples may view the prospect of eventually converting or raising children in their partners' faith.

✧   ✧   ✧

When it comes to marriage, the most striking demographic difference between Jews and Mormons is the age at which they get married. The av-erage age of first marriage for Mormons according to my study is twenty-three, and for Jews it's twenty-seven. Because the sample of both groups was relatively small, we tried to confirm these statistics looking at other studies.

If we look at data taken from the 2006 General Social Survey (the last time researchers asked the question about age at first marriage), Jews mar-ried at 25.8 and Mormons at 22.6.[5] If we look at the whole decade of the 1990s, Jews were at 25.8, and Mormons were at 21.6.

This does seem to imply that the average age of marriage has been creeping up for Mormons. The 2000–2003 U.S. Census Bureau data seem to support this finding. It showed Utah with the lowest average age of marriage in the country—about twenty-four years of age for men and twenty-two for women, about three years younger than the national average, but climbing. (There are plenty of non-Mormons in Utah, of course, so this is an inexact measure.)

Meanwhile, according to the 2000 National Jewish Population Survey, "American Jews, both men and women, tend to marry later than Americans generally. In every age group under 65, proportionally fewer Jews than all Americans have ever married, with the largest gap being among those age 25–34." The survey authors suggest: "High educational levels and concentra-tion in high status jobs among Jews provide a partial explanation for their delayed marriage and family formation."[6] Perhaps, but even high-income and highly educated Mormons marry young.

Regardless, my data show that the later the age of marriage, the higher the likelihood that it will be an interfaith one. There is a strong effort made by the LDS Church to get young people to think about mar-riage early on, especially during college. Brigham Young University has a very active marriage market, with students moving quickly from dating to engagement. Observers would point out that young adult Mormons are more likely to adhere to the church's ban on premarital sex than young adult Jews, and so the former have more of an incentive, as it were, to marry earlier. Others might suggest that the availability of sex within marriage at an early age will help reduce the temptation of premarital sex.

The church elders realize that marriage and family are crucial to involvement in the faith and try as soon as possible to get their members married and settled into a particular community. (The LDS Church is divided geographically into wards, and each family is assigned to one.) It does not want members to experience those "odyssey years" when "emerging adults" tend to drift in and out of relationships and in and out of religious institutions. That is when you start to lose them.

Indeed, it seems that unlike most other faith communities in the United States, the LDS Church's demands are *most* intense on members in their early twenties—men are asked to serve a two-year mission and women may serve an eighteenth-month one. As Allison Pond wrote in the *Wall Street Journal* at the end of 2011: "The most important converts to Mormonism might be the missionaries themselves. Studies indicate that returned missionaries maintain strong levels of religious activity, with more than 80 percent attending services each week and paying tithes to the church. Returned missionaries also tend to have high educational levels and marriage rates."[7]

Indeed, Pond, a former analyst at the Pew Forum who now writes for the *Deseret News*, a Utah newspaper, argues that the missionary experience may replace entirely the emerging adulthood phase. "With Americans today fretting about prolonged adolescence, particularly among young men, the Mormon mission experience is a radical anomaly. It forces inexperienced young men and women, some barely out of high school, to grow up extraordinarily quickly. They minister primarily among the middle and lower classes, where they may find themselves giving marital advice, talking someone through the stages of grief or even leading a congregation. They wrestle with their own doubts and questions, make mistakes and experience the satisfaction of watching lives change."

Jewish institutions, on the other hand, do not seem for the most part to talk about marriage early on. Jewish youth groups do exist and certainly serve as a pool for making same-faith friends and even finding romantic partners. But few Jews in high school ever hear about marriage as a priority.

After the bar mitzvah at twelve or thirteen, most Jewish institutions do not have any kind of formal schooling or other particular religious requirements. Aside from teen youth groups and college Hillels, Jewish leaders mostly seem to be waiting for young Jews to simply return to their doors when they get married sometime in their late twenties. Emerging adulthood, though they may not call it that, is embraced by most Conservative and Reform families, who want their children to have a variety of educational, professional, and geographical opportunities, unencumbered by the needs of a mate.

When I spoke to Jack Wertheimer of the Jewish Theological Seminary about the LDS strategy of encouraging early marriage, he suggested that this would not work for Jews. "Given how sophisticated younger Jews are," he told me, "it has to be done a lot more subtly than that."

I'm not sure that young Mormons, especially the college-bound ones, are not as "sophisticated" as young Jews. The comment seems to smell of some of the usual condescension that urban elites reserve for those hicks in Utah; it also suggests a discomfort on the part of Jewish leadership with looking to other religious groups for ideas.[8] There are, no doubt, real differences between Jews and other groups but that doesn't mean there is nothing to be learned from poking our heads outside the bubble every once in a while.

It is worth studying both some of the structures and attitudes of the LDS Church that have so far allowed it to remain largely endogamous while at the same time not isolating its members from the rest of the country.

Let's begin with the other side. How did Jews become the religious group with one of the highest interfaith marriage rates in the country? Historically, interfaith marriage was not a significant problem for Jews. Anti-Semitism was so pervasive in most times and places for the past few thousand years that non-Jews were neither inclined nor allowed in many cases to wed Jews. But America has been different. As Jonathan Sarna, a professor at Brandeis University, has written, the issue of Jews marrying out in America came up as early as 1656 "when one of America's first known Jews, Solomon Pietersen, married a local Protestant and raised his daughter in her mother's faith."[9] Sarna estimates the interfaith marriage rate for Jews in the colonial period to have been between 10 and 15 percent. Jewish families realized they were in a very small minority, with few eligible mates for their children, and so such accommodations were practical. Moreover, they wanted to promote peaceful relations with their neighbors—intermarriage could bring them closer together and objecting to it could drive them further apart.

After the American Revolution, Sarna writes, "amidst the heady atmosphere of freedom characteristic of that era, intermarriage rates between Jews and Christians rose sharply." More than a quarter of all marriages involving Jews are thought to have been interfaith. Sarna cites the letter one immigrant wrote to her parents in Hamburg: In America, unlike Europe, "anyone can do what he wants. There is no rabbi in all of America to excommunicate anyone."[10]

The nineteenth century brought with it a different dynamic. Not only did great waves of immigration in the second half of the 1800s mean a higher number of potential marriage partners for Jews, but anti-Semitism also grew, which meant that intermarriage wasn't a popular option for gentiles either.[11] A study of intermarriage in New York between 1908 and 1912 suggests that the rate was a little over 1 percent.

Sarna explains that up until the last half-century, most religious groups in the United States have discouraged intermarriage, and successfully so. Jews might have been somewhat more endogamous than Protestants and Catholics, but they were hardly an anomaly. "From a Jewish point of view, this had very important ideological implications. It meant that American culture—the norms and expectations of society—reinforced Jews' own traditional sense that out-marriage was wrong and in-marriage was right." But then everything changed. Starting in the 1960s, the rate of interfaith marriage began to climb for all groups. Marriage among members of different Protestant denominations was hardly considered a leap anymore. Rates of Catholic intermarriage and Orthodox intermarriage skyrocketed. (And so did interracial marriage, by the way.) Jews, in some ways, were merely along for the ride.

✦   ✦   ✦

So how did Mormonism retain its countercultural attitude on this issue? Well, for one thing, there is still plenty of anti-Mormon sentiment in America, which may aid in isolating the population the same way it isolated Jews for centuries. A 2007 Pew poll showed that only 53 percent of Americans have a favorable opinion of Mormons. That's roughly the same percentage who feel that way toward Muslims. By contrast, more than three-quarters of Americans have a favorable opinion of Jews and Catholics.

What could cause these anti-Mormon feelings? Mormons don't drink, smoke, or gamble. Members give at least 10 percent of their income to the church and often volunteer more than twenty hours a week in some religious capacity. The church stocks soup kitchens across the country and internationally (both its own and those of other faiths) with food from its farms and warehouses. Rather than behaving like an insular cult, members are integrated into the society around them, sending their kids to public schools and assuming leadership positions locally and nationally. Even though many Mormons serve as proselytizing missionaries, this does not mean that they constantly bombard their neighbors with invitations to join up.

But few Americans have Mormon neighbors. And they feel deeply uneasy with some of Mormonism's tenets (or some tenets, like polygamy, that they believe are still a part of the faith). A lot of what we call religious tolerance depends on social contact, not theological understanding, and there are only about six million LDS members in the United States, mostly concentrated in the western states (though increasingly less so). If you press Baptists, they will acknowledge finding Catholics' belief in transubstantiation implausible at best; Jews have a little trouble getting over the virgin birth. But we all get along, for the most part, because we know each other and live similar lives as Americans, whatever faith we profess.

In other words, as the Mormon population continues to spread—and the church has made a concerted effort to encourage migration to the cultural and political centers of the country—anti-Mormon sentiment may not be strong enough to keep LDS interfaith marriage rates down.

But there may be other factors that will. Aside from pushing members to go on missions and marry in their early twenties, the church has additional policies that can work to discourage interfaith marriage. For one thing, it is a lay-run church. Everyone is eligible for a leadership position, and they rotate regularly. So while Jews or Catholics or many Protestants may simply decide that they're going to remain on the sidelines of church life, this is not as much of an option for Mormons. In the same way that clergy of another faith might feel the obligation to marry inside the church, lay Mormons may as well. Not only do they understand how much of their lives will be tied up with duties to the church, but they may also worry about the example they are setting for others in the community.

One obvious distinction between Mormons and Jews, as we discussed in the previous chapter, is their inclination to proselytize. This has enormous implications for interfaith marriage. First, as we found in our survey, as many as a quarter of same-faith couples were once interfaith couples. Faiths that are more interested in gaining members may bring more members in after marriage. The church, however, doesn't see conversion as the spouse's explicit responsibility. Representatives of the church will visit the nonmember partner and speak to him or her about converting just like any other potential member. In the meantime, though, nonmembers are welcome to participate in most aspects of church life, though they are not allowed into the Temple. And their marriage cannot be "sealed" in the church, meaning that the interfaith couple will be prevented from living on together in eternity.

Interestingly, in our survey, roughly one-third of same-faith Mormon couples (7 of 19) started out as interfaith. It's not a large number, but a 1977 article on Mormon interfaith marriage by Brent Barlow came to an almost identical conclusion. According to Barlow, 34 percent of those who married out eventually saw their spouse convert to Mormonism. Certainly these statistics support the notion that over time many non-Mormons convert once they are already married.[12] This, in turn, seems to affect the way Mormons see the non-Mormons in their midst.

While our survey found that, in general, men and women were about equally likely to convert to the religion of their spouse, Barlow found evidence that for Mormons this is not the case. The study is obviously dated, but he found that non-Mormon women were almost twice as likely to convert to Mormonism as non-Mormon men were. It's not clear why this would be the case, and Barlow doesn't speculate. But trying to raise children as Mormons is certainly much easier if the mother is of the same faith. Our earlier findings suggest that children of interfaith couples are about twice as likely to be raised in the faith of their mother as that of their father. In other words, if the numbers were going to be lopsided, it works out well for the Mormon Church that they're tilted this way.

Barlow made one other point that is worth highlighting here. More educated Mormons were actually more likely to marry inside the faith. He writes that "nearly half (45 percent) of the endogamous Mormons in his study had graduated from a four-year college, while only 10 percent of the exogamous ones had obtained the same level of education."[13] This suggests that while some may suspect discouraging interfaith marriage is a matter of keeping church members isolated from the wider world and unaware of other options, that does not seem to be the case.

✦ ✦ ✦

In 1993, Susan Buhler Taber published a book called *Mormon Lives*, a study of one particular ward in Maryland and Delaware that she observed over the course of an entire year. She includes in the book an extensive interview with the man who was then the bishop of the ward (and is a prominent historian), Richard Bushman. He tells the story of one of his daughters, who had become inactive in the church and got engaged to a non-Mormon named Charles. "We immediately liked and admired him, but he was not a church member. We felt he was good for Clarissa. He had integrity." But Bushman and his daughter had a disagreement over whether champagne would be served at the wedding. Bushman says, "It was also a problem because Charles felt like this was Mormonism creeping into his life."[14]

Bushman and his wife agreed that they would attend the wedding ceremony but would not go to the party afterward if alcohol were served. "That was a horrible thing," he told Taber. "I came down to my study one morning and prayed that God would give me the words to say that would somehow help them understand why I couldn't give way on this, words that would bring them around. But the only thing I could pray for was that I would find a way to assure my daughter that I loved her." He acceded to the couple's wishes. "My first-born was to be married outside the temple, and there was to be champagne at the reception, and yet I felt it was right. I was telling her she was more important to me than champagne."

Jewish leaders might read this story and conclude that this is the beginning of the end for Mormon endogamy. If a prominent Conservative Jewish leader allowed his child to marry out and attended the wedding and the reception (where they, say, served scallops wrapped in bacon during cocktail hour) and gave as his explanation that he simply loved his child more than some religious prohibition, his colleagues would hang their heads. But Bushman was not removed from his position. Nor does Taber report any other negative consequences for the family.

There are certainly rare occasions in which the Mormon Church has excommunicated members—typically members who have committed adultery or a felony. But interfaith marriage does not seem to be an offense that rises to this level. Richard Popp, an archivist at the University of Chicago and a Mormon, wrote an article about his marriage to an evangelical Lutheran minister. "I'm sure that my ward is not representative, but a full third of the families at that time included a non-member spouse . . . I also became aware of many couples I assumed were stalwart, dyed-in-the-wool, pioneer-stock Mormons, one or both of were, in fact, converts of some years."[15]

The Mormons I interviewed seem to confirm a general acceptance of mixed couples and nonmembers in their midst. When I ask Ahmed, a Muslim, whether he ever feels pressured to convert to Mormonism when he accompanies his wife, Maria, to church in Washington, DC, he tells me no. But the leaders of his ward do seem to regularly engage him on theological questions. They ask him what he thinks of the particular message he heard that morning, and they don't object when he expresses some sort of doubt and don't mind passionate discussion either.

The church's view of conversion is that if someone honestly investigates Mormonism, they will eventually accept it, which may explain the kind of calm persistence that many nonmembers experience from Mormons. Tom Holman, a BYU professor who has written extensively about marriage and romantic relationships, says:

> My experience has been that those who are not members of our church who are married to LDS members are treated with respect and love and kindness. If there is an interest, we will talk to them about our faith. [Nonmembers] are discussed in church leadership meetings. There is a sister in our ward married to a nonmember husband. There is a missionary leader is assigned as home teacher to him. They're treated well, invited to participate to the extent they can and invited to investigate church.

Holman emphasizes, "The leadership says: do not try to force the issue."

Perhaps because the general assumption seems to be that nonmembers are simply members who haven't converted yet, my interviews suggest that children of these mixed couples do not seem to be treated any differently in their religious schooling. Not only are families required to attend ward meetings on Sundays, they also participate in family home night, in which they are encouraged to pray together and participate in some other wholesome activity, like playing board games. High school students also must attend "seminary," a daily religious school program offered either before school or (in areas where there is a large population of Mormons) during release time from school hours.

It is interesting that the Mormons have not followed the model of other religious groups in the United States by developing their own religious schools. For many faith leaders, the avoidance of secular schools (either public or private ones) was seen as a way to limit the influence of other faiths or American culture generally on their kids. But there is something about the Mormon cultural attitudes that have stopped the leadership from going down this path. The LDS attitude toward education—integration into the larger society while maintaining a deep connection to the faith community—seems to foreshadow its approach to intermarriage.

In all of this comparison of Jews and Mormons, I have purposely avoided mention of one great difference separating them. Judaism, in the eyes of many Jews and non-Jews, is not simply a system of religious beliefs. It is an ethnicity, a race, a people. It's the reason that Jews who have not been to synagogue in years, Jews who don't believe in God, and Jews who have had no religious education still identify themselves as Jews. It's the reason that one author of a book on his search for God describes himself at the beginning as a "gastronomical Jew."[16]

In 1997, Elliott Abrams, author of *Faith or Fear: How Jews Can Survive in a Christian America*, participated in an online conversation at about intermarriage with Eric Liu, author of *The Accidental Asian*.[17] It was an odd exchange, to say the least. Sure, rates of Asian intermarriage are high, and some recent immigrants might object to the way the American melting pot has affected the cultural legacy of their children, but there is almost no concern about passing on religious norms. For one thing, many of the Asian immigrants in the United States are actually Christians, and they do not find that the United States places any undue pressure on them to leave their churches.

Abrams launched the dialogue by noting the high rates of interfaith marriage and explaining the low statistical likelihood that children of such marriages will identify as Jewish. Moreover, he writes that even in marriages where a spouse does convert, the same problem often arises:

> Today it is common to hear that all Jews are "Jews by Choice," and those who use that phrase are talking about the fact that we all live in a free and open society. Children of mixed marriages especially tend to accept

something like a Christian definition of religion, in which personal faith is the key and community solidarity is of much less importance—80 percent say that religion is a "purely private matter" and 81 percent say that "belonging to a Jewish community" is not important.[18]

This certainly makes sense and seemed to be confirmed in the interviews I've conducted. Those who marry outside their faith and the children of interfaith couples seem to view religion as a choice, a decision people have to make on an individual basis. And there is no question that Americans in general have been moving toward that understanding of religion—hence the high conversion rates in the country generally. But I wonder how many Christians would agree with Abrams's characterization of their faith as "purely private" or with the notion that belonging to a religious community is unimportant to them. Certainly most of the leaders of the evangelical churches, Catholic parishes, and Mormon wards I have visited would suggest that the creation and maintenance of a community is vital to the strength of their faith and that individuals who can maintain faith without that support are few and far between.

Abrams explains that the problem with the new view of Judaism by choice is that "this is not the traditional Jewish view, which posits a *community* of Jews living in a covenant with God that imposes special obligations on them. The Jewish view has always been that every Jew has an obligation to instruct his or her children in Judaism, not in the virtues of free thinking. Judaism imposes obligations binding on one *and* on one's offspring." In other words, it is an obligation imposed by virtue of one's bloodline. Again, before we let this distinction be made so easily, it should be noted that many Christians feel a strong obligation to bring up their children in the tenets of their faith—not because their children are "born" Christians, but because the parents believe Christianity to be true. They do not sit around waiting for their children to sample all the faiths available and then arrive at the truth of Christianity.[19]

Even nonbelievers often seem to find value in belonging to religious communities. Elaine Howard Ecklund, a professor at Rice University, found that a little less than one in five atheist scientists had attended religious services more than once in the past year.[20] Many of those interviewed said they wanted that kind of "community" for their family.

It does seem unlikely, though, that most Conservative or Reform American Jews will return to the idea of Judaism as the obligation to a particular race or ethnicity, that they will simply adhere to that community's strictures as a result of having been born into it.

Jonathan Sarna, who acknowledges that Jews (with the exception of the Orthodox) "have never been very good at being countercultural," accepts that Jews are not going to go against the "zeitgeist" on this issue. He offers up one alternative: "The kids of people who are talking about how racist it is to promote endogamy are people who I think have accepted the idea of having very special rules to protect endangered species." In other words, he thinks that the justification Jews might use to explain why they should be the exception to our melting-pot society is that there are so few of them in number, they will simply disappear and that something valuable will disappear with them. Semantically, it's an interesting argument, and I'd be curious to see how it played in focus groups. But ultimately, I think the question the community needs to answer is "What is that something important that will disappear with Jews?" It's not gefilte fish or chopped liver. It has to be some tradition of religious beliefs and practices.

So what will Judaism look like in our modern multicultural society, in which allegiances to race and ethnicity are seen as bigoted and backward? One option is presented by Shaul Magid, a professor of religious studies at Indiana University, who writes that in this new society where anti-Semitism is not an issue, in this "post-ethnic America," "[r]eligious syncretism and hybridity . . . are now taken for granted, even celebrated as part of Jewish 'creativity.' Religious and cultural experimentation are less on the margins of Jewish society; they are understood now as a reflection of the new constitution of Jewishness that is emerging . . . ."[21]

Jewish creativity hardly seems like a particularly compelling cause. I guess you could "celebrate" it, but I'm not sure that it's much of a rallying cry for Judaism's future. It is hard to imagine where religious belief or practice of any sort fits into this conception of Judaism. But why must this be the direction of post-ethnic Judaism? Why does post-ethnic Judaism have to look more like being Chinese and less like being a Mormon?

No doubt this line of questioning will be seen as simplistic by religious leaders of all stripes, but particularly by Jewish ones. From biblical commentaries to legal opinions to novels to synagogue membership regulations, gallons of ink have been spilled in the modern era trying to answer the question "What is a Jew?"

And certainly life in America has only complicated it further. In many parts of the world, race and religion are still inextricable from one another.

Faith is not simply a choice that people make. Indeed, even if Jews in America start to think of themselves more as adherents to a set of religious beliefs than as a particular race or ethnicity, it's not clear that others would follow suit. In other parts of the world, Jews are considered a people, and anti-Semitism is undoubtedly a racial animus. What would it mean for the State of Israel, for instance, if Jews began to think of themselves as less of a tribe and more of a religious group like Christians?

✦   ✦   ✦

I interviewed a couple of Israeli immigrants to the United States who themselves were not particularly observant. When they lived in Israel they led mostly secular lives. But they wanted their non-Jewish spouses to convert to Judaism so that if they ever wanted to return to Israel, their families could live there as full-fledged citizens. This often puzzles their spouses, who are on the one hand being asked to agree to a set of beliefs and practices, but on the other hand are told they are just doing it so they can belong to a people.

Barak, an Israeli, met Nancy when he was working in London as a security guard and she was studying abroad. Nancy had been raised in Pittsburgh without much faith, she says. Her mother was Catholic and her father attended a Hungarian Reformed Church, but only occasionally. After they had dated for four years, Nancy began to wonder whether Barak was ever going to propose. Finally they had a discussion about marriage, and he asked if she would consider converting to Judaism. "I was kind of taken aback," she recalls, "because I had never thought about it before." She describes both Barak and herself as fairly secular and says she doesn't think he believes in God. "I think for him the cultural aspect is what was really important—the idea that he would want his children to have a chance to be accepted by the Jewish family, and to move to Israel when they wanted and be accepted as part of the community."

Nancy did eventually agree to convert. "I can't remember the nature of the conversation about it," she says, "but I think I said, 'I'd rather convert than change my last name.'" The couple has been married for two years and living in the United States now. But she has not converted yet. She says she is looking for the right synagogue and rabbi to mentor her through the process, but she is confident that she will. Nancy says she would not feel as comfortable converting to another faith. But, she tells me, "I'm fairly secular and Judaism seems to me to have a lot of cultural base as well as religious space."

While Nancy clearly thinks religious conversion is a time commitment—the conversion class will probably last a year—she doesn't seem to worry about what it really means. Perhaps Barak has given her the impression that it's simply not a big deal, just something that he wants so that his kids can live in Israel, but nothing more. Presumably a rabbi might attempt to disabuse her of this notion if she ever decides to go through with the process. But it will also be interesting to see how Barak views his own Jewish identity after living in the United States for a few years. Many Israelis find themselves at sea in this country. As Barak says, living in Israel, "[Judaism] was all around me. I don't know if you realize it so much, but it is all around you." Even secular Jews in Israel feel Jewish.

We have already discussed how in part because Judaism is not a proselytizing faith by nature, Jewish spouses are not inclined to encourage their non-Jewish spouses to convert. Of the twelve same-faith Jewish couples in our survey, three of them began as interfaith ones. Again, these numbers are too small to draw any real conclusions. The notion that non-Jewish spouses seem disinclined to convert seems borne out by the number of synagogues that have large percentages of interfaith couples in them. (If the synagogue doesn't care, why bother?) Much of the Jewish leadership seems to believe that Jews need to do more to encourage these non-Jewish spouses to consider conversion.

But it is not simply that these men and women are not being asked to convert; it is also that when they are, conversion is presented in a peculiar way. Most Jews are not as interested as Barak is in the question of whether their families can settle in Israel. But many non-Jews simply want their spouses and children to "belong." More than one convert I interviewed told me they were initially worried about whether it would be an obstacle to conversion that they didn't believe in God. And they were relieved to find out it wasn't. Maybe the Jewish spouses simply didn't want to put too much pressure on the non-Jewish ones. They wanted to make becoming Jewish seem easy. But setting the bar so low does not encourage the spouse to really investigate Judaism in any serious way. Conversion is just a means to an end, and the end is getting the whole family to be culturally Jewish, or even nominally Jewish.

Even when they are not asked to convert, many non-Jews get the impression that raising children Jewish is something to be done for the sake of the continuity of a people, for the maintenance of ethnic traditions, rather than out of any belief that there is something valuable in Jewish tradition.

More than one Jew I interviewed told their spouse that they had to raise their children Jewish because of the impact of the Holocaust on the Jewish people.

It's possible that this will induce enough guilt in the non-Jew for it to work. But what has been gained? How does the Holocaust turn into a lesson or a value that a non-Jew or a convert to Judaism can pass on to his or her children? It's not even clear how a Jewish parent can impart the value of Judaism to his children relying only on a history of persecution.

Joke as Jews like to do about the centrality of guilt to their religious and cultural traditions, this is not the way to sell one's faith in America's religious marketplace. If there is something to be learned from the way the Mormon Church has approached interfaith marriage, it is not only that certain policies, structures, and teachings of the church work to encourage endogamy. They do. But interfaith marriage is not unheard of among Mormons. In fact, there are people at the highest levels of church leadership who come from interfaith homes or whose own children are in interfaith marriages.

Over time, though, a significant portion of these marriages become same-faith ones. And it is because of the church's attitudes toward interfaith couples and nonmembers in general that this is the case. I would describe it as a calm and quiet confidence that there are important truths to be found in the LDS faith, that their community is one that people should *want* to join. There is a sense that religious views do not necessarily change overnight, but sometimes only after years of marriage or a decade or more of involvement with a community. Mormons understand that conversion is not something you ask about once and then drop. People change, and they become more receptive to religious messages at different points in their lives. It is not devious or threatening to try to engage nonmembers in such discussions regularly as long as you are not mean-spirited or hectoring. When we think of conversions to Mormonism, we often picture missionaries we don't know knocking at our doors, but those married to Mormons are just as likely to encounter the church's doctrines (and perhaps, more attractively to some, the church's community) through their spouses and their friends.

Jewish leaders have so far focused mostly on the problems they have had convincing young Jews to marry inside the faith. But they have not paid as much attention to what happens after intermarriage. There is an acknowledgement that pushing more conversion would be a good idea. But Jews are so new to this idea that they are not quite sure how to go about it. When they do, they are often timid and deeply concerned about offending non-Jewish spouses. Or they simply want to make it seem like Judaism is something that is compatible with a spouse's agnosticism or secularism. This is understandable, but America is a thriving religious marketplace and if Jews are going to compete, they will need to have more confidence in their message.

Rabbi Jay Rosenbaum was one of the few Jewish leaders I spoke with who seemed to genuinely understand this challenge. He told me that he recently returned from a month working in India. Since returning he has spoken to a lot of Hindu immigrants who are concerned about the faith of their children.

He asks them, "Do you assume that because you came from India that your kids by osmosis are going to feel attached to Hinduism? [Just because] you have memories of this from your childhood? That is not going to happen." He tells them about the Jewish experience. "This is not 1950 where everyone spoke Yiddish and lived in the same Jewish neighborhood. This is America. It's the most open society in the history of the world."

He advises parents who want their children to keep the faith, whatever that faith is, to be "intentional" about it, to "model it in your own life." Though much of Rabbi Rosenbaum's focus is on making Judaism attractive to children so that they will not want to marry out in the first place, his words are equally important for those who are interested in encouraging non-Jewish spouses to convert or encouraging interfaith couples to raise children Jewish. The rationale, he says, cannot be "if you don't [carry on the Jewish tradition] you'll be interrupting a chain of 3,000 or 4,000 years. That will not cut it." Rather, he explains, "It has to be joyful. It has to be something consistent and regular. And it has to be something meaningful personally."

Rosenbaum's choice of words is interesting. Without making too much of it, he seems to be encouraging a de-emphasis of the racial/ethnic notion of Judaism—in America we don't keep up a connection with something simply because our parents and grandparents did. He is also using a vocabulary that most Christians would be comfortable with. It is the idea of having a "personal" experience with religion, perhaps even with God, that attracts new members and keeps the old ones in the fold.

Conclusion

———◆———

IN HER INSIGHTFUL NOVEL ABOUT THE WAYS IN WHICH ALLEGATIONS
of sexual abuse against a priest rock a Boston Catholic family, author Jennifer Haigh zeroes in on the relationship between the accused priest's brother Mike and his Lutheran wife, Abby. Mike, who believes his brother is probably guilty, still has a strong attachment to the Catholic Church and wants his children raised in it. When Mike points out that "some people" in the parish think that his brother is innocent, Abby replies, "Some people don't think at all." The exchange, which takes place as they prepare for their oldest son's First Communion, goes downhill from there:

> Stupid brainwashed Catholics, he could hear her thinking. She didn't say it—not this time—but Mike heard it all the same. . . .
>
> "Honey, stop. You're just winding yourself up." He took the paper away, folded it closed. "I know you're upset. But this has nothing to do with us."
>
> Something in her face changed. "Oh really? We have three children, last time I checked. Three *boys*, Mike. Do you really want to raise them in this kind of church?"

"Don't start," Mike said. "We already decided that, remember? When we had them baptized."

"I gave in," she said. "I shouldn't have. That was my mistake. I'm serious," she added, somewhat unnecessarily. Abby was always serious.

He inhaled deeply, staying cool. "Maybe so, but what's done is done. They're baptized. End of story."

Abby closed one eye.

"Wait a minute. We have options here. Just because we made one bad decision—" She broke off. "What I'm saying is, let's not go any further down that road than we already have. . . .

"You knew the deal when we got married," he said, keeping his voice calm. "The kids are Catholic. When they grow up, if they want to, they can choose something else. Abby, look at me." He waited until she did. "We agreed on this."

The argument continues in this excruciating way for several more paragraphs. No resolution is reached for the obvious reason that such a deep divide cannot be bridged. We can see in this conversation the ways in which an external factor—a church's scandal—can rip apart an agreement that was reached before marriage. But it is also possible to glimpse how the seeds of this disagreement were there all along. Mike knows—presumably from previous conversations—what Abby really thinks of Catholicism. The arrangement about raising their kids notwithstanding, it seems that Abby has always had misgivings about his church.

Catholic-Protestant couples are not particularly exotic these days. Yet even a divide between Christians can tear at the fabric of a marriage. And even when couples actually reach an agreement about religion for their family—something many couples don't even bother with—it is no guarantee that their feelings will not change. In part because we have come to think of marriage as such an individual decision, we often underestimate the ways in which a religious community can still tug at us.

But marriage, and interfaith marriage especially, is often a story of competing loyalties. The biblical command in Genesis that a man should leave his parents and cleave to his wife is often read at wedding ceremonies, but its full impact is rarely felt on the wedding day. Though we may talk about committing ourselves fully to our spouses, we recognize that marriage is often a matter of navigating between a desire to honor a husband or wife and to hold dear the family and the attachments we were raised with.

Indeed, some religious texts speak about a person's relationship with his faith in terms that sound similar to the way we talk about our spouses. Abraham is told by God to leave his family, his people, and his land to start a new nation. Jesus tells his followers to leave their families behind them in order to join with him. Faith in its purest form requires total devotion. Even in the watered-down form in which many Americans practice it, faith demands some loyalty.

But it is easy for many of us to put these demands out of our heads, at least for a time. We place our religious lives on hold for years, often at precisely the phase when we are choosing a mate. After leaving our childhood homes, we get out of our family's habit of attending religious services. We move from one place to another. Our friendships change. Our jobs change. Nothing remains stable, and commitment to a religious institution, religious practices, or even religious belief can get lost in the shuffle.

This period of instability eventually comes to an end, but sometimes not for a long time. And the way it comes to an end is important too. We start to date and find that a romantic relationships can be all-consuming, leaving little room for attachment to a religious community or a commitment to faith.

Our culture encourages us to think of our spouses as "soul mates," to make our husbands and wives into our closest—and sometimes only—confidants, the fulfillers of our heart's deepest longings. In a 2007 op-ed in the New York Times, marriage historian Stephanie Coontz writes that this was not always the case. "From medieval days until the early 19th century, diaries and letters more often used the word love to refer to neighbors, cousins and fellow church members than to spouses. When honeymoons first gained favor in the 19th century, couples often took along relatives or friends for company. Victorian novels and diaries were as passionate about brother-sister relationships and same-sex friendships as about marital ties."

Indeed, she notes that "[u]ntil 100 years ago, most societies agreed that it was dangerously antisocial, even pathologically self-absorbed, to elevate marital affection and nuclear-family ties above commitments to neighbors, extended kin, civic duty and religion."

While the institution of marriage may have experienced a marked decline in recent decades—both in terms of the percentage of the population who marries and the likelihood that such a marriage will last—the relationship between husband and wife has most definitely become more "pathologically self-absorbed."

In a piece written on the twentieth anniversary of the famous *New York Times* "Vows" column, one of its regular authors, Lois Smith Brady, reflects on how the institution of marriage has shifted in her lifetime. "The way people look at marriage, and live it, has changed over the years. It's like farming, once considered drudgery and hard work, but now seen as a soulful utopian adventure." She gushes: "Young people are so beautifully ambitious about marriage these days. I recently interviewed a couple . . . who said they wanted to spend their lives finding each other's 'inner voices.'" But is seeing marriage as a "soulful utopian adventure" a positive development? Maybe for the wedding dress manufacturers.

For those who are concerned that young people choose their mates wisely and with a view to the long-term happiness and stability of the marriage, though, this approach can be less than ideal.

The trends that are leading to a higher rate of interfaith marriage show no signs of slowing. The age of marriage continues to rise—even in communities, like the LDS Church, that have historically maintained younger averages than the rest of the country. We might expect some pushback, if only because younger women are becoming more aware of declining fertility as they try to bear children later in life. But there is no evidence for it yet, and the pressure to bear children (let alone more than one or two) in twenty-first-century America is almost nonexistent. In other words, there is presumably some upper limit to the rising age of marriage, but the trend is unlikely to reverse itself any time soon.

Neither religious leaders nor parents of twenty- and thirty-somethings seem inclined to encourage young adults to start thinking about marriage any sooner. Parents, especially, continue to see the marriage of their children as a personal choice—one in which they should not intervene. Religious leaders have more of a sense that the choice of a spouse can impact a community. But they tread lightly. Talking with, say, high school students, about what to look for in a marriage partner would be a decidedly countercultural activity.

Religious communities, by their own admission, are having a great deal of trouble attracting young adults. Whether it is because singles living away from home have never had a particularly strong attachment to church, as sociologists like Rodney Stark have told me, or because this generation has some peculiar aversion to "institutions" of any sort as David Kinnaman of the Barna Group argues, America's congregations have a gaping generational hole. The lack of religious engagement among young adults is both a cause and effect of interfaith marriage. But it also shows no signs of turning around.

Finally, our cultural attitudes about the importance of diversity continue to intensify. Our educational and political leaders keep suggesting that bringing people together from a diversity of backgrounds—whether it is racial, ethnic, gender, sexual orientation or some combination of the above—make for better schools, more effective workplaces, and even morally superior environments. Religion has gotten lumped in with all these other immutable personal traits—what I referred to earlier as the racialization of religion—despite the fact that Americans' faith views seem to be so much in flux and religion-switching is at an all-time high. And the celebration of diversity has carried over into marriage.

But religion is not race and a marriage is not a public school.

Even if religion can be seen as an accident of birth—an idea that can frequently be heard even in certain fairly religious quarters these days—it is not simply a superficial characteristic the way race or ethnicity are. And religious leaders must work to make this difference clear.[1]

Religion is supposed to embed values within us—sets of principles that are not to be taken lightly or easily discarded. If people are to be soul mates—if, as many say, the important thing is to find a partner who shares one's values—then religion is something that must be taken into account. Religion makes values specific. It offers a set of texts, a code of behavior, and even a group of leaders who can make those values into something more substantive and more of a basis for action than "be a nice person."

Similarly, the goals of a marriage are not the same as those of social institutions. Obviously husbands and wives will differ on what they hope to get out of marriage, but surely it's some combination of achieving personal happiness and building a family, and religion is a factor in both of those. There is nothing about having diverse perspectives in a marriage that will make it inherently better—in fact, it may be less likely to succeed in the long run.

When you add up these cultural and religious attitudes, it is easy to see why interfaith marriage is growing by leaps and bounds. We like diversity; we believe members of other faiths are not only decent, but can get to heaven; we see marriage as a largely individual decision; we will meet our spouse and marry him or her with little forethought about his or her religious beliefs; when we find a potential partner, we believe the relationship between spouses will be an all-consuming one and that our families and communities do not have any kind of competing claims on our loyalties; we think religion is important but it is for kids and parents, not for young, single adults.

✧   ✧   ✧

The inexorable rise in interfaith relationships will change the face of religious institutions in America. Many will simply experience a decline in membership as couples decide that it is easier to push religious questions to the back burner. Even those couples who wanted to raise their children with faith—and who try to do so when those children are young—will simply throw their hands up as the children grow older. This is true for many same-faith couples as well, who have bought into the notion that they can have little influence over the adolescents living in their home (despite the research that shows parents, not peers, are the single biggest influence on teenage behavior).[2] But interfaith parents will have more trouble presenting a united front on religious practice and are likely to give up more easily.

More religious institutions will undoubtedly make accommodations for interfaith couples. Though most Americans report that their congregations are welcoming of interfaith families, some religious leaders will try to do more, like hosting social or educational events for these families. Others may try to offer more premarital counseling to present the implications of interfaith marriage before the wedding ceremony. And a few may even do more to encourage conversion on the part of the nonmember spouse.

Finally, those congregations that maintain a hard line against interfaith marriage may find themselves growing even more orthodox. Not only will interfaith couples themselves stay away, but members of the religious group who do not appreciate the message that congregants should in-marry will begin to look elsewhere. The lack of diversity and the warnings against it may simply grate on those with more liberal sensibilities.

This kind of religious sorting gives me a sense of foreboding. Our chattering classes may like to talk about a religious America and a secular America (I myself may have done it once or twice), but religion in America has long existed on a kind of continuum, and I think that is healthy. In fact, individual religious congregations usually have their own spectrums. It is good, I think, for the more and less religiously observant to see each other and interact with one another. As individuals, our inclinations to be more and less religious may change over time, and it is good for us to see that religion needn't be an all-or-nothing prospect. It would be a poor development if we came to think that once we had started to practice faith less frequently we would have to give it up altogether. Or if we had to worry that we wouldn't be welcomed back into the fold. A religious perspective on life can bring us great comfort and happiness or a sense of purpose, even at times when we don't expect it. And there is much to be said for encountering it regularly, even if we are not strong believers.

Similarly, interfaith marriage brings us into contact with people from other backgrounds. And this interaction is good for many reasons. Sure, the children of a Jewish-Muslim marriage will have a great theme for a college application essay. But the negotiations that take place every day between this husband and wife, the push and pull that their own friends and extended families will get to witness, may also promote tolerance and understanding in those communities. What such marriages mean in terms of the prospects of peace in the Middle East is another question. But insofar as the intermixing of Americans can produce warmer feelings toward those of other faiths, it is a good thing.

While such interfaith marriages will usually take place between people who have decided that adherence to faith is not the most important priority in their lives, these couplings may also be an educational experience for both spouses. Ironically, interfaith marriage may awaken people to the fact that religions are not all the same, that the particulars of practice and belief do matter, and that not all interfaith conflicts can be solved with the placement of a menorah next to a manger.

The appropriate stance for religious institutions to take on the question of interfaith marriage will depend in large part on their theological views. But there are certain sociological lessons that can inform their approach. To begin with, religious groups that are concerned foremost with marital stability will have to counsel members of interfaith couples that a rocky road may lie ahead for them. For those religious leaders, on the other hand, who are more worried about obedience and adherence to religious texts, the line may have to be drawn more strictly—intermarried couples may simply not fit into the community.

To encourage in-marriage, religious leaders cannot simply focus on childhood education and the attendance of families at religious services or the practice of religious rituals in the home. These do not, on the whole, prevent marriage outside the faith. The crucial years, it seems, are those of young adulthood. Though it may be tempting to allow singles in their twenties and thirties to disengage as they work on a process of self-discovery, these are the vital years for making long-term religious decisions. This demographic may be hard to reach, and some of them may eventually return of their own accord. But that is hardly guaranteed. And marrying someone of another faith might close off the possibility of return altogether.

Most religious institutions have already given much consideration to the question of young-adult outreach. And religious leaders have grown legitimately frustrated in trying to engage with this group. I cannot offer any specific program that will solve this problem. The lives of young adults are in flux these days in a way that would have been hard to imagine fifty or sixty, let alone a hundred years ago. But I hope religious institutions will not give up trying to speak to this group both about faith and marriage and thinking about the two more intentionally. Their voices remain vital.

✦   ✦   ✦

So how should religious institutions think about interfaith couples in their midst? As we saw in the previous chapter's description of the LDS Church, it is actually possible to advocate in-marriage—even denying the possibility of living eternally with one's family—while at the same time welcoming intermarried couples in the community. Regularly engaging nonmember spouses in conversations about the faith is important. So is understanding that conversion is a possibility. A surprisingly large number of same-faith couples begin as interfaith ones.

Too much pressure can, of course, damage a church's relationship with both member and nonmember spouses. The attitude that bringing someone into the fold rests ultimately with a higher power seems also to be effective. It frees the member spouse from the burden of pressuring his or her partner to join the faith.

And what about the children? Ostracizing the children in interfaith families or suggesting to them that their parents have somehow failed usually backfires. Numerous parents and adult children of interfaith families I interviewed still hold grudges against religious institutions that tried this tactic.

Not only is it important to welcome the children of interfaith families where it is within theological bounds, it is particularly important to welcome their mothers. Whatever the scriptural perspective on matrilineal or patrilineal descent, it is important to note that children of interfaith marriages in the United States are more than twice as likely to practice the mother's faith as the father's. Religious leaders may have their own opinions about how a faith is passed down, but this seems to be the sociological reality in America.

Religious institutions are only part of the equation here. Couples and their families must explore the issues of interfaith marriage for themselves.

These matches are not for the faint-hearted. They bring less satisfaction to spouses, on average. And, in certain combinations, they can result in a higher likelihood of divorce. Unfortunately, many couples fail to discuss their religious differences before marriage. In fact, only a small percentage of interfaith couples actually discuss an issue as important as the faith of their children until well after the wedding.

But it does not seem to be because they don't care about faith. As many as 40 percent of interfaith couples try to raise their children in one faith. When children are young, the practices of interfaith and same-faith couples are not significantly different. But things get harder as kids get older.

It seems like a long road between those first dates and having kids who are independent enough to object to going to church, but as any parent will tell you, the years will fly by. Couples who are considering marriage need to start thinking about religion as early as possible. Working out how different faiths are theologically compatible is not of great importance. Arguments about transubstantiation and infant baptism are fairly rare. Couples need to think in practical terms about their faith differences—how it will affect the way they spend their time, their money, and the way in which they want to raise kids.

Whatever cultural taboos are at work in preventing people from discussing religion with potential spouses—faith is an immutable trait (like race) and we shouldn't discriminate; faith is a personal choice and we shouldn't be nosey; it's not very romantic or spontaneous to ask someone you're dating whether you plan to send your kids to Sunday school—we should help couples get over them.

Encouraging couples to speak more freely about these issues both before and during marriage is a challenge to religious institutions and perhaps to society at large. But it is also a challenge for parents. There are some parents who have no problem taking on such a role, but their numbers, if anything, seem to be dwindling. The highest aspiration most parents have for their children is that they find a spouse who brings them personal fulfillment. It's a worthy goal. But personal fulfillment does not always mean the same thing in the long term as in the short term. Our children may be getting married later—and that too may make parents more reluctant to offer advice—but offering some guidance on what makes a long and happy marriage is still an important task. The truth that marriage is a struggle between the desires of another individual and the demands of a community—with each deserving careful consideration—is an idea that the old can still pass on to the young.

NOTES

$\textbf{\textemdash\!\!\!+\!\!\!\textemdash}$

Preface

1. In July of 2010, I conducted an original survey of 2,450 Americans that was focused specifically on interfaith marriage. To my knowledge, it is the most detailed examination ever done of Americans' attitudes toward, and experiences with, marriages between spouses of different religions. Because they are the focus of the study, interfaith couples were oversampled, which simply means that the survey includes more people in interfaith marriages than would be expected in a true random sample of the population. However, results from the national population account for this oversampling through the use of weighting, a standard statistical technique that ensures the results are not distorted by the disproportionate share of respondents in interfaith marriages. The survey was done online by YouGov, a firm specializing in internet surveys. YouGov draws from an extremely large panel of respondents who have opted into doing periodic surveys. The firm draws statistically valid samples of the American population through a system of "matching," whereby YouGov statisticians calibrate the demographic characteristics of each sample to correspond to known characteristics of the U.S. population (as reported by the U.S. Census Bureau). The result is a nationally representative sample of Americans. In addition to the main survey of 2,450, I also conducted a shorter follow-up survey with 704 respondents who had been married previously, in order to ask about their prior marriages.

2. Christian Smith and Patricia Snell, *Souls in Transition: The Religious and Spiritual Lives of Emerging Adults in America* (New York: Oxford University Press, 2009), 140.

3. Marriage among people of different faiths is, of course, not a uniquely American phenomenon. Many European countries also have high rates of intermarriage. Using data from the International Social Survey Programme

(ISSP), we can calculate that the intermarriage rates for the United Kingdom and France are 36 percent and 34 percent respectively. These numbers represent marriage across religious families but not across traditions. The evangelical-mainline distinction is not made in European countries. There are other countries where the numbers are extraordinarily low. In Cyprus it is 2 percent, and in Croatia it is 9 percent. In the case of the latter, one might surmise that intermarriage is unlikely to happen simply because there is very little religious diversity. In the case of the latter, though, one might suppose that a history of ethnic strife has led the religious groups to maintain a high wall of separation among them. All of which is to say that a comparison between the United States and Europe when it comes to interfaith marriage—or matters of religion at all—is not enormously enlightening.

4. Robert Putnam and David Campbell, *American Grace* (New York: Simon and Schuster, 2010), 150.

5. Results of some studies like the American Religious Identification Survey notwithstanding, it is difficult to calculate intermarriage rates for Buddhists because estimates for this population vary widely—from 2 million to 10 million in the United States. What people mean when they identify as a Buddhist also seems to vary even more than for other religious populations.

Introduction

1. Unless otherwise specified, the names of the members of interfaith couples have been changed. Because Judy's family is a prominent one, they have allowed me to use their real names.

2. Putnam and Campbell, *American Grace*, 526.

3. Barry A. Kosmin, Egon Mayer, and Ariela Keysar for the Institute for the Study of Secularism in Society and Culture, "The American Religious Identification Survey (ARIS) 2001." http://commons.trincoll.edu/aris/surveys/aris-2001/.

4. Will Herberg, *Protestant, Catholic, Jew* (Chicago: University of Chicago Press, 1955).

5. See, for instance, *Going Solo*, by Eric Klinenberg, *Singled Out* by Bella DePaulo, or the article "All the Single Ladies," in the November 2011 *Atlantic* by Kate Bolick. The last has been optioned for a television show. Eric Klinenberg, *Going Solo: The Extraordinary Rise and Surprising Appeal of Living Alone* (New York: Penguin Press, 2012). Bella DePaulo, *Singled Out: How Singles Are Stereotyped, Stigmatized, and Ignored, and Still Live Happily Ever After* (New York: St. Martin's Press, 2006).

6. As we will see in later chapters, this idea works better in principle than in practice. In America, it is usually the mother who is in charge of children's religious education, and so more often it is her religion that is passed down.

7. D'Vera Cohn, Jeffrey S. Passel, Wendy Wang, and Gretchen Livingston, "New Marriages Down 5 Percent from 2009 to 2010: Barely Half of U.S. Adults Are Married—A Record Low," Pew Research Center, December 14, 2011. http://www.pewsocialtrends.org/2011/12/14/barely-half-of-u-s-adults-are-married-a-record-low/.

8. My survey asked in what year the respondent married his or her current spouse, and then we calculated, based on his or her age, how old the respondent was when he or she married.

9. David Murrow, *Why Men Hate Going to Church* (Thomas Nelson Books, 2005).

10. Similarly, the 2001 American Religious Identification Survey estimates that roughly 1 in 5 Muslims are in "mixed religion households" (which includes cohabitation) and a slightly lower percentage of Muslims have married outside their religion. Given the high percentage of the Muslim population who are themselves immigrants, this number is also likely to rise quickly as future generations become more assimilated. Kosmin, Mayer, and Keysar, "American Religious Identification Survey (ARIS) 2001."

11. Judy and Bob's son, Terry, is obviously the outlier here. Children of interfaith couples raised in both faiths don't regularly become members of the clergy. We will discuss shortly results of the Faith Matters survey, which suggest that children of parents who are of different faiths tend to have slightly lower rates of religious service attendance and religious identification. But we don't have any way of measuring whether those children were consciously raised in two faiths.

12. Philip Weiss, "What Would a Jewish Veep Say About Intermarriage," *New York Observer*, May 1, 2000.

13. Lee Strobel, *Surviving a Spiritual Mismatch in Marriage* (Grand Rapids, MI: Zondervan, 2002).

Chapter 1

1. The 1990 National Jewish Population Survey set off a large-scale panic in the Jewish community about declining numbers when it reported that more than half of Jews were intermarrying. Citing the study in a 2005 article in *Commentary*, Jack Wertheimer noted, "Nearly three-quarters of children raised in intermarried families go on to marry non-Jews themselves, and only 4 percent of these raise their own children as Jews."

2. Kalman Packouz, *How to Prevent an Intermarriage* (n.p.: published by the author, 1976, revised 2008) http://www.preventintermarriage.com/download.html. Accessed July 6, 2012.

3. All Bible translations are taken from the New Revised Standard Edition unless otherwise noted.

4. The standards for conversion have provoked a bitter fight in the Jewish community, particularly with regard to Israel. Jews from anywhere in the world

may emigrate to Israel and become citizens, but the question of who qualifies as a Jew has vexed Israeli authorities. Currently it is Orthodox rabbis who hold the power to make this decision, and they have declared that they will not accept anything less than an Orthodox conversion—and only ones performed by particular rabbis.

5. National Jewish Population Survey of 2000–2001, "Orthodox Jews: A United Jewish Communities Presentation of Findings," February 2004. http://www.jewishfederations.org/local_includes/downloads/4983.pdf.

6. Strobel, *Surviving a Spiritual Mismatch*, 20–21.

7. Strobel, *Surviving a Spiritual Mismatch*, 20.

8. Strobel, *Surviving a Spiritual Mismatch*, 15–16.

9. Again we are discussing this from a strictly theological perspective. Obviously it would be fairly difficult to be a Jew in America today and not encounter gentiles.

10. Russell M. Nelson, "Celestial Marriage," The Church of Jesus Christ of Latter-day Saints. October 2008. http://www.lds.org/general-conference/2008/10/celestial-marriage?lang=eng&;query=eternal+marriage. Modified February 21, 2012.

11. Nelson, "Celestial Marriage."

12. Lewis J. Patsavos and Charles J. Joanides, "Interchurch Marriages: An Orthodox Perspective," *International Academy for Marital Spirituality Review* 6 (2000): 215–33.

13. Patsavos and Joanides, "Interchurch Marriages."

14. Patsavos and Joanides, "Interchurch Marriages."

15. Emilie Lemmons, "Church Teachings: Interfaith Marriages," United States Conference of Catholic Bishops. http://foryourmarriage.org/catholic-marriage/church-teachings/interfaith-marriages/. Accessed July 6, 2012.

16. "Degree on Ecumenism: *Unitatis Redintegratio*," Documents of the Vatican Council. http://www.vatican.va/archive/hist_councils/ii_vatican_council/documents/vat-ii_decree_19641121_unitatis-redintegratio_en.html. Accessed July 6, 2012.

17. "On the Powers and Privileges Granted to Bishops," *Pastorale Munus. Motu Proprio of Pope Paul VI*, November 30, 1963. http://www.papalencyclicals.net/Paul6/pasmunus.htm. Last modified March 2012.

18. "Apostolic Letter of Pope Paul VI on Mixed Marriages," *Matrimonia Mixta*, Catholic Doors Ministry. http://www.catholicdoors.com/misc/marriage/mixed.htm. Accessed July 6, 2012.

19. "Apostolic Letter of Pope Paul VI."

20. Lemmons, "Church Teachings: Interfaith Marriages."

21. Lemmons, "Church Teachings: Interfaith Marriages."

22. Lemmons, "Church Teachings: Interfaith Marriages."

23. Alex B. Leeman, "Interfaith Marriage in Islam: An Examination of the Legal Theory Behind the Traditional and Reformist Positions," *Indiana Law Journal* 84 (2009): 743–71.

24. Qur'an 2:221, 5:5, 60:10, M. H. Shakir, trans., *The Holy Qur'an*, 9th ed. (New York: Tahrike Tarsile Qur'an, Inc., 2004).

25. Mashood A. Badern, "Interfaith Marriage in Islam: An Examination of the Legal Theory Behind the Traditional and Reformist Positions," *International Human Rights and Islamic Law* 144 (2003).

26. Khaleel Mohammad, "Defense of Inter-faith Marriage." IrshadManji.com. https://www.irshadmanji.com/sites/default/files/Eng_BothPages.pdf. Accessed July 6, 2012.

27. I have not mentioned Eastern religions here because they do not have a theologically or textually based prohibition on intermarriage—which is not to say there are no cultural taboos or that families welcome the idea of children marrying out. In America, certainly, recent immigrants are likely to pressure their children into marrying inside the faith. But because Hinduism and Buddhism allow for the idea that there are different paths to God, broadly speaking, marriage to someone pursuing another path does not hinder one's road to salvation or enlightenment. And one would be hard pressed to find Hindu or Buddhist leaders who object on religious grounds to mixed marriages.

28. Putnam and Campbell, *American Grace*, 151.

Chapter 2

1. Mark Regnerus and Jeremy Uecker, *Premarital Sex in America: How Young Americans Meet, Mate, and Think About Marrying* (New York: Oxford University Press, 2011), 1.

2. *National Survey of Family Growth*. Centers for Disease Control and Prevention. http://www.cdc.gov/nchs/nsfg.htm. Last updated December 5, 2011. Accessed July 11, 2012.

3. Parents of young people in minority religions are certainly more likely to be concerned.

4. Regnerus and Uecker, *Premarital Sex in America*, 249.

5. Regnerus and Uecker, *Premarital Sex in America*, 249.

6. Holly Finn, "My Fertility Crisis, *Wall Street Journal*, July 23, 2011, Review Section. http://online.wsj.com/article/SB10001424053111903461104576458134196248312.html.

7. Simon May, *Love: A History* (New Haven, CT: Yale University Press, 2011), 3.

8. For more on this age span, see *Emerging Adults in America: Coming of Age in the 21st Century*, edited by Jeffrey Jensen Arnett and Jennifer Lynn Tanner (Washington, DC: American Psychological Association, 2006). For a religious perspective on emerging adulthood, see Smith and Snell, *Souls in Transition*. For more on how emerging adults view romantic relationships, see Kay S. Hymowitz, *Manning Up* (New York: Basic Books, 2011).

9. Robert Wuthnow, *After the Baby Boomers* (Princeton, NJ: Princeton University Press, 2007), 53.

10. David Kinnaman, *You Lost Me: Why Young Christians Are Leaving Church and Rethinking Faith* (Grand Rapids, MI: Baker Books, 2011).

11. Katherine S. Newman, *The Accordion Family: Boomerang Kids, Anxious Parents, and the Private Toll of Global Competition* (Boston: Beacon Press, 2012), 65.

12. The same could be said of certain areas of the South—Atlanta and Charlotte are two cities with this reputation—but a history of religiosity in the South might counterbalance this trend.

13. Sikhism is a monotheistic religion founded around 1500 in the Punjab region of India.

14. While it is true that students who attend college do report a drop-off in religious attendance, young adults who do not go to college can experience an even more significant decline. It is possible that there are two different dynamics at work here. Young adults who experience the college-related decline are finding their faith challenged, but they are ultimately returning to solid middle-class lives, which are likely to include church attendance. Young adults who skip college may simply be falling further and further off the middle-class track and never return to religious life. My own survey found no distinctions in interfaith marriage based on level of education, but it is possible that those with lower levels of education end up in interfaith marriages for reasons that are different than those with higher levels of education.

15. Munira Ezzeldine, *Before the Wedding: Questions for Muslims to Ask Before Getting Married* (Irvine, CA: Izza Publishing, 2003).

16. Sharon Jayson, "Living Together No Longer 'Playing House,'" *USA Today*, July 28, 2008.

17. Putnam and Campbell, *American Grace*, 137.

Chapter 3

1. The term communion derives from the Latin word *communio*, meaning sharing in common. If you don't have enough in common, you can't take communion.

2. Daniel Garland, Jr., "Why Can't Non-Catholics Receive Communion at Mass?" *Irish, Catholic, and Dangerous* (blog). October 4, 2007. http://iris-handdangerous.blogspot.com/2007/10/why-cant-non-catholics-receive.html. Accessed July 11, 2012.

3. Susanna Kim, "Brides Tighten Garters: Average Wedding Cost Drops to $26,501," *ABC News*, June 23, 2011. http://abcnews.go.com/Business/brides-tighten-garters-average-wedding-cost-drops-26501/story?id=13888184#.T6gE2O0sE2o. Accessed July 11, 2012.

4. Joan C. Hawxhurst, ed., *Interfaith Wedding Ceremonies: Samples and Sources* (Kalamazoo, MI: Dovetail Publishing, 1996).

5. Hawxhurst, ed., *Interfaith Wedding Ceremonies*, 63.

6. "Officiants Directory," *Winter 2008 New York Wedding Guide. New York Magazine*. http://nymag.com/weddings/listings/officiants/. Accessed July 11, 2012.

7. Jim Keen, *Inside Intermarriage: A Christian Partner's Perspective on Raising a Jewish Family* (New York: URJ Press, 2006).

8. Hawxhurst, ed., *Interfaith Wedding Ceremonies*, 69.

Chapter 4

1. Faith Matters Survey 2006 [computer file]. Roper Center for Public Opinion Research Study USMISC2006-FAITH Version 2. Saguaro Seminar [producer], 2006 (Storrs, CT: The Roper Center for Public Opinion Research, University of Connecticut [distributor], 2011).

2. It used to be that infants were baptized as soon as possible, but with the decline in infant mortality many families wait, sometimes for months, so they can schedule a party around the event or just because they haven't gotten around to it. Once families worried that babies who died before they could be baptized ended up in what the church called "limbo," which wasn't hell but wasn't heaven either. A few years ago, a Vatican-affiliated commission referred to limbo as a "hypothesis," leaving Catholics free to hope that these babies will go to heaven.

3. Smith and Snell, *Souls in Transition*, 284.

4. In this case, we simply asked a general question about whether they do these things for "any of their children."

5. It is important to note, though, that sociological studies of children and adolescents suggest that parents are still the most important influence on their children—ahead of friends, teachers, and religious leaders.

6. I should stipulate that in some faiths, home-based rituals are simply more important than in others.

7. Cox's book on his own experience as a Christian bringing up a Jewish child is well worth reading for interfaith couples. His views as a Christian (and a theologian) of Jewish holidays will resonate with Jews and Christians alike. *Common Prayers: Faith, Family and a Christian's Journey Through the Jewish Year* (New York: Houghton Mifflin, 2001).

8. From a theological perspective, many Christian leaders would disagree with this formulation, but the idea that your birth does not determine whether you are Christian finds its support primarily in Galatians 3:27–29: "For all of you who were baptized into Christ have clothed yourselves with Christ. There is neither Jew nor Gentile, neither slave nor free, nor is there male and female, for you are all one in Christ Jesus. If you belong to Christ, then you are Abraham's seed, and heirs according to the promise."

Chapter 5

1. Margaret Moorman, *Light the Lights* (New York: Scholastic Books, 1994).
2. Michael G. Lawler, Barbara Markey, Lee M. Williams, Lisa A. Riley, Gail S. Risch, C. Timothy Dickel, *Ministry to Interchurch Marriages: A National Study* (Omaha, NE: Creighton University Center for Marriage and Family, 1999), 8.
3. Maureen and Bob love this story so much they have allowed me to use their real names here.
4. Jane Kaplan, *Interfaith Families: Personal Stories of Jewish-Christian Intermarriage* (Westport, CT: Praeger Publishers, 2004), 110–11.
5. These are their real names.
6. There is reason to believe this interpretation is correct, but it is not a common part of the education of Jewish children about the Passover story.
7. I should say up front that it is a little bit confusing talking to leaders of the Messianic movement about interfaith marriage. They will regularly refer to marriages between Messianic Jews and Christians as mixed marriages. My reaction, I acknowledge, is often frustration, combined with a little annoyance. I remember going to visit an evangelical college a number of years ago and being told that there were Jews who attended. I found that hard to believe since students had to sign a statement claiming Jesus as their savior in order to enroll. When I expressed my skepticism, I was told, "Oh, they're Messianic Jews." Chalk it up to my own parochialism if you like, but I generally think of people who believe Jesus is the Messiah as Christians. And Messianic Jews married to Christians are not couples I would classify as interfaith.

Chapter 6

1. Please note that the results on this question were gathered from a follow-up to our original survey.
2. The question asked about the respondent's "ex-spouse." There may have been more than one, but since it was already an intrusive question, we opted not to be more specific (and imply that they had been serially divorced).
3. Albert I. Gordon, *Intermarriage: Interfaith, Interracial, Interethnic* (Boston: Beacon Press, 1964), 348.
4. Evelyn L. Lehrer and Carmel U. Chiswick, "Religion as a Determinant of Marital Stability," *Demography* 30, no. 3 (August 1993): 385–404.
5. Kosmin, Mayer, and Keysar, "American Religious Identification Survey (ARIS) 2001."
6. Philip M. Rosten, "The Mischling: Child of the Jewish-Gentile Marriage," B.A. Honors Paper, Department of Social Relations, Harvard University, April 1960.
7. It is important to keep in mind that marital satisfaction is a number reported by a single respondent to a survey. We are not putting a number on the

overall happiness of a couple together, but merely one person's perspective on the relationship.

8. Jeffrey Passel, Wendy Wang, and Paul Taylor, "One-in-Seven New U.S. Marriages is Interracial or Interethnic: Marrying Out," Pew Research Center, June 4, 2010. http://www.pewsocialtrends.org/2010/06/04/marrying-out/. Accessed July 11, 2012.

9. A 2008 survey of couples who married after 1980 found that the percentage of interracial couples who had divorced by the tenth year after their wedding exceeded that of same-race couples. The biggest disparity, the authors found, occurred among marriages initiated between 1985 and 1989, where 55 percent of interracial marriages ended in divorce by their tenth year, compared to 35.6 percent of same-race marriages. Couples that included a non-Hispanic black husband and a white wife were twice as likely to divorce as couples with white husbands and wives. Couples that included Asian husbands and white wives were 59 percent more likely to divorce. Jenifer L. Bratter and Rosalind B. King, "'But Will It Last?' Marital Instability Among Interracial and Same-Race Couples," *Family Relations* 57 (April 2008), 160–71.

10. These same factors could work to explain why interracial marriage remains relatively uncommon.

11. "U.S. Religious Landscape Survey: Religious Affiliation: Diverse and Dynamic, February 2008," The Pew Forum on Religious and Public Life. http://religions.pewforum.org/pdf/report-religious-landscape-study-full.pdf. Accessed July 11, 2012.

12. Lehrer and Chiswick, "Religion as a Determinant."

13. I have divided religious attendance into thirds. "High attendance" includes those who attend more than once a week to those who attend two or three times a month; "Medium attendance" includes those who attend once a month to those who attend once or twice a year; "Low attendance" includes those who never attend to those who attend less than once a year. The reason for splitting religious attendance this way is that it produces the closest thing to an even division of the population into thirds.

14. Christopher Ellison, Amy Burdette, W. Bradford Wilcox, "The Couple That Prays Together: Race and Ethnicity, Religion, and Relationship Quality Among Working-Age Adults," *Journal of Marriage and Family* 72 (August 2010): 963–75.

15. David C. Dollhaite and Nathaniel M. Lambert, "Forsaking All Others: How Religious Involvement Promotes Marital Fidelity in Christian, Jewish and Muslim Couples," *Review of Religious Research* 48, no. 3 (2007): 305.

16. Once again, please note that we are reporting the marital satisfaction level of the respondent only, not the couple as a whole.

17. Margaret L. Vaaler, Christopher G. Ellison, and Daniel A. Powers, "Religious Influences on the Risk of Marital Dissolution," *Journal of Marriage and Family* 71, no. 4 (November 2009): 917–34.

18. Her real name.

19. An evangelical denomination that originated in nineteenth-century England. Today, it is characterized by a strict adherence to biblical texts, a lack of professional clergy, and the lack of set liturgy.

20. R. R. Reno, *Fighting the Noonday Devil* (Grand Rapids, MI: Wm. B. Eerdmans Publishing, 2011), 26.

Chapter 7

1. Ben Barrack, "All-American Muslim Star: Shocking Truths and Lowe's Good Call," *Human Events*, December 15, 2011. http://www.humanevents.com/article.php?id=48166. Accessed July 11, 2012.

2. "Muslim Americans: Middle Class and Mostly Mainstream," Pew Research Center, May 22, 2007. http://pewresearch.org/assets/pdf/muslim-americans.pdf. Accessed July 11, 2012.

3. Putnam and Campbell, *American Grace*, 526.

4. "Mapping the Global Muslim Population: A Report on the Size and Distribution of the World's Muslim Population," Pew Research Center, October 7, 2009. http://www.pewforum.org/Mapping-the-Global-Muslim-Population.aspx. Accessed July 7, 2011.

5. "Muslim Americans: No Signs of Growth in Alienation or Support for Extremism," Pew Research Center, August 2011. http://www.people-press.org/files/2011/08/muslim-american-report.pdf. Accessed July 11, 2012.

6. "Asian Americans: A Mosaic of Faiths," Pew Research Center, July, 2012. http://www.pewforum.org/Asian-Americans-A-Mosaic-of-Faiths.aspx. Accessed September 25, 2012.

7. "Muslim Americans: Middle Class and Mostly Mainstream." Arab-Americans opposed it more than other Muslim ethnic groups.

8. "Muslim Americans: No Signs of Growth in Alienation or Support for Extremism," Pew Research Center, August 2011. http://www.people-press.org/files/2011/08/muslim-american-report.pdf. Accessed July 11, 2012.

9. "Muslim Americans: No Signs of Growth in Alienation."

10. David E. Campbell and Robert D. Putnam, "Islam and American Tolerance," *Wall Street Journal*, August 12, 2011.

11. Campbell and Putnam, "Islam and American Tolerance."

12. Israel Zangwill, *The Melting Pot* (New York: Macmillan, 1912), 37.

13. Adam B. Ellick, "Speed-Dating, Muslim Style," *New York Times*, February 11, 2011.

14. Ezzeldine, *Before the Wedding*.

15. Syma Mohammed, "Why British Muslim Women Struggle to Find a Marriage Partner," *The Guardian*, January 18, 2012.

16. Qanta Ahmed, "Islam, Interfaith Marriage Go Hand in Hand," *USA Today*, February 12, 2012.

17. Mohammad, "Defense of Inter-faith Marriage."

18. "Mapping the Global Muslim Population: A Report on the Size and Distribution of the World's Muslim Population," Pew Research Center, October 7, 2009. http://www.pewforum.org/Mapping-the-Global-Muslim-Population.aspx. Accessed July 7, 2011.

19. Almost half of the world's Jewish population of 13 million resides in the United States. Arnold Dashefsky, Sergio DellaPergola, and Ira Sheskin, eds., *World Jewish Population, 2010: Current Jewish Population Reports*. Number 2-2010. http://www.jewishdatabank.org/Reports/World_Jewish_Population_2010.pdf. Accessed July 11, 2012.

Chapter 8

1. James B. Twitchell, *Shopping for God* (New York: Simon and Schuster, 2007), 29–30.

2. Masorti is the movement in Israel that is most closely identified with the Conservative movement in the United States.

3. Jack Wertheimer, "Current Trends in American Jewish Philanthropy," *American Jewish Yearbook 1997* (New York: American Jewish Committee, 1997), 62–63.

4. "The 2005 Boston Community Survey," report by the Steinhardt Social Research Institute at Brandeis University, November 2006. http://www.cjp.org/local_includes/downloads/16072.pdf.

5. "The National Jewish Population Survey 2000–01: Strength, Challenge and Diversity In The American Jewish Population." United Jewish Communities. Updated January 2004. http://www.jewishfederations.org/local_includes/downloads/4606.pdf.

6. Sue Fishkoff, "Study Suggests That Outreach to the Intermarried Pays Dividends," *Jewish Exponent*, November 22, 2006.

7. Jewish Policy and Action Research, "Population Growth," Jewish United Fund/Jewish Federation of Metropolitan Chicago. http://www.juf.org/pdf/ealert/pop_study.pdf. Accessed July 11, 2012.

8. Jewish Policy and Action Research, "Population Growth"; "The 2005 Boston Community Survey: Preliminary Findings," report by the Steinhardt Social Research Institute, Brandeis University, November 2006. http://www.cjp.org/local_includes/downloads/16072.pdf. Accessed July 11, 2012.

9. Charles Radin, "Conservative Jews Set a Conversion Campaign," *Boston Globe*, December 7, 2005.

10. Lisa Katz, "Inviting Non-Jews to Convert to Judaism." http://judaism.about.com/od/conversiontojudaism/a/convert_invite.htm. Accessed July 11, 2012.

11. Sylvia Barack Fishman, *Double or Nothing: Jewish Families and Mixed Marriage* (Hanover, NH: University Press of New England, 2004), 148–49.

12. Fishman, *Double or Nothing*, 149.

13. There are 144 evangelicals in interfaith marriages.

14. It is admittedly not clear what "Nones" mean when they report a conversion attempt: Were they trying to convert their spouses to agnosticism or atheism? Or are they referring to a previous point in their lives, when they had a religious affiliation?

Chapter 9

1. Yes, some Mormons have engaged in the controversial practice of posthumously baptizing Jews who perished in the Holocaust, but LDS Church leaders have responded to public pressure and told church members that they are only to perform such baptisms for their own ancestors.
2. This is different, by the way, from the way some fundamentalist Christians say they "love Jews" because of their "special" relationship with God.
3. In her recent book, *Faith and Money* (Cambridge: Cambridge University Press, 2011), Lisa A. Keister includes LDS members in a chapter with Jews and Mainline Protestants because of the three groups' relatively high levels of wealth and educational attainment.
4. My own survey did not include enough Mormons or Jews to make such a statistically definitive statement. A higher percentage of Buddhists had married non-Buddhists, but Buddhism in America is very disparate—immigrants from different Asian countries have brought different strains; Buddhism for many self-described Buddhists is not even a religion but a set of cultural concepts; the community boundaries are often fuzzy; and marriage outside of the group is hardly unusual let alone frowned upon. Estimates of the number of Buddhists living in America range from 2 to 10 million, so it's a little hard to get a grasp on any demographic issues.
5. Note, however, that the 2006 GSS only had 21 Jews and 17 Mormons total—our survey has more of each.
6. "National Jewish Population Survey 2000–01."
7. Allison Pond, "From American Idol to Mormon Missionary," *Wall Street Journal*, December 30, 2011.
8. This is not the first time I've experienced this, by the way. In a book I wrote ten years ago, I tried to compare Yeshiva University with other religious colleges in the country and received similar reactions.
9. Jonathan D. Sarna, "Intermarriage in America: The Jewish Experience in Historical Context," *Ambivalent Jew: Charles Liebman in Memoriam* (New York: Jewish Theological Seminary, 2007), 126.
10. Sarna, "Intermarriage in America," 128.
11. Sarna, "Intermarriage in America," 130.
12. Brent A. Barlow, "Notes on Mormon Interfaith Marriages," *Family Coordinator* 26, no. 2 (April 1977): 143–50.
13. Barlow, "Notes on Mormon Interfaith Marriages," 143–50. A 2012 Pew survey of Mormons similarly found a correlation between higher levels of education and greater commitment to Mormon orthodoxy.

14. Susan Buhler Taber, *Mormon Lives: A Year in the Elkton Ward* (Urbana: University of Illinois Press, 1993), 181.

15. Richard Popp, "Two Faiths, Two Baptisms," *Dialogue: A Journal of Mormon Thought* 23 (1990): 125–28.

16. Eric Weiner, *Man Seeks God: My Flirtations With the Divine* (New York: Twelve, 2011).

17. Eric Liu, *The Accidental Asian: Notes of a Native Speaker* (New York: Vintage Books, 1999).

18. Elliott Abrams, *Faith or Fear: How Jews Can Survive in a Christian America* (New York: Simon and Schuster, 1997).

19. I might add that belonging to a community seems to be one of the most significant values for Americans these days. Hence the use of the word "community" in almost every context—the computer programmer community, the pet rescue community, the mental health community, the families of cancer victims community, etc.

20. Elaine Howard Ecklund and Kristen Schultz, "Atheists and Agnostics Negotiate Religion and Family," *Journal for the Scientific Study of Religion* 50, no. 4 (December 2011): 728–43.

21. Shaul Magid, "Be the Jew You Make: Jews, Judaism, and Jewishness in Post-Ethnic America," *Sh'ma*. http://www.shma.com/2011/03/be-the-jew-you-make-jews-judaism-and-jewishness-in-post-ethnic-america/. Accessed July 11, 2012.

Conclusion

1. One idea that occasionally comes up in my conversations, particularly ones with younger evangelicals, is that they are only Christian by accident of their birth. I could have been a Muslim born in Pakistan, they tell me.

2. See Smith and Snell, *Souls in Transition*, 284.

INDEX